Cucina Ebraica

Cucina Ebraica

FLAVORS *of the* ITALIAN JEWISH KITCHEN

BY **Joyce Goldstein**

PHOTOGRAPHS BY Ellen Silverman

CHRONICLE BOOKS

SAN FRANCISCO

First Chronicle Books LLC paperback edition, published in 2005.

TEXT COPYRIGHT © 1998 by Joyce Goldstein.
PHOTOGRAPHS COPYRIGHT © 1998 by Ellen Silverman.
ILLUSTRATIONS COPYRIGHT © 1998 by Rachel Goldstein.

ISBN 0-8118-5013-7

The Library of Congress has cataloged the previous edition as follows:

Goldstein, Joyce Esersky.
Cucina ebraica: flavors of the Italian Jewish kitchen / by Joyce Goldstein;
photography by Ellen Silverman.
P. CM.
Includes bibliographical references and index.
ISBN 0-8118-1969-8 (hardcover)
1. Cookery, Jewish. 2. Cookery, Italian. 3. Jews, Italy, Social life and customs.
TX724.G657 1998
641.5'676'0945—DC21
97-45054
CIP

Manufactured in China.

Designed and typeset by Anne Galperin
Prop styling by Betty Alfenito
Food styling by Anne Disrude
Cover Design by Jay Peter Salvas

Distributed in Canada by Raincoast Books
9050 Shaughnessy Street
Vancouver, British Columbia V6P 6E5

10 9 8 7 6 5 4 3 2 1

Chronicle Books LLC
85 Second Street
San Francisco, California 94105

www.chroniclebooks.com

Table of Contents

Introduction

In 1957 I traveled to Italy for the first time and fell madly in love with the countryside, the art and architecture, the people, the culture, and the food. In other words, I became a fanatic Italophile. While traveling I had picked up rudiments of the language, using a pocket dictionary and considerable chutzpah. When I went back to graduate school in art and architecture, I enrolled in a basic Italian class so that I would have some grammar to go with the nouns and adjectives, in anticipation of a return.

In the meantime, my passion for Italy raged unabated. I read Italian poems aloud. I painted in the style of the Trecento. I learned how to apply gesso, red bole, and gold leaf to dyptichs and tryptichs that would reveal angels in Umbrian and Tuscan landscapes. Inspired by reading Elizabeth David, I cooked Italian dinners. And, thinking of myself as Gioia, I secretly prayed that my mother's maiden name, Salata, was Italian, thereby linking me to the country of my dreams. Now I realize that the name was Sephardic and that her branch of the family somehow ended up in Russia, but back then I kept thinking they had gone the wrong way. Why, I wondered, didn't they stop in Italy, where their name would have meant "salted"?

In 1959 my dreams became reality. My former husband and I went to Italy to study art and architecture, and for about six weeks we lived in Perugia. The Fulbright committee, probably not by coincidence, billeted us with an Italian Jewish family named Coen. Guido, its head, was in his early seventies. His chatty wife, Clara, who was in her late fifties, and his two sisters, eighty-two-year-old Albertina and eighty-four-year-old Livia, made up the rest of the household. World War II had so decimated the Italian Jewish population of the region that the synagogue was now located in a room in the Coen home. I had to pass through it every day on my way to the bathroom. Once a week, the rabbi came from Florence to perform services and special holiday ceremonies. On his visits, he would take over the balcony where he would proceed to kill chickens according to kosher law.

Being in the Coen's home-cum-synagogue put me in touch with my Jewishness in a way I hadn't known before. Both my parents were born in Russia and came to the United States as children. They made conscious efforts to bury the past. I was raised to be an American, and, even more specifically, a New Yorker. Our family was not at all religious. We rarely attended temple except for an occasional bar mitzvah or wedding. Yet we were Jewish. For the first seventeen years of my life I lived in the Brooklyn shtetl of Crown Heights. From the 1930s to the late 1940s, the neighborhood was filled with Jewish businesses: bakeries, dairy stores, kosher butchers and poultry markets, delicatessens, and the famed Dubrow's cafeteria, now vanished. Like most New Yorkers, the Jewish cuisine I was exposed to was Ashkenazic. Being in an Italian Jewish home about to learn about Italian Jewish food, from people who had been through Nazi persecution and the war and had survived, filled me with a sense of wonder and anticipation. It made me humble, grateful, and anxious to make an emotional connection.

While my husband studied Italian at l'Università per Stranieri, I explored Perugia, a stunning hill town with narrow, winding streets, overhanging porticos, and stepped alleyways, and sketched the breathtaking Umbrian countryside. At some point during the day I would spend time with Livia and Albertina, watching them prepare what I thought was going to be special Italian Jewish food. Albertina fancied herself to be quite a cook. Livia, who had been active in the resistance and had smuggled many Jews out of Italy, was her reluctant assistant. Alas, they were terrible cooks. Every day for lunch we had plain boiled spaghetti with watery tomato sauce. Occasionally, Albertina would present her *capolavoro*, her culinary masterpiece, *insalata russa*, with cold, overcooked vegetables bound in an oily mayonnaise. At night we ate a weak chicken broth with pastina, a little dry meat, and a few overcooked vegetables. The overcooking did seem familiarly Jewish, but the flavors were definitely Italian. My first attempt to discover the good food of the Italian Jews hit a snag in Perugia.

Later, when we settled in Rome, we found some wonderful restaurants specializing in *cucina ebraica* in the ghetto off the Via Portico d'Ottavia. I did not, however, understand what made their dishes particularly Jewish. They seemed to be Italian, and were served in many other Roman restaurants that didn't bill themselves as Jewish. In fact, most of the so-called Jewish restaurants were not kosher; pancetta appeared on the menu, and dairy and meat items were served at the same time. But obviously certain dishes in the restaurants'

repertoires had Jewish roots. These were the complex *fritto misto* assortments, tiny potato *gnocchi*, interesting salt-cod dishes served with polenta, fish with herbal marinades, hearty stews, ricotta fritters, and, of course, the most well-known Jewish dish of all, *carciofi alla giudia*, chrysanthemumlike deep-fried Roman artichokes. I asked questions, took notes, and tasted carefully.

When we returned to the United States, after the warmth and golden light of Rome, New York seemed dark and oppressive. I realized that I was no longer a New Yorker; I had been reborn as a spiritual Italian. So we moved to San Francisco, which felt Mediterranean in color, landscape, and mood. My passion for Italy continued unabated. I taught Italian cooking for eighteen years and cooked Italian food at home and daily at my restaurant, Square One.

In 1989, I decided to offer an Italian Passover dinner in our private dining room, as I didn't think I could fill the entire restaurant. The so-called Italian Seder was such a hit that every year we were able to fill the entire restaurant, up until 1996 when I closed Square One. Because I wanted these meals to be authentic and memorable, I intensified my research on Italian Jewish food.

It was in Italy that I taught myself to cook. I asked questions in restaurants and at the markets and requested recipes from friends. Knowing that I wouldn't be in Italy forever, I also searched for cookbooks to bring home, but in those wonderful learning years of 1959 and 1960, very few cookbooks were available, mostly just weighty classics like *Il talismano della felicità* by Ada Boni and Pellegrino Artusi's *La scienza in cucina e l'arte di mangiar bene*. Unlike Americans, Italians were not cookbook crazy, and it was just about impossible to find books that focused on regional cuisine. Years later, when my son, Evan, returned from an Italian vacation with a few cookbooks on the food of the Veneto, I was thrilled. The books were part of a new series being published in Padua by Franco Muzzio, and the chapters on *cucina ebraica* caught my eye. I noted that some Venetian Jewish dishes resembled those I had eaten in Rome, but many of the other recipes were distinctly Sephardic.

Since that time, I've built a nice library of Italian regional cookbooks, and as I have browsed through them in search of old and new ideas, I have discovered additional recipes attributed to Italian Jewish cuisine. A few dishes actually remind me of "home," such as a meat loaf with hard-boiled eggs running down the middle that I thought was Brooklyn Jewish cuisine but turned out to be Italo-Sephardic in origin. There are recipes for *stufatino di zucca gialla*, a stew of yellow squash with meat that resembles a classic tsimmes; *polpettine di pesce*, fish balls seasoned with cinnamon and cloves—not exactly gefilte fish but tasty—and *cavolo ripieno*, or stuffed cabbage, a family favorite. *Spuma di tonno*, a tuna spread for bread; *fegato alle uova sode*, chopped liver pâté; and *grigole*, or gribines, the cracklings from goose, duck, or chicken fat—a childhood weakness—also appear, as do *haroset*, the Passover

Seder condiment of dried fruits, nuts, and wine, and chicken soup with rice and chopped hard-boiled eggs. Many dishes are finished with *bagna brusca*, an egg-and-lemon sauce that most of us think of as Greek or Turkish but is really Sephardic. It acts as a thickener in dishes that non-Jews would enrich with cream or butter.

To my surprise, many recipes that I had previously identified as regional Italian classics turned out to have an Italian Jewish connection, including pasta with tuna, *zuppa pavese*, *baccalà mantecato*, *salsa verde*, and *triglie alla livornese*. I discovered that most Italian dishes for fennel and eggplant were originally cooked only by Jews, both these vegetables having been shunned by other Italians when they were first introduced in the markets. And many recipes for artichokes and yellow squash, the *zucca barucca* of the Veneto, were also Jewish in origin.

My studies are ongoing. Every time I visit Italy I'm on the lookout for that special dish, a new book that refers to the food of the Italian Jews, an acquaintance who turns out to be an Italian Jew with a story to tell.

The Jews in Italy

Although most of us think of Italy as the cradle of Catholicism, in fact, the oldest Jewish community in the world is in Rome. Jews have been in Italy since the second century B.C., arriving from settlements in Palestine when Judah Maccabeus formed an alliance with Rome. After the destruction of the Temple in Jerusalem in A.D. 70, more Jews came to the city, many as prisoners of war. A relief on the Arch of Titus in the Colosseum depicts the carrying away of the menorah from the Temple. (For years, no Jew would ever walk under this arch. In 1947, when the United Nations announced the formation of the

Jewish state of Israel, Roman Jews met at the Forum to celebrate and dance under the arch.) At the end of the first century, some thirty thousand Jews lived in Rome, settled around Trastevere and the Isola Tiburina.

Italian Jews fall into three major strains. The Italkim are Jews who have been in Italy since the second century B.C. The Sephardim came from Spain and Portugal after the Spanish Inquisition of 1492. The Sephardic and Marrano Jews (the latter, Jews who were forced to convert to Catholicism in order to survive but secretly held on to their beliefs) brought tomatoes, peppers, potatoes, corn, and pumpkin—the foods of the New World carried home by Iberian explorers—to Italy. Finally, there are the Ashkenazim, who came from Central Europe in the early fourteenth century. They settled in the north of Italy: the French Jews in Piedmont, the German Jews in Friuli and Trieste, others in Mantua and Ferrara. They represent a minority among Italian Jews. In the ghetto in Venice, well-concealed synagogues called *scuole* (schools) represent the different Jewish communities: the Scuola Tedesca and Canton (French) for the Ashkenazim, the Scuola Spagnola for the Sephardim, the Scuola Italiana for the Italkim, and even the Scuola Levantina for the Eastern and Arabic Jews.

When we talk of Jews in Italy, we are not talking about a huge population, however, nor of large Jewish centers. At its height, the Jewish population in the whole of the country numbered perhaps a few hundred thousand. After wars, famines, the ravages of disease, and emigration, about forty thousand Jews remain in Italy today, predominantly in the large urban centers of Rome, Milan, Turin, and Florence. *Italy, Jewish Travel Guide*, by Annie Sacerdoti and Luca Fiorentino, traces Jewish settlements all over the country, from the distant past to the present. I was surprised to learn that many of the best-known Italian Jewish communities were actually quite small. For example, Pitigliano, a revered Jewish town in the Maremma known as "Little Jerusalem," became a refuge for Jews fleeing the Papal States in 1569 and 1593. The town was protected by the Medici family and even boasted a matzoh factory. When Edda Servi Machlin, author of *The Classic Cuisine of the Italian Jews*, lived there from the early 1930s to the early 1950s, the total population was three thousand and the Jews numbered about three hundred.

Under the Este regime, from the thirteenth to sixteenth centuries, the Jews in the Emilia-Romagna city of Ferrara numbered two thousand in a community of twenty-five thousand. (By 1938, there were only some nine hundred Jews in Ferrara.) Livorno enjoyed a sizable Jewish population due to the efforts of Grand Duke Ferdinand I de Medici. He invited all merchants of any nation to settle in Livorno and Pisa. His motives were economic: he wanted to develop Livorno, a small town of only fifteen hundred residents. He offered freedom of trade and religion and protection from the Inquisition. In 1601, 114 Portuguese Jews arrived. A steady immigration increased the total population to 711 Jews in 1622, three thousand in 1689, forty-three hundred in 1784, and five thousand in 1800.

THE EARLY DAYS

Having struggled through respected historian Cecil Roth's epic *History of the Jews in Italy*, I can say that no clear line of tolerance or oppression existed. The story of the Jews in Italy is as complicated as Italy's own very complicated chronicles. One has to keep in mind that for much of its history, Italy was not one nation. Until the Risorgimento in 1848, it was divided into small independent states or principalities, ruled by a variety of idiosyncratic noblemen and, of course, the Papacy. There was great diversity of political and religious practices and socioeconomic conditions. These ever-evolving local policies were echoed in the states' treatment of the Jews. What befell them depended upon where they lived and who was in power at the time.

The early Romans were relatively tolerant of the Jews, who had settled not only in Rome but also in Sicily (Syracusa, Messina), in Campania (Pompeii, Pozzuoli), in Apulia (Taranto and Otranto), and in Ferrara and Milan in the north. With the Edict of Milan in 313, which recognized Catholicism as the official religion, the climate changed. As the empire's power declined, the Papacy became stronger, and from the first to the thirteenth centuries the mood swings and attitudes of the Pope controlled the fate of the Jews, for better or for worse.

Despite the Papacy, with the rebirth of the Holy Roman Empire under Charlemagne, the Jews were granted civil and commercial rights. Under the feudal lords, they were barred from trade and art guilds. As the Church forbade Christians to be moneylenders, this activity was reserved for the Jews, along with the sale of used clothing, or *strazzaria*—literally "rag trade," a term still used today. Moneylending gave the Jews an important commercial and financial role in the economy.

In the earliest times, the largest Jewish communities were in the south, in Rome, Apulia, Calabria, Sardinia, and especially Sicily, where the Jewish population was estimated by some to have reached one hundred thousand. According to Roth, however, that figure was greatly exaggerated, and he put the total at about twenty thousand. The exact number is less important than the fact that there was a sizable Jewish population in a place of such significance to those interested in food and culture. From the eighth to the fourteenth century, under the Ottomans and then the Normans, the Jews in southern Italy thrived. They established schools for Jewish studies and were active in the silk and cloth trade and in the practice of medicine. The majority were artisans: weavers, dyers, cobblers, silver workers, blacksmiths, and carpenters. Sicily was a busy center for all Mediterranean trade, and the comings and goings of the Arabs, Normans, and Aragonese influenced customs and cuisine. The Arabic presence at the table is reflected in sweet-and-sour dishes, the classic combination of pine nuts and raisins that pervades Italian Jewish recipes. The Arabs introduced rice, eggplants, artichokes, and many spices to the island.

The harmony was too good to last. Restrictions against the Sicilian Jews began in 1296. Jewish doctors could no longer treat Christians. Jews were not permitted to hold public office or have Christian servants. The synagogues were not allowed to have any visible outer decoration. In 1392, after

Martin of Aragon ascended to the throne, religious persecutions of the Jews increased. Conditions deteriorated until the expulsion edict of King Ferdinand in 1492.

In north and central Italy it was a fluid story as well. In an eerie preview of Nazi Germany, after the Fourth Lateran Council in 1215, Jews were required to live in separate quarters, and in 1222, under the rule of Emperor Frederick II of Hohenstaufen, who wanted to show his loyalty to the Pope and the Lateran Council, Jews were forced to wear a blue badge in the shape of a T, and the men were required to grow beards as a distinguishing mark. Although the rules would change over the years—yellow circles, yellow or red skullcaps—the law stipulating the wearing of a "badge" would remain in effect in various of the Papal States for centuries.

In 1348, the plague raced through Europe, causing a new wave of persecutions against the Jews. Because they lived in separate quarters in the cities and followed strict religious hygienic practices, Jews did not suffer as much as the rest of the population during the epidemic, with the result that in Germany and northern Europe, Jews became victims of slander, accused of poisoning the wells. There were many massacres and Ashkenazic Jews who could flee headed for Venice, Ferrara, Padua, and Mantua.

The height of the Renaissance was a better period for the Jews. Some communities were tolerant and Jews prospered, actively pursuing banking and moneylending, medicine, printing, trade of precious metals and gems, and fabrics and clothing. Under enlightened rulers such as the Este family in Ferrara, the de'Medicis in Florence, and the Visconti court in Milan, Jews were protected and busy as advisors, scholars, and bankers. But at the same time, other cities were sites of oppression and reduced employment opportunities.

After the Spanish Inquisition, in the years of Columbus's travels, Spanish and Portuguese Jews were hastening their enforced departure from their homelands. They settled in Livorno, Ancona, and Venice, bringing their recipes, along with New World foods like tomatoes, pumpkin, corn, potatoes, and peppers. Jews were also forced to leave southern Italy and the islands of Sicily and Sardinia, which had been under Spanish rule. Some settled in the Marches, in the cities of Ancona and Pesaro, but most went to Rome, which is how so many Sephardic and Arab-inspired dishes entered the Roman culinary repertoire.

THE GHETTO

In the early 1500s, along with the emigration of the southern Italian Jews northward and the sizable influx of Sephardic Jews, Jews from the German states (Ashkenazim) arrived in Italy. This sudden wave of people caused overcrowding in many cities and brought about the institution of segregation. In 1516, the first ghetto of about seven hundred Jews was established in Venice in an isolated part of the city (now called the Cannaregio) which had been the site of a foundry. The word *ghetto* originates from the Venetian hard g pronunciation of *getar*, which means "to smelt." The Giudecca, a term now synonymous with the Jewish quarter, is the long, narrow island in the Venetian lagoon. It was reputed to have been where the Jews lived from the eleventh to the thirteenth century, but recent studies have revealed that the name may derive from *zudega*, Venetian dialect for the verb *giudicare*, meaning "tried" or "judged." In communities other than Venice, however, the Jewish quarter was often called the *giudecca*.

In 1555, under the reign of Pope Paul IV, ghettos were established throughout Italy, and the lives of the Jews were drastically restricted. (Livorno, under Ferdinand I of Tuscany, was the only major city without a ghetto.) They lived in poverty in terribly overcrowded conditions, and the limitations of space resulted in buildings growing taller and taller, up to nine stories, to accommodate the growing population. These structures are the forerunners of the *grattacieli*, or "skyscrapers." The population of the Roman ghetto grew from two thousand in 1555 to seven thousand by the late seventeenth century. By 1938, there were twelve thousand Jews in and around the Roman ghetto. (Today, after the war and emigration, about fifteen thousand Jews live in Rome.)

But there were also towns that didn't permit Jews to live in them at all. In 1569, all Jews were expelled from the Papal States, except for Rome and Ancona, and many Jewish communities disappeared altogether. Jews from Ravenna, Fano, Orvieto, Spoleto, Viterbo, and the Castelli Romani moved to cities where there were ghettos to accept them. In the seventeenth and eighteenth centuries segregation continued. Jews were relegated to the margins of society. Their livelihood in moneylending was threatened, as Christians were eventually permitted to open pawnshops. Then in 1775, in a move that would only worsen conditions for the Jews, Pope Pius VI issued the *Editto sopra gli ebrei*, reinforcing the persecutory measures of his predecessors. According to Cecil Roth, the new laws, among other restrictions, forbade the Jews "to pass the night outside the Ghetto under pain of death. They were not to buy, possess, copy, translate, sell or otherwise dispose of any book on the Talmud. . . . The distinguishing yellow badge was to be worn by men and women alike, both inside the Ghetto and outside. They were not to sell or distribute meat, bread or milk to Christians. They were not to have shops or lodging houses outside the Ghetto. . . . They were not to avail themselves of the services of their [Christian] neighbors as servants, nurses or midwives, or even to light the fires on the Sabbath."

In 1796, with the invasion of Napoleon's armies, the ghettos were liberated. While the habits of years and years of anti-Semitism were hard to erase, in general, life improved for the Jews. From worse to better. Under Napoleon's reign, Jews were allowed to attend public schools and participate in government, but with his downfall in 1815, the Jews suffered a setback and a return to a life of ghetto restrictions. From better to worse, again.

With the Risorgimento in 1848, Italy was finally unified. In 1849, the ghettos were closed for good and the Jews were finally emancipated. Instead of concealing their temples behind anonymous facades, they built impressive synagogues in Florence, Turin, Rome, Milan, Alessandria, and Vercelli. Annie Sacerdoti and Luca Fiorentino, authors of *Italy, Jewish Travel Guide,* describe the transformation: "The Emancipation changed the face of Italian Judaism. Assimilation began, as did the abandoning of the old customs of their fathers, which had been conserved for centuries. In order to consider themselves Italians, the Jews completely integrated themselves into the surrounding environments and often negated, whether consciously or not, their heritage." Cecil Roth notes that assimilation was easy because "there was in the Italian Jew no element of the foreigner. Established in the country for . . . two thousand years, he was as much a native as any other components of the Italian people."

Occasionally while walking in Italy, I am suddenly taken aback when faced with a physical reminder of the ghetto. In Lecce, I noticed a sign stenciled on a building that said Via Sinagoga, yet there was no synagogue in sight. I am still shaken by seeing the signs for Sotoportego or Campo del Gheto Novo in Venice. There is a Via dei Giudei in Messina and also in Bologna, where the main street in the ghetto was aptly named Via dell'Inferno. There was a Corso della Giudecca in Ferrara, a Via Giudea in Trani. In Modena, up until a few years ago, the Via Emilia was called Portico degli Ebrei, and a main street in the ghetto was Via Squallore.

While the segregation they represent is over, gates gone, restrictions lifted, the ghettos as places still exist. Some continue to be a center of Jewish community life. In the ghetto in both Venice and Rome are Jewish museums, containing menorahs, oil lamps, spice boxes, rimonims (for holding the Torah), Torah pointers, fabrics, and ketubahs (marriage documents). Both *quartieri* have a Jewish bakery and many retail shops selling clothing, jewelry, and Jewish artifacts. For the moment, the bakery in Venice on the Calle del Forno still makes matzoh and traditional sweets, but it may close, as the baker's son does not want to remain in his father's business, with its long hours and low pay. While there are no Jewish restaurants in the Venetian ghetto, one can have lunch, with sufficient advance notice, in the Jewish Home for the Aged.

The Forno del Ghetto on Rome's Via Portico d'Ottavia does a brisk business with locals and tourists, selling cheesecake and dried fruit-encrusted "pizza." Restaurants specializing in Jewish food, as well as kosher butcher shops and markets, are found in and around the Roman ghetto and across the Tiber into Trastevere. The most famous restaurant is Piperno, but there is also Paris in Trastevere and da Giggetto and Portico on the Via Portico d'Ottavia. Also on the Via Portico d'Ottavia is a fabulous discount housewares store owned by the Limentani family, relatives of Donatella Limentani Pavoncello, whose lovely cookbook has provided me with delicious family recipes.

ASSIMILATION AND FASCIST ITALY

After the unification of Italy, the largest Jewish communities were to be found in Rome and in the industrial north, in Turin, Milan, Vercelli, and Alessandria. Between the closing of the ghettos and 1938, the Jews lived in relative harmony in Italy, with little anti-Semitism. Cecil Roth, however, regretted the trend toward assimilation. "Jewry had withstood . . . the onslaught of long generations of oppression, but, as elsewhere, it proved unable to resist the insidious blandishments of the new world of opportunity and equality. . . . Synagogues that were formerly open for service twice a day now had difficulty in assembling the necessary quorum once a week. . . . The great synogogal libraries that had been assembled by the devotion of past generations, were neglected or dispersed. . . . Intermarriage, with its corollary of secession from Judaism at least on the part of the next generation, grew alarmingly."

A modest Jewish revival began after 1890. With a powerful new rabbi in Florence, a new Jewish religious magazine, the *Revista israelitica*, and the periodical *Israel*, there was a rebirth of Jewish intellectual life. While Jews didn't return to the orthodoxy of the past, they did revive some pride in being Jewish.

Until Alexander Stille's outstanding and prodigiously researched book, *Benevolence and Betrayal*, in which he traces the lives of five Jewish families under fascism, there hadn't been many books written about the quality of Jewish life in Fascist Italy, except for Giorgio Bassani's memorable *The Garden of the Finzi-Contini*. Modern Italy had been a tolerant country, and the Jews were totally assimilated into the fabric of everyday life. According to Cecil Roth, after emancipation, "there was no part of the world where religious freedom was more real or religious prejudice so small." Most Jews thought of themselves as Italian first and Jewish second. Very few were orthodox in their beliefs and behavior. Like the father in *The Garden of the Finzi-Contini*, some Jews were even members of the Fascist party. Stille writes that "what distinguished the story of Italian Jews from that of Jews elsewhere in Europe was the long coexistence between Jews and fascists in Mussolini's Italy. Italian fascism was in power for sixteen years before it turned anti-Semitic in 1938. Until then Jews were as likely to be members of the Fascist Party as were other conservative-minded Italians. . . . The people of the ghetto were mainly shopkeepers and workers who wanted to be left alone to earn a living and take care of their families. Many of them joined the Fascist Party to avoid trouble with their jobs. Many Italians, Jews and non-Jews, joked that

the initials of the party, PNF (Partito Nazionale Fascista), stood for *per necessita familiare*, 'for family necessity.'"

Stille points out that the "close bond between fascist Italy and its Jews had a whole series of important consequences—both positive and negative—in the lives of individuals. It changed the Jews' sense of national and religious identity. It affected the decision they made about whether to stay or emigrate after 1938. During the German occupation it altered the perceptions of the dangers they faced and the way they reacted to them. After the war it influenced the decisions of most Italian Jews to remain in Italy rather than emigrate to Israel or the United States, as most German and Eastern European Jews did." Italian first, Jewish second.

The spirit of assimilation extended to cuisine. No longer did all Italian Jewish families keep a kosher home. Referring to the Foa family of Turin, Stille says, "Although the Foas and their relatives celebrated Passover each year, none of them was particularly religious or placed special importance upon being Jewish. . . . Most at the Passover seder thought more about the delicious food than about the Hebrew ceremony few of them could remember or understand." In *The Garden of the Finzi-Contini*, Bassani describes a repast served by the wealthy Ferrarese family to their guests: "The tray was heavily laden, with buttered sandwiches of anchovy paste, smoked salmon, caviar, pâté de foie gras, ham; with little vol-au-vents filled with minced chicken in béchamel; with tiny *buricchi*, which had surely come from the prestigious little kosher shop Signora Betsabea . . . had run on the Via Mazzini." The ham and chicken in béchamel are clear violations of the kosher laws. "Signora Betsabea" was in reality a famed Ferrarese ghetto shopkeeper named Nuta Ascoli. He sold goose salami and sturgeon caviar and was known for his fabulous *buricche*. His recipes were eventually given to a Signor Bianconi. Some of them have been orally transcribed in books that I have used as reference.

Stille notes that "while most Jews in the north were cosmopolitan and highly assimilated and far from religious orthodoxy, those in the Roman ghetto were barely literate, deeply religious and powerfully linked to the traditions of their community." That is why so many of the traditional recipes in this book come from the Roman ghetto and are still served there today.

THE WAR AND ITS AFTERMATH

The discrimination against the Jews began subtly in 1930, with the strengthening of relations between Mussolini and Hitler. The writing was on the wall, but because the Jews were so assimilated, they couldn't believe that what was happening in the rest of Nazi-dominated Europe would happen to them. As usual, things went from better to worse. After condemning anti-Semitism on several occasions, Mussolini, in 1938, published the *Manifest of Italian Racism*. In it, Fascism aligned itself with the Nazi ideology and, as if all those years of emigration and assimilation had not existed, announced the existence of a Pure Italian Race. Italian Jews were now forbidden to attend schools, join the army, or participate in public service.

In 1940, when Italy entered the war as Hitler's ally, fascist squads were authorized to sack the Jewish communities, and the synagogues of Turin, Padua, and Ferrara were devastated. Many of the Jews who had not joined the flight to Palestine or the United States were confined in camps. Others became active with the *partigiani* in the resistance. Organizations like Delegazione Assistenza Ebrei Emmigranti (Delasem) helped Italian and foreign Jews alike. In 1943, the roundups and deportations to Nazi concentration camps began. Jews frantically tried to find shelter anywhere they could—in the Alps, with sympathetic Italian friends and families, in convents and monasteries.

In 1945, the nightmare ended, but not without major loss to the Italian Jewish community. Some seventy-five hundred had died in the gas chambers, nine thousand had emigrated, and six thousand had converted. Gradual awareness of the extent of the Nazi devastation, of the death of six million other Jews, only deepened their despair. After the war the Italian constitution reinstated all of the rights taken away under Fascism. Jews were allowed to return to schools, to their professions, and to reopen their businesses. Some were able to recover their possessions.

It has been a long road back. Today, Italy's largest Jewish communities are in Rome and Milan. Although their numbers are small, they have maintained their identity and have grown a bit by welcoming Libyan Jewish refugees in Rome and Iranian Jewish refugees in Milan. In the 1970s, a period of restoration and documentation of the Jewish communities began. Pride in their history was strengthened. Synagogues underwent restoration. Museums were expanded and upgraded, as the bright new wing in the Venice ghetto museum demonstrates. And, fortunately for us, cookbooks were published.

For a Catholic country, Italy is rather anticlerical. Scarcely any Italian will confess to a strong belief in religious dogma, Catholic or Jewish. In 1955, Leslie Fiedler wrote an article, "Roman Holiday," in *Commentary*, as part of a series called An End to Innocence. In Rome at Passover, he set out with his wife and sons to find the communal Seder. His vision was romantic; he wanted a connection to the emotional past, a reaffirmation of religious traditions. Instead he found, much to his disappointment, a badly cut, perfunctory ceremony and a mediocre meal. "It was a completely Roman, non-Paschal meal: broth with pasta, slices of roast veal, and finally artichokes alla giudea . . . the last disconsolate touch."

While that Seder may have been a letdown, I can't ever think of *carciofi alla giudea* as "disconsolate." Italian Jewish food sings of family, it tastes like home should taste. I often jokingly say that if more people were cooking such dishes today, we would have less divorce and fewer unhappy families. This is, of course, an exaggeration, but it is my hope that my grandchildren will cook this food for their families, like their Nonna Gioia—the one who wanted to be Salata.

About the Recipes

This book does not pretend to be a comprehensive study of the food of the Italian Jews. Instead, it is a personal selection of some of my favorite Italian Jewish recipes, those that I thought the home cooks of today would be interested in preparing. In my studies, I found many fascinating traditional recipes, such as brain-filled ravioli, home-cured goose breast, and goose salami, but I have not included them. Although many home cooks might be intrigued by the existence of such foods, and even be likely to buy them if they were available, I don't think they would take the trouble to make them.

Overall, the recipes were selected according to taste and practicality. Most of them are traditional recipes from the past. I chose only a handful of recipes from contemporary Italian Jewish cookbooks, because almost any Italian recipe can be made to work in the kosher kitchen with careful menu planning. In other words, kosher chocolate mousse and smoked-salmon pasta were not of interest to me. I looked for recipes with a long history.

In this era of overmanipulated restaurant-inspired cuisine, it is refreshing to find a repertoire of true home cooking, Mama food, food with soul. Dishes infused with flavors derived from using the freshest ingredients (and not too many of them in one dish) and without much technical sleight of hand. Most of the recipes in this book are simple to prepare. Furthermore, most are economical. While in some major northern Italian cities there were prosperous Jewish families, most of the Italian Jews in the ghetto of Rome or Venice, or in the Italian south, were not wealthy, so the recipes reflect a sense of thriftiness. They also display creativity in the way that a few humble ingre-dients or leftovers are transformed into something special.

MIGRANT CUISINE AND CULINARY ASSIMILATION

When you realize that Italy was divided into inde-pendent states up until 1848, you will understand why there is no single Italian cuisine. Italian food is truly regional food. The differences among the dishes of Lombardy, the Veneto, and Apulia are often as great as the differences among the dishes of Spain, France, and Greece. Jewish Italian food, which is the regional table as cooked by Jews accord-ing to the laws of kashrut, reflects these regional dif-ferences. With a history of intermittent religious persecution, Jews were often forced to move from their homes and homelands. As they roamed from country to country, region to region, their recipes were adapted to reflect the local cuisine and easily gathered ingredients, so that many familiar Italian classics have not only Jewish origins, but Sephardic ones as well. These recipes have such a long history that they have been fully assimilated into the regional repertoire, thus becoming an integral part of Italian cuisine. Non-Jewish Italians and Italian Jews assemble them in the same way. The primary differ-ence is that Jews serve them in meals prepared according to kosher laws.

In order to distinguish certain traditional recipes as Jewish, they are sometimes given names of biblical figures such as Rachel, Rebecca, Ezekiel, and Moses. Or they are designated *all'ebraica, alla giudia*, or occasionally even *alla grega*, referring not to the Greeks but to Sephardic origin. In *La cucina nella tradizione ebraica*, published by the Associazione Donne

Ebrei d'Italia (ADEI-WIZO), a Jewish Women's association, and edited by Giuliana Ascoli Vitali-Norsa, most of the recipes are identified as Italian, Sephardic, or Ashkenazic and then by region: *alla padovana*, *alla romana*, *vecchia ricetta veneziana*, *all'uso marchigiano*. I have focused on the Jewish foods of Rome, Sicily, the Veneto (Padua, Vicenza), Trieste, Emilia-Romagna (Mantua, and especially Ferrara, where a Jewish dialect is spoken to this day), and Tuscany and the Maremma, especially the communities of Livorno and Pitigliano.

RECIPES FROM THE ORAL TRADITION

The recipes in this volume have come from a variety of sources, including photocopies of families' stained recipe cards and conversations with restaurant cooks and owners, but mainly they have been taken from Italian books. No matter what the source, however, the majority of recipes have been transcribed from oral descriptions, and, from my experience, not tested. Most of the recipes are filled with errors: missing steps, missing ingredients, no timing, odd proportions. They are a proverbial minefield.

How could this happen? In part it happened because books put together in an earlier time were not as technical nor as detailed as they are today. Now we measure every grain of salt, designate the size of the pan, prescribe the amount of heat on the stove, and specify the timing down to the minute. Authors used to take home cooks at their word. When asked about how a dish was made, people gave measurements and directions from memory. Very few recipes were transcribed as cooks worked in the kitchen.

In the old days, recipes never had to be written down. The family repertoire was generally small and the ingredients available were limited. The same dishes were prepared over and over again, so recipes were committed to memory and passed on within the family, from mother to daughter. If they were written down at all, they were "sketches," with just enough information to jog the memory of someone who had made the dish before or had seen it prepared. Measurements were vague—a handful of this, a small glassful of that—and cooking directions obtuse—"roast until done." "Assemble dough in the usual manner." Great for those who had seen it, but a total mystery to the rest of us.

Since many of the transcriptions were inaccurate, or poorly translated, I've had to become a culinary detective and trace the recipes back to other sources or test them until they work. It's not that the dishes are technically difficult, only that information gaps need to be filled. Then, too, recipes describing the same dish with minor modifications often have a different name, from city to city, region to region, family to family. I learn of a dish, I get excited and think it's a new discovery, and it turns out to be one I already knew, but with a different name.

Although I respect tradition, I have not been a slave to the recipes. For example, I confess to taking some liberties with cooking times to accommodate modern tastes. I do not call for boiling soup noodles for two hours or fish for over an hour. But whenever long simmering results in a delicious dish with melting textures, I have stayed with the recommended cooking time. I have also kept some vegetable cooking times longer than is currently in vogue if improved flavor was worth the loss of crunch.

Now to raise a sensitive issue. After testing the recipes carefully, I found that many produced very bland food. That is not a crime, of course, but nor is it a reason for a cookbook. Authenticity is important, but I want a recipe only if it produces delicious food. So I've streamlined directions and techniques when practical, and, more often than not, I've increased the amount of herbs, spices, garlic, and other seasonings to bring the recipes more in line with the contemporary palate. Whenever these changes have been made, I let you know, just in case some of you may want to cook the dishes the old way.

The Kosher Laws and the Sabbath

If you just look at the recipes in this book, you may think they are simply Italian. What makes them Jewish is how they are served, the structure of the kosher meal, and the laws of kashrut, which deal with what is permitted *(kosher)* and what is forbidden *(treyfe)*.

Because the Bible says that one must not cook a lamb in its mother's milk, meat and dairy are kept separate in the kitchen and at the table. In a kosher household, different sets of plates and cooking utensils are used for dairy meals and meat-based meals. They cannot even be put into the dishwasher at the same time. No milk products can be served at a meat meal. This means that grated Parmesan cannot be sprinkled on a meat soup or pasta, and no creamy besciamella is layered with a meat-sauced lasagna.

Vegetable stocks are used for making risotti, soups, or other dishes on a dairy menu. No butter- or cream-based pastries are offered at the end of a meat meal. Instead, pastries made with chicken or goose fat, oil, or nondairy margarine are served.

No shellfish are allowed and only fish with scales can be eaten. Therefore swordfish, sturgeon, monkfish, ray, skate, turbot, shark, eel, all crustaceans, octopus, and squid are forbidden. Only animals who chew their cud and have cloven hooves are permissible, so no pork, rabbit, or game may be served. Game birds brought down by hunters and all animals who have died of natural causes are forbidden because they have not been slaughtered in the ritual manner.

Pareve, neutral foods such as fish, vegetables, fruits, and grains, can be taken with meat or dairy products. And if this is not complicated enough, the Ashkenazim and the Sephardim have separate sets of rules. For example, although the Sephardim can eat rice during Passover, the Ashkenazim cannot.

THE SABBATH

According to the orthodox laws of the Sabbath, no work can be done after sundown on Friday. The night is celebrated with the lighting of the candles, the breaking of bread, and the blessing of the wine. It is a rich and festive meal. But since no cooking, which is, of course, work, is permitted until sundown on Saturday, the Saturday midday meal has to be prepared before sunset on Friday.

In the days of no refrigeration, freezers, or microwave ovens, these religious rules inspired great ingenuity. Cooks came up with creative culinary solutions. Dishes were cooked slowly over very low heat, and buried in the hamin, or "oven," for many hours, even overnight. A versatile assortment of preparations was created that tasted good while warm but was also delicious served at room temperature.

Here are five sample Sabbath menus. The final one is for Sabato Bescialach, a Sabbath holiday celebrated by Italian Jews during which a passage in the Torah is read that describes the parting of the Red Sea.

Sabbath Menu I
Stroncatelli in Brodo   *Handmade Pasta in Broth*
Pesce e Indivia   *Fish and Bitter Greens*
Pollo Arrosto all'Arancia, Limone, e Zenzero
Roast Chicken with Orange, Lemon, and Ginger
Carote alla Giudia   *Braised Carrots, Jewish Style*
Polpettine di Spinaci   *Spinach Croquettes*
Pizza Dolce   *Sweet Pizza*

Sabbath Menu II

Riso del Sabato   *Sabbath Rice*

Baccalà al Pomodoro

Salt Cod with Tomato Sauce

Spinaci con Pinoli e Passerine

Spinach with Pine Nuts and Raisins

Budino di Mandorle e Cioccolata

Almond and Chocolate Pudding

Sabbath Menu III

Quadrettini di Patate in Brodo

Potato Dumplings in Broth

Concia   *Zucchini with Mint and Vinegar*

Triglie alla Mosaica   *Red Mullet, Jewish Style*

Rotolo di Vitello coi Colori

Veal Stuffed with Peppers and an Omelet

Piselli in Tegame   *Braised Peas*

Bocca di Dama   *Almond Sponge Cake*

Sabbath Menu IV

Quadrucci in Brodo con Spinaci

Pasta Squares in Broth with Spinach

Indivia e Alici   *Curly Endive with Anchovies*

Stracotto di Manzo   *Braised Beef in Red Wine*

Cuscussù alla Livornese

Livornese Couscous with Meatballs, White Beans, and Greens

Crostata di Marmellata di Visciole e Mandorle

Sour Cherry Jam and Almond Tart

Sabato Bescialach Menu

Carciofi alla Romana

Artichokes with Mint and Garlic, Roman Style

Hamin per Sabato

Sabbath Pasta Dish from Emilia-Romagna

Spinaci con Pinoli e Passerine

Spinach with Pine Nuts and Raisins

frutta fresca   *fresh fruit*

The Jewish Holidays

Here are some brief descriptions of the major Jewish holidays, along with suggested menus using recipes in this book. Although Italian Jews continue to recognize many of these holidays, they are not celebrated today with the religious zeal and orthodoxy of the past. There are so few kosher food shops and so few Jewish neighborhoods, that the holiday celebrations are essentially invisible to outsiders. Getting ready for Passover still prompts a major housecleaning at the bakery on the Via Portico d'Ottavia in Rome, but life for the majority of Italian Jews has become highly secular.

ROSH HASHANAH: THE JEWISH NEW YEAR

This holiday occurs on the first day of Tishri, usually in late September or early October. The New Year celebrations, which last for two days, include a bounty of sweet foods.

Rosh Hashanah Menu I

Stroncatelli in Brodo   *Handmade Pasta in Broth*

Triglie alla Mosaica   *Red Mullet, Jewish Style*

Polpettone di Pollo   *Chicken Loaf*

Zucca in Agrodolce   *Sweet-and-Sour Squash*

Sfratti   *Nut-Filled Cookie Sticks*

Rosh Hashanah Menu II

Stroncatelli in Brodo   *Handmade Pasta in Broth*

Pesce Freddo alla Salsa di Noce

Fish with Walnut Sauce

Delizie di Pollo con Peperoni

Chicken Morsels with Peppers

Sformato di Spinaci   *Spinach Pudding*

Pan di Spagna alle Nocciole

Hazelnut Sponge Cake

Rosh Hashanah Menu III

Risotto con Regagli   *Rice with Giblets*

Pollo Arrosto all'Arancia, Limone, e Zenzero

Roast Chicken with Orange, Lemon, and Ginger

Stufadin di Zuca Zala

Braised Meat with Butternut Squash

Verze Sofegae   *Suffocated Cabbage*

Mele Cotogne in Giulebbe   *Quince in Syrup*

Pizza Dolce   *Sweet Pizza*

YOM KIPPUR: THE DAY OF ATONEMENT

On the tenth day of Tishri, after Rosh Hashanah, this day of fasting and praying is celebrated. The meal before the fast must be filling, simple, and not highly seasoned, to avoid making the diners thirsty. The fast might be broken with this menu.

Yom Kippur Break-the-Fast Menu

Stroncatelli in Brodo   *Handmade Pasta in Broth*

Triglie con Pinoli e Passerine

Mullet with Pine Nuts and Raisins

OR

Pesce in Saor   *Marinated Fish*

Budino di Pollo all'Ebraica   *Jewish-Style Chicken Pudding*

Zucca Disfatta   *Melted Golden Squash*

Torzelli   *Deep-fried Curly Endive*

Roschette Dolce   *Ring-Shaped Cookies*

Bocca di Dama   *Almond Cake with Yom Kippur variation*

SUKKOT: THE FEAST OF THE TABERNACLES

This holiday starts on the fifteenth day of Tishri, usually in early October, and lasts for eight days. The sukkah, a hut built with branches, symbolizes God's protection and is a representation of the huts the Jews lived in while in the wilderness. It is built for the holiday and is where meals are taken. Four symbolic plants listed in the Torah are part of the holiday rituals. They are the *etrog* (citron), a palm frond, a myrtle branch, and a willow branch. Sukkot is a harvest festival.

Sukkot Harvest Menu

Rape e Riso   *Broth with Broccoli Rabe and Rice*

Pizza Ebraica di Erbe   *Double-Crusted Vegetable Pie*

Scaloppine di Vitello alla Lattuga

Veal Scallops with Lettuce

Cavolo Ripieno per Simhà Torà   *Stuffed Cabbage*

Carote alla Giudia   *Braised Carrots, Jewish Style*

Pomodori con l'Uva   *Tomatoes with Grape Juice*

Finocchi alla Giudia   *Braised Fennel, Jewish Style*

Frutta Caramellata   *Caramelized Fresh Fruit*

Bianco Mangia   *Almond-Filled Pastries I*

Dolce di Tagliatelle   *Noodle Pudding*

HANUKKAH: THE FESTIVAL OF LIGHTS

This joyful holiday begins on the twenty-fifth day of Kislev, which usually falls in December, and lasts eight days. It celebrates the 165 B.C. uprising of a small group of Jews, the first time Jews resorted to arms to preserve their religion. When they arrived at the Temple of Jerusalem, all of the oil for the lamps was gone except for one container, which held enough for only one night. Miraculously, however, the oil lasted for eight days. To celebrate the miracle of the oil, many fried foods are served during this holiday.

Hanukkah Menu I
Riso del Sabato   *Sabbath Rice*
Pollo Fritto per Hanucca   *Fried Chicken for Hanukkah*
Caponata alla Giudia
Sweet-and-Sour Eggplant, Jewish Style
Frittelle di Zucca   *Squash Fritters from the Veneto*

Hanukkah Menu II
Ceci con Pennerelli   *Chickpea and Veal Shank Soup*
Baccalà al Pomodoro   *Salt Cod with Tomato Sauce*
Torzelli   *Deep-fried Curly Endive*
Scodelline   *Almond Pudding*
Pan di Spagna alla Nocciole   *Hazelnut Sponge Cake*

Dairy Menu for Hanukkah
Quadrucci in Brodo con Spinaci
Pasta Squares in Broth with Spinach
Melanzane in Insalata   *Grilled Eggplant*
Roba Fritta   *Mixed Fry*
Bolo   *Ring-Shaped Sweet Bread*

PURIM: THE FESTIVAL OF QUEEN ESTHER

This day of celebration, which falls on the fourteenth day of Adar, usually in March, commemorates Queen Esther of Persia's clever triumph over the evil minister Haman, who had decreed death to all Jews. Although in most of the Sephardic and Ashkenazic world this is a vegetarian and dairy meal, in Italy meat is served.

Purim Menu
Quadrucci in Brodo con Spinaci
Pasta Squares in Broth with Spinach
Buricche   *Pastry Turnovers*
Agnello Arrosto al Rosmarino, Aglio, e Limone
Roast Lamb with Rosemary, Garlic, and Lemon
Testine di Spinaci   *Spinach Stems*

Carciofi alla Romana
Artichokes with Mint and Garlic, Roman Style
Orecchie di Amman   *Haman's Ears*
Scodelline   *Almond Pudding*

PESACH: PASSOVER

The holiday begins on the fourteenth day of Nissan, usually in April, and lasts eight days. It celebrates the exodus of the Jews from Egypt, which occurred in such haste that their bread dough did not have time to rise. To commemorate this event, no leavened foods (*hametz*) may be eaten. Matzoh is the main bread product served, but it is made from wheat flour that is ground just before baking so that it will not have time to ferment. Special china and silverware are used for this holiday and a major spring cleaning is usually undertaken to rid the house of any traces of *hametz*.

Ritual dinners called Seders occur the first and second nights of the holiday. At the Seder, Jews recite the story of the Exodus from a book called the Haggadah. The centerpiece of the table is the Seder plate, which is divided into sections to hold the ritual foods: the *karpas*, a mild green herb such as parsley or romaine represents new growth and is dipped in salt water symbolizing the tears of the slaves; the *maror*, or bitter herb, which is usually horseradish or chicory, recalls the bitter times of slavery; the *betza*, or roasted egg, stands for the sacrificial offering to God in the Temple, required as an expression of Thanksgiving; the *zeroah*, or roasted lamb bone, depicts the sacrifice of a lamb by the slaves on the eve of the Exodus—a symbol of religious freedom; and finally, the *haroset*, a fruit-and-nut paste, represents the mortar used by the Jews to construct the pyramids.

Two Seder menus follow, one for each of the two nights.

A First Seder Menu

Uova Inhaminade   *Long-Cooked Eggs, Trieste Style*

Brodo con Polpette e Uova per Pesach
Passover Soup with Chicken Dumplings and Eggs

Triglie alla Mosaica   *Red Mullet, Jewish Style*

Capretto e Carciofi all'Uova e Limone
Kid and Artichokes with Egg and Lemon

Carciofata di Trieste   *Spring Vegetable Stew*

Scodelline   *Almond Pudding*

Torta di Carote del Veneto
Carrot Cake from the Veneto

A Second Seder Menu

Brodo con Polpette e Uova per Pesach
Passover Soup with Chicken Dumplings and Eggs

Uova Inhaminade   *Long-Cooked Eggs, Trieste Style*

Scacchi   *Passover Meat and Matzoh Pie*

Pollo Arrosto all'Arancia, Limone, e Zenzero
Roast Chicken with Orange, Lemon, and Ginger

Carciofi alla Giudia
Crispy Fried Artichokes, Jewish Style

Crochette di Patate   *Potato Croquettes*

Piselli in Tegame   *Braised Peas*

Pan di Spagna alle Nocciole
Passover Hazelnut Sponge Cake

Frutta Caramellata   *Caramelized Fresh Fruit*

SHAVUOT: FESTIVAL OF THE GIVING OF THE TORAH

Falling on the sixth day of Sivan, usually in late May or early June, this festival celebrates God giving the Torah, including the Ten Commandments, to the Israelites at Mount Sinai. This overwhelming event made every one of the Israelites direct witnesses to God's existence. Following the Revelation, Moses ascended Mount Sinai, where he was given the two stone tablets of the Covenant on which were engraved the Ten Commandments. All else that God told him he recorded on a scroll, the Torah. This is traditionally a dairy meal.

Shavuot Menu

Sformato di Spinaci   *Spinach Pudding*

OR

Rotoli di Spinaci e Ricotta
Pasta Rolls with Spinach and Ricotta Filling

Pizza Ebraica di Erbe   *Double-Crusted Vegetable Pie*

Bomba di Riso   *Baked Rice Casserole*

Pesce al Sugo di Carciofi
Fish with a Sauce of Artichokes

Tonno Fresco con Piselli   *Fresh Tuna with Peas*

Cassola   *Ricotta Soufflé Pancake*

Antipasti
APPETIZERS

Crostini di Spuma di Tonno   *Crostini with Tuna*

Crostini di Mascarpone, Gorgonzola, e Nocciole   *Crostini with Cheeses and Hazelnuts*

Crostini di Peperoni   *Crostini with Roasted Peppers*

Crostini di Funghi   *Two Crostini with Mushrooms*

Polpettone di Tonno Cotto   *Tuna Loaf*

Fegato alle Uova Sode   *Chopped Liver, Italian Style*

Uova Inhaminade   *Long-Cooked Eggs, Trieste Style*

Roschette   *Savory Pastry Rings*

Rebecchine di Gerusalemme   *Polenta and Anchovy Fritters*

Buricche   *Pastry Turnovers*

Pizza Ebraica di Erbe   *Double-Crusted Vegetable Pie*

Pizza di Ricotta   *Ricotta Pie with Potato Crust*

Torta di Carciofi   *Artichoke and Egg Tart*

Antipasti

In Italian Jewish cooking, antipasti, the small bites of food traditionally served at the start of the Italian meal, are meant to stimulate the appetite, just as they are on every Italian table. This chapter includes assorted spreads for *crostini*, little filled pastries called *buricche*, polenta fritters, and vegetable pies. The pies could, of course, be served as the centerpiece of a lunch or supper, but they are customarily offered at the beginning of a meal. Along with the fritters and pastries, one might set out slices of *polpettone di tonno cotto*, tuna loaf accompanied with a lemon-caper mayonnaise.

At the Jewish markets in Italy, such cold cuts as goose salami and *carne secca*, air-dried beef similar to the famed northern Italian *bresaola* but prepared in the kosher manner, are available and would be part of the antipasto table. Slices of cooked chicken or turkey sausage and *bresaola* can stand in for these delicacies.

Recipes in other chapters can also be served as appetizers. Among them are *testine* (marinated spinach stems), sweet-and-sour pumpkin squash, and *concia* (marinated zucchini). White beans with tuna, even potato croquettes or miniature *bombe di riso*, called *supplì*, would be appropriate starters.

Crostini di Spuma di Tonno
CROSTINI WITH TUNA

In Italy, most recipes that call for tuna are referring to canned tuna packed in olive oil. The best is *ventresca di tonno*, rich undercut (belly) packed in high-quality olive oil. (Of course, you can use fresh tuna and sauté it in olive oil.) This recipe for tuna pâté evolved from a description in Giuseppe Maffioli's *La cucina padovana*. The spread can be bound with mayonnaise instead of butter, but it will not have the unctuous texture of traditional Jewish tuna pâté.

SERVES 6 TO 8

½ pound canned olive oil-packed tuna, preferably Italian

5 tablespoons unsalted butter, at room temperature

Grated zest of 1 lemon

2 olive oil-packed anchovy fillets, drained and finely minced (optional)

Fresh lemon juice to taste

Freshly ground black pepper to taste

12 slices coarse country bread, toasted or grilled

3 tablespoons capers, rinsed and coarsely chopped

3 tablespoons coarsely chopped pitted green olives

Place the tuna (undrained) in a food processor and pulse to break it up. Add the butter, lemon zest, and anchovies (if using) and process until you have a smooth, creamy puree. Season with lemon juice and pepper. The anchovies should provide enough salt.

Spread on the bread slices and top with the capers and olives.

VARIATION:

Author Milka Passigli describes a recipe that combines ½ pound canned olive oil-packed tuna, ½ pound mascarpone cheese, and ½ cup unsalted butter, at room temperature. Mix them together in a food processor, season to taste with salt and freshly ground black pepper, and serve spread on toasted or grilled bread. Garnish with chopped fresh flat-leaf parsley. Alternatively, add 1 cup mashed potato in place of the cheese.

Crostini di Mascarpone, Gorgonzola, e Nocciole
CROSTINI WITH CHEESES AND HAZELNUTS

Crostini don't have to be complicated to be good. Here's a simple but rich spread for toasted bread inspired by a recipe in Milka Belgrado Passigli's *Le ricette di casa mia*. Many of the book's recipes are based on family traditions but updated for the modern kitchen. Therefore, I don't think it sacrilegious to top this with a thin slice of ripe pear.

SERVES 6

¼ pound mascarpone cheese

¼ pound Gorgonzola dolcelatte cheese

¼ cup hazelnuts, toasted, peeled, and coarsely chopped

12 slices coarse country bread, toasted or grilled

Combine the cheeses in a food processor. Add the nuts and pulse briefly. You do not want to overprocess or the texture will be lost. Spread the mixture on the bread and serve.

 Crostini di Mascarpone, Gorgonzola, e Nocciole

Crostini with Cheeses and Hazelnuts

Crostini di Peperoni
CROSTINI WITH ROASTED PEPPERS

In the original recipe, as related to Milka Passigli by her friend Olga, onions and peppers are boiled in water for an hour, then pureed. To my palate that's not a kind way to handle peppers, as too much of their flavor is lost. So to accentuate their lively taste and bring up their sweetness, I have substituted roasted peppers.

SERVES 6 TO 8

3 tablespoons olive oil, or as needed

2 onions, chopped

4 medium or 3 large roasted red peppers, chopped

Fresh lemon juice to taste

Salt and freshly ground black pepper to taste

*4 tablespoons capers, rinsed and chopped, and/or
3 tablespoons chopped fresh flat-leaf parsley or basil*

12 slices coarse country bread, toasted or grilled

Chopped fresh flat-leaf parsley or basil for garnish

Warm the 3 tablespoons olive oil in a sauté pan over medium heat. Add the onions and cook, stirring, until very soft, 12 to 15 minutes.

Transfer to a food processor and add the roasted peppers. Pulse to a coarse puree. Add the lemon juice, salt, and pepper. Beat in a little more oil if the puree is too dense. Add the capers and/or parsley or basil. Spread the mixture on the bread slices and top with additional chopped parsley or basil.

Crostini di Funghi
TWO CROSTINI WITH MUSHROOMS

Wild mushrooms such as porcini or chanterelles will result in a wonderfully intense spread. If, however, all you can find at the market are cultivated white or brown mushrooms, the mixture will still be tasty if you increase the garlic and add a pinch of hot pepper. Another way to heighten the flavor is to add a few softened slices of dried porcini and their strained soaking liquid. Here are two versions of the mushroom spread, one made with *besciamella*, a classic cream sauce, and one made without, depending on whether the meal is meat or dairy.

EACH RECIPE SERVES 6

MUSHROOM CROSTINI I

3 tablespoons unsalted butter or olive oil

1/2 pound fresh mushrooms, chopped

1 cup Classic Cream Sauce, page 162

*2 tablespoons dried porcini (optional) soaked in
hot water for 30 minutes, strained, with liquid reserved
and mushrooms chopped*

Salt and freshly ground black pepper, to taste

Freshly grated nutmeg, to taste

12 small slices coarse country bread, toasted or grilled

Grated Parmesan cheese for garnish

Warm the butter or olive oil in a large sauté pan over high heat. Add the fresh mushrooms, stirring occasionally, until they give off their liquid, about 6 minutes. Add the *besciamella* and the porcini and soaking liquid (if using). Season with salt, pepper, and nutmeg.

Spread the warm mixture on the bread slices and top with a dusting of Parmesan. Slip under a preheated broiler until glazed, 3 to 4 minutes. Serve hot.

Mushroom Crostini II

3 tablespoons olive oil

½ pound fresh mushrooms, chopped

2 cloves garlic, finely minced

Pinch of red pepper flakes

Salt and freshly ground black pepper to taste

12 small slices coarse country bread, toasted or grilled

Chopped fresh flat-leaf Italian parsley for garnish

Warm the olive oil in a sauté pan over medium heat. Add the mushrooms and cook, stirring often, until they give off a little liquid, about 8 minutes. Add the garlic and red pepper flakes and cook for a few more minutes to blend the flavors. Transfer to a food processor and pulse until coarsely pureed. Season with salt and pepper.

Spread the warm mixture on the bread slices. Sprinkle with chopped parsley and serve at once.

Polpettone di Tonno Cotto
Tuna Loaf

Not only do Italian Jewish cookbooks have sections for foods served at Passover and other holiday repasts, but one for dairy meals as well. Tuna loaf is a very old recipe that appears in the roster of dairy dishes in nearly all of the Jewish anthologies. It can be served as part of an antipasto assortment or as a luncheon dish. Makes a great sandwich, too.

Serves 6

9 ounces olive oil-packed tuna, preferably Italian (see recipe introduction, page 24)

¼ cup grated Parmesan cheese

¾ cup fresh bread crumbs, soaked in milk and squeezed dry

3 eggs

Salt and freshly ground black pepper to taste

Mayonnaise flavored with capers, lemon, and anchovies (page 162-3) or Tuna Sauce (page 166)

Place the tuna (undrained) in a food processor and pulse to break it up. Add the Parmesan cheese, bread crumbs, and eggs and process until you have a smooth puree. Season with salt and pepper. Form the tuna into a sausage shape and wrap in cheesecloth or plastic wrap.

Bring a saucepan of lightly salted water to a gentle boil, slip the tuna "sausage" into the water, adjust the heat, and poach until set, about 25 minutes. Remove from the water, let cool, and chill well.

To serve, slice the loaf and serve chilled with the mayonnaise or tuna sauce.

Note: Edda Servi Machlin, in her ground-breaking book, *The Classic Cuisine of the Italian Jews*, poaches her tuna loaf in a mixture of water and milk, then uses some of the poaching liquid to make a sort of mayonnaise flavored with capers and anchovies.

Fegato alle Uova Sode

CHOPPED LIVER, ITALIAN STYLE

Although this spread resembles the traditional Jewish American chopped chicken liver found in delicatessens, it includes the very Italian addition of *vino*. The recipe has been adapted from a description in Giuseppe Maffioli's *La cucina padovana*, and is probably Ashkenazic in origin. To keep this kosher, flame-singe the livers before sautéing and cook them until there is no trace of pink remaining.

SERVES 6

½ cup olive oil or, preferably, rendered chicken or duck fat

2 or 3 onions, finely chopped

*1 pound chicken, duck, or goose livers,
well trimmed of connective pieces and any dark spots*

⅓ cup dry white wine

6 hard-boiled eggs

Salt and freshly ground black pepper to taste

*Toasted or grilled coarse country bread slices,
crackers, or matzohs for serving*

Using 2 sauté pans, divide the olive oil or chicken or duck fat evenly between them. Add the onions to one pan and sauté over medium heat until they are dark golden brown, 15 to 20 minutes.

Meanwhile, in the other pan, sauté the livers over medium heat until they are medium-cooked, 5 to 7 minutes. There should still be quite a bit of pink, but they should not show any signs of blood. During the last few minutes of cooking, add the white wine and allow most of it to evaporate. Remove from the heat and chop the livers coarsely. Reserve the pan juices.

Peel and chop the hard-boiled eggs. (If you decide to chop these in a food processor, pulse them briefly in very small batches; you do not want to lose the chunky texture.)

In a bowl, combine the warm onions and livers and the chopped eggs. Add all of the pan juices and mix well. Season with salt and pepper. If the mixture seems a little dry, add more melted fat or olive oil. Serve with bread, crackers, or matzohs.

Uova Inhaminade

LONG-COOKED EGGS, TRIESTE STYLE

The recipe for eggs cooked with onion skins is Sephardic in origin. Greek, Turkish, and Italian Jews traditionally serve these at Passover. The name comes from the word *hamin*, which means "oven." Traditionally the eggs were placed in a heavy casserole that was then buried in the smoldering ashes of a wood-burning oven for eight to twelve hours. The same results can be achieved by cooking them on top of the stove over very, very low heat. A faint oniony taste infuses the eggs, and they become pale brown and develop an incredibly creamy texture. Eat them plain or serve them with sliced cucumbers and radishes or with bread and *caprino* (goat) cheese.

In a variation that the Italians call *uova turche* (Turkish eggs) or *uova inhaminade al caffè* (eggs baked with coffee), 1 ½ cups coffee grounds are added along with the onion skins.

SERVES 8

3 cups brown or red onion skins

8 eggs, at room temperature

1 bay leaf

4 whole cloves

8 black peppercorns

1 1/2 cups coffee grounds (optional)

1/4 cup olive oil

Layer some of the onion skins on the bottom of a heavy pot. Place the eggs atop the onion skins. Add the bay leaf, cloves, and peppercorns, then add more onion skins and the coffee grounds (if using). Add cold water to cover and the olive oil, then cover the pot tightly. Place the pot over very low heat and cook at a bare simmer for 6 hours. Check the eggs occasionally, and add water as needed to keep them covered. When the eggs are ready, plunge into cold water and peel.

Roschette
Savory Pastry Rings

These savory pastries, a specialty of Livorno, have the texture of bread sticks but are formed into rings. They resemble the Egyptian *semit* or Apulian *taralli*. Author Carol Field, in her excellent *Italy in Small Bites*, has a version of this recipe using *1/2* cup oil and *3/4* cup water. She suggests a double rising for better texture, and the use of an egg wash to promote a golden finish more quickly.

Makes About 24 Rings

2 teaspoons active dry yeast

1 1/4 cups warm water

4 tablespoons olive oil, plus olive oil for brushing

3 3/4 cups all-purpose flour

2 teaspoons salt

Semolina flour for dusting

1/4 cup aniseeds

1 egg yolk lightly beaten with a little water

Combine the yeast and warm water in the bowl of a stand mixer and let stand until foamy, about 10 minutes. Add the 4 tablespoons oil, then beat in the flour and salt with the paddle attachment until the dough comes together. Switch to the dough hook and knead for about 5 minutes until almost smooth.

Turn out onto a work surface dusted with semolina flour and knead until smooth and elastic, 3 to 5 minutes. Pat into a 4-by-14-inch rectangle and brush with olive oil. Cover with a tea towel and let rise until doubled, about 1 1/2 hours.

Preheat an oven to 400 degrees F. Lightly oil 2 baking sheets or line with parchment paper. Uncover the dough, dust with semolina flour, and sprinkle with the aniseeds.

Working from a long side, cut the rectangle into 4 equal pieces. Then cut each piece crosswise into 6 equal strips. You should have 24 pieces in all. Using your palms, roll and stretch each strip until it is almost 6 inches long. Form each strip into a ring and pinch the ends together. Place the rings on the prepared baking sheets. At this point, the circles can be covered again and allowed to rise for 45 minutes, or they can be baked immediately (see recipe introduction).

Brush the circles with the egg yolk-water mixture. Bake until golden, about 20 minutes. Serve warm.

 Rebecchine di Gerusalemme

Polenta and Anchovy Fritters

Rebecchine di Gerusalemme
Polenta and Anchovy Fritters

Versions of these anchovy-filled polenta sandwiches appear in almost every book on the cuisine of Italian Jews, but nowhere can I find a reliable story about the origin of the name. I doubt that these fritters were ever served in Jerusalem. Instead, the name Gerusalemme seems to be the Italian way to let you know that the dish originated in the Jewish community, just as the name Rebecca, or in this case the diminutive Rebecchine, indicates a Jewish origin.

While most traditional polenta recipes call for pouring the cornmeal in a fine stream into boiling water and advise you to stir the grain like crazy to prevent lumps, I find that combining the polenta with cold water in the pot and then gradually bringing it to a boil while whisking occasionally is foolproof in the prevention of dreaded lumps.

Serves 6 to 8

1 cup polenta (not instant)

4 cups water

Salt

¼ pound salt-packed anchovies (about 12 anchovies)

Olive oil for sautéing

Vegetable oil or pure olive oil for deep-frying

1 or 2 eggs

All-purpose flour for dusting

Combine the polenta, cold water, and 1 teaspoon of salt in a heavy-bottomed saucepan and place over medium heat. Bring to a gentle boil, whisking occasionally. Adjust the heat to maintain a simmer and cook, stirring often, until very thick and no longer grainy on the tongue, about 30 minutes. If the polenta becomes quite thick but is still grainy, stir in some hot water and continue to simmer until cooked through and soft. Pour out onto an oiled baking sheet, forming a layer ½ inch thick. Let cool, then chill until fully set.

Fillet and rinse the salted anchovies, then chop them coarsely. Place them in a sauté pan with 2 tablespoons olive oil over low heat. Cook, stirring often with a fork, until the anchovies soften and melt, about 5 minutes. It is imperative that they do not burn. Remove from the heat.

Using a cookie or biscuit cutter 2½ to 3 inches in diameter, cut the chilled polenta into rounds. Spread half of them with the anchovy puree. Top them with the remaining rounds.

Pour vegetable or olive oil into a wide, deep sauté pan to a depth of 2 inches. Place over medium-high heat and heat to 375 degrees F. Meanwhile, break 1 egg into a shallow bowl and beat until blended. Spread some flour on a plate.

Working with a few polenta sandwiches at a time, dip them into the beaten egg and then into the flour. (Some cooks reverse the order, dipping them first in flour, then in egg.) Slip them into the hot oil, a few at a time, and fry, turning once, until golden, about 4 minutes total. Remove with a slotted skimmer to paper towels to drain. Serve warm.

Note: If you don't like anchovies, you can cut the cooked polenta into fingers, dredge them lightly in flour, and fry them in the same manner. Or you can sandwich the polenta rounds with slices of Fontina or mozzarella cheese, dip them in egg and then flour, and then deep-fry.

Buricche

Pastry Turnovers

Buricche, sometimes spelled *burricchi* and also called *pasticci*, are highly popular in Sephardic cuisine, where they are called *borekas*. If the name seems familiar, it is because these filled pastries are related to the well-known Turkish *borek*. The dough can be either a simple one or one that results in a rich, layered flaky pastry. As you can buy puff pastry, I have given you just the recipe for plain oil-based dough. You also can make these with a *pasta frolla salata*, the same pastry used for the *Torta di Carciofi* (Artichoke and Egg Tart, page 37) and *Pizza Ebraica di Erbe* (Double-Crusted Vegetable Pie, page 34).

These turnovers are an ideal example of the thriftiness of the Italian Jewish kitchen, where little bits of leftovers are used and made "special." Leftover cooked meat, poultry, chopped chicken liver, fish, mashed cooked eggplant seasoned with onion and tomato, and the like are all possibilities. Be sure to season the fillings highly, as their flavors are muted by the crust. Two different fillings are given here, each sufficient to fill half the pastry recipe. The chicken filling, which is in the style of Ferrara, is possibly the one that was stuffed into the *buricche* served by Signora Betsabea in Giorgio Bassani's *The Garden of the Finzi-Contini*.

Makes About 48 Small Turnovers

For the meat filling:

2 tablespoons rendered chicken fat or olive oil

1 onion, finely chopped

3 tablespoons chopped fresh flat-leaf parsley

1 teaspoon minced garlic

3/4 pound ground beef

1/2 teaspoon ground cinnamon (optional)

1/4 teaspoon freshly grated nutmeg

Salt and freshly ground black pepper to taste

1/3 cup pine nuts

1/3 cup raisins, plumped in hot water
for 30 minutes and drained

1 egg, lightly beaten

3 to 4 tablespoons fine dried bread crumbs

For the chicken filling:

3 tablespoons rendered chicken fat

1 onion, finely chopped

3/4 pound ground chicken or turkey

1/4 cup water or chicken broth

3 slices bread, soaked in chicken broth and squeezed dry

1 egg, lightly beaten

Salt and freshly ground black pepper to taste

Freshly grated nutmeg to taste

For the pastry:

1 cup vegetable oil or olive oil

1 cup warm water

1 teaspoon salt

5 to 6 cups all-purpose flour, or as needed

1 egg yolk, lightly beaten with a little water

To make the meat filling, melt the chicken fat or warm the oil in a large sauté pan over medium heat. Add the onion and sauté, stirring often, until softened, about 8 minutes. Add the parsley, garlic, ground beef, cinnamon (if using), nutmeg, salt, and pepper. Cook, stirring occasionally, until the beef is cooked through, about 10 minutes. Remove from the heat and add the pine nuts, raisins, egg, and bread crumbs, mixing well. Let the filling cool for at least 30 minutes. It can be made up to 8 hours ahead. (This filling can also be used in a double-crusted meat pie, encased in strudel crust, or used to fill *scacchi*, the matzoh pie on page 150.)

To make the chicken filling, melt the chicken fat in a large sauté pan over medium heat. Add the onion and sauté, stirring often, until softened, about 8 minutes. Add the chicken or turkey, stir well, and sauté for 5 minutes. Add the water or broth and cook until the liquid is absorbed and the meat is tender, about 8 minutes longer. Remove from the heat and add the softened bread and the egg, mixing well. Season highly with the salt, pepper, and nutmeg, as chicken and turkey can be bland. Let the filling cool for at least 30 minutes. It can be made up to 8 hours ahead.

To make the pastry, in a large bowl, combine the oil, warm water, salt, and as much of the flour as needed for the mixture to come together in a workable dough. Cover with a tea towel and let stand at room temperature for about 20 minutes. (You do not have to chill this dough.)

Preheat an oven to 350 degrees F. Lightly oil 2 baking sheets or line them with parchment paper.

The dough should be rather springy. The trimmings can be rerolled but the dough will need to rest between rollings. Divide the dough into 3 or 4 pieces. On a lightly floured work surface, roll out 1 piece as thin as possible. Using a cookie cutter or glass 3 inches in diameter, cut out rounds. Place about 1 tablespoon of the filling on each round, fold over to form a half-moon, and pinch the edges to seal. Place the rounds on a prepared baking sheet, spacing them well apart. Repeat until all the dough and filling are used.

(The turnovers can be assembled up to 1 day in advance and refrigerated until baking. They can also be frozen on the baking sheets, transferred to lock-top bags, and frozen for up to 3 months. Bake without thawing; increase the baking time to about 40 minutes.)

Brush the pastries with the egg yolk–water mixture. (Some versions of this recipe suggest sprinkling the turnovers with sesame seeds.) Bake until golden, about 30 minutes. Remove from the oven and serve warm.

Variations:

The turnovers also can be filled with a fish mixture. Possible combinations include finely chopped cooked fish mixed with a little chopped anchovy and grated raw or cooked chopped onion (optional) bound with egg; flaked cooked fish, a thick *besciamella* (see page 162), some slivered almonds, chopped parsley, and a little grated lemon zest (optional); or canned tuna, chopped black olives, capers, lemon zest, and olive oil.

Pizza Ebraica di Erbe

Double-Crusted Vegetable Pie

Called a Jewish-style pizza, this dish probably has its origins in the Italian south. Here the word pizza is related to the Greek *pitta*, a name for filo pies and a term still in use in Apulia, where many dishes reflect a Greek heritage. This recipe calls for *pasta frolla salata*, a short pastry that gives it a wonderful richness.

Serves 8

For the pastry:

2 ½ cups all-purpose flour

½ teaspoon salt

8 to 10 tablespoons chilled unsalted butter or margarine

1 egg, lightly beaten

2 to 4 tablespoons water, or as needed

For the filling:

Juice of 1 lemon

3 large or 5 medium artichokes

Olive oil

1 large onion, diced

1 large bunch fresh flat-leaf parsley, chopped (about ⅓ cup)

1 pound beet greens or spinach, coarsely chopped

2 pounds English peas, shelled (about 2 cups shelled)

1 tablespoon salt

½ teaspoon freshly ground black pepper

½ teaspoon freshly grated nutmeg, or to taste

2 eggs, lightly beaten

Olive oil or lightly beaten egg for coating pastry

To make the pastry, stir together the flour and salt in a bowl or in the container of a food processor. Cut in the butter or margarine until the mixture resembles coarse meal. Blend in the egg and as much water as needed for the dough to come together into a rough ball. Divide the dough in into two pieces, one slightly larger than the other, and flatten each portion into a disk. Place the disks in a plastic bag and refrigerate for 1 hour.

To make the filling, have ready a large bowl filled with water to which you have added the lemon juice. Working with 1 artichoke at a time, remove the stems and all the leaves until you reach the pale green heart. Pare away the dark green areas from the base. Cut the artichoke in half lengthwise and scoop out and discard the choke from each half. Then cut each half lengthwise into ¼-inch-thick slices and drop into the lemon water to prevent discoloration.

Pour enough olive oil into a large sauté pan to form a film on the bottom and place over medium heat. Add the onion and parsley and sauté 3 to 4 minutes. Drain the artichokes and add to the pan along with the greens and peas. Reduce the heat to low, cover, and cook slowly until the mixture is almost dry, 10 to 15 minutes. Remove from the heat, let cool, and season with the salt, pepper, and nutmeg. Mix in the eggs.

Preheat an oven to 375 degrees F.

On a lightly floured work surface, roll out the larger pastry disk into an 11-inch round about ⅛ inch thick. Carefully transfer to a 9-inch tart pan with a removable bottom. Spoon in the filling. Roll out the remaining pastry disk in the same way into a 10-inch round. Carefully place over the filling. Trim any excessive overhang, then turn under the pastry edges and pinch together. Cut a few steam vents in the top crust, then brush with olive oil or beaten egg.

recipe continues on page 36

 Pizza Ebraica di Erbe
Double-Crusted Vegetable Pie

Bake until the crust is golden, 30 to 40 minutes. Remove from the oven and place on a rack to cool. Serve warm or at room temperature.

Notes: If you are worried about the bottom crust becoming soggy, sprinkle a thin layer of fine dried bread crumbs over the pastry before adding the filling. Alternatively, blind bake the bottom crust for 15 minutes, lining it with pie weights, let cool, and then add the filling.

This vegetable filling is suitable for making *scacchi*, the matzoh pie on page 150. Use it in place of the meat filling, and substitute vegetable broth for the meat broth.

Pizza di Ricotta
Ricotta Pie with Potato Crust

La cucina nella tradizione ebraica is a seminal cookbook assembled by an association of Jewish women in Padua in 1987. While leafing through it, I found this delicious recipe for ricotta pie. Like the vegetable-filled pie on page 34, the recipe closely resembles a dish from Apulia, *pitta di patate*. I adapted it, and prefer baking the potatoes, rather than boiling them, as I think this makes for a firmer crust. It will not, however, become fully crisp in either case. The chewy potato character will always dominate. *Pizza di ricotta* is typically served as an appetizer at a dairy-based meal, although it also makes a fine main dish.

Serves 8

13 to 14 ounces (about 1 3/4 cups) ricotta cheese

1 pound boiling or baking potatoes

1 2/3 cups all-purpose flour, or as needed

1 teaspoon salt

1/2 cup sliced, pitted green olives

Freshly ground black pepper to taste

1/4 cup grated Parmesan cheese

1 tablespoon chopped fresh marjoram or summer savory

Spoon the ricotta cheese into a sieve placed over a bowl and refrigerate for 2 hours to drain off the liquid.

Meanwhile, if cooking the potatoes on the stove top, peel them and place in a saucepan with salted water to cover generously. Bring to a boil and boil until tender, about 30 minutes. Drain well and pass through a ricer or food mill placed over a bowl, or simply mash. Alternatively, place the baking potatoes in an oven preheated to 400 degrees F and bake until very soft, about 1 hour. Cut in half and scoop out the potato flesh, passing it through a ricer or food mill or mashing it. While still warm, add the 1 2/3 cups flour and the salt to the potatoes and knead them in to make a firm, smooth dough, adding more flour as needed to achieve the correct consistency.

Preheat an oven to 375 degrees F. Lightly oil a 10-inch pie plate.

On a lightly floured work surface, roll out the dough into an 11-inch round about 1/4 inch thick. Carefully press it into the prepared pie plate. Turn under the edges and press on to the plate rim. (Alternatively, roll out, place on an oiled baking sheet, and fold up the edges like a pizza crust.) Spread the ricotta over the crust, then distribute the olives evenly over the ricotta. Sprinkle with the pepper, Parmesan cheese, and chopped marjoram or savory.

Bake until golden, 30 to 45 minutes. Remove from the oven and place on a rack to cool slightly. Serve warm, cut into wedges.

Torta di Carciofi

ARTICHOKE AND EGG TART

This is my adaptation of a recipe from *La cucina nella tradizione ebraica*. Because this tart is very rich, a small slice will suffice. Make sure the artichoke hearts are not overcooked, or they will not slice easily. The eggs can be boiled for 6 or 7 minutes, as they will continue to cook in the tart. Chill them after peeling for easy slicing.

SERVES 8

For the pastry:

1 ½ cups all-purpose flour

Pinch of salt

6 tablespoons chilled unsalted butter

1 egg, lightly beaten

1 to 2 tablespoons water, or as needed

For the filling:

Juice of 1 lemon

6 jumbo or 8 large cooked artichoke hearts

*3 or 4 hard-boiled eggs, peeled and sliced
(see recipe introduction)*

Salt and freshly ground pepper to taste

Freshly grated nutmeg to taste

2 to 2 ½ cups heavy cream, or as needed

2 eggs

To make the pastry, stir together the flour and salt in a bowl. Cut in the butter with knives or a pastry blender until the mixture resembles coarse meal. Blend in the egg and as much water as needed for the dough to come together into a rough ball. Flatten into a disk, place in a plastic bag, and refrigerate 1 hour. Select a 9- or 10-inch deep-dish pie pan, a fluted tart pan with a removable bottom, or a 9-inch springform cake pan.

On a lightly floured board, roll out the pastry into a 12-inch round ⅛ inch thick. Carefully transfer the dough round to the pan and trim the edges. Fold under and crimp. Chill.

Preheat an oven to 375 degrees F.

While the pastry is chilling, prepare the filling: Have ready a large bowl of water to which you have added the lemon juice. Working with 1 artichoke at a time, remove the stem and all the leaves until you reach the pale green heart. Peel away the dark green area from the base. Drop into the lemon water. Bring a saucepan of water to a boil. Drain the artichokes, add to the boiling water, and cook until just tender, about 15 minutes. Drain and, when cool enough to handle, cut in half lengthwise and scoop out and discard the chokes. Slice the halves lengthwise.

Arrange the artichokes in the pastry shell. Top with the slices of hard-boiled egg. Sprinkle with salt and pepper and a generous grating of nutmeg. In a bowl, whisk together 2 cups cream and 2 eggs until well blended, then season with a little salt and pepper. Pour the cream mixture over the eggs and artichokes. If the liquid does not cover the egg slices, add more cream as needed to cover.

Bake until golden, 30 to 40 minutes. Remove from the oven and place on a rack. Let cool for 10 to 15 minutes, then slide the tart onto a serving plate. Serve warm, cut into wedges. This is also delicious served at room temperature, but you must be sure that the hard-boiled eggs were covered with the cream mixture, or as the tart sits, the eggs will develop hard edges where they are exposed to the air.

Minestre
Soups

Stroncatelli in Brodo   *Handmade Pasta in Broth*

Brodo con Polpette e Uova per Pesach   *Passover Soup with Chicken Dumplings and Eggs*

Zuppa di Azzime   *Passover Matzoh Soup*

Indivia Rehamina   *Curly Endive Soup*

Ceci con Pennerelli   *Chickpea and Veal Shank Soup*

Rape e Riso   *Broth with Broccoli Rabe and Rice*

Crema di Carciofi Ester   *Artichoke Soup*

Pasta e Fagioli alla Veneta   *Venetian White Bean Soup with Pasta and Beef Sausage*

Minestra di Esau   *Lentil Soup with Meatballs*

Quadrettini di Patate in Brodo   *Potato Dumplings in Broth*

Zuppa di Pesce Passato   *Puree of Fish and Potato Soup*

Minestre

Given the mystique of the curative powers of chicken soup and the idealized image of the Jewish mother forever offering a steaming bowl at the first sign of stress or illness, it is surprising that the written repertoire of Italian soup recipes is not more extensive. I suspect that because the serving of soup was such an everyday occurrence, many recipes were not transcribed. I have found soup recipes made with artichokes or asparagus but surprisingly none for eggplant, fennel, or butternut squash and pumpkin, vegetables much beloved by the Jews and used by them in so many other dishes.

The thrifty Jewish housewife of the past turned all bones and meat or poultry trimmings into broth, while the kosher laws made vegetable broth a pantry staple for dairy-based meals. Even fish bones and trimmings were simmered to extract as much flavor as possible, then pureed and thickened with potato for a rich-tasting *zuppa*.

Most Italian Jewish soups are broths embellished with rice, pasta, broken matzohs, potato dumplings, a few peas, chopped spinach or cooked greens, bits of chicken or meat trimmings, tiny meatballs, fried or toasted bread, or eggs, hard-boiled or uncooked, beaten or whole. In *zuppa pavese*, boiling broth is carefully ladled over raw eggs and fried bread in a soup bowl, the heat of the broth cooking the eggs just enough. The remaining soups are rich with hearty legumes such as chickpeas, lentils, and white beans. Some of the vegetable purees are thickened with *besciamella*, the classic cream sauce, and others with the equally classic egg-and-lemon *bagna brusca*.

Stroncatelli in
Brodo
Handmade Pasta in Broth

Stroncare means "to break." Here, in this old recipe from Ancona, the homemade pasta strands are broken into pieces and, according to one version in *La cucina nella tradizione ebraica*, boiled in meat stock for about two hours! I doubt that so long a time is needed to cook fresh egg pasta. If you don't want to roll the pasta ropes by hand, put the dough through a pasta machine, but don't roll it too thin. You want a thick-cut fettuccine. For a real shortcut, use spaghetti broken into pieces and cook it for 10 minutes. Then you can call this *minestra spezzata*, meaning "broken-up pieces."

Serves 8

3 ¹/₂ to 4 cups all-purpose flour

4 jumbo eggs

Olive oil for working dough plus 2 tablespoons

1 small head celery, cut into 1-inch lengths

4 tablespoons tomato paste

Salt and freshly ground black pepper to taste

About 2 ¹/₂ quarts flavorful meat broth

In a large bowl, mound the flour, make a well in the center, and break the eggs into the well. Using a fork, beat the eggs until blended, then gradually pull the flour into the well. When all the flour has been incorporated, you will have a rather stiff dough. Turn out onto a lightly floured work surface and knead well until the dough is elastic, about 15 minutes, then cut it into several pieces. Dip your fingers into the olive oil, and roll the pieces back and forth on the work surface until they form spaghetti-like ropes. Cut the ropes into 2-inch lengths. These are the *stroncatelli*.

Warm the 2 tablespoons olive oil in a saucepan over medium heat. Add the celery and cook, stirring occasionally, until pale gold, 8 to 10 minutes. Stir in the tomato paste and a little water and cook until the celery is very tender, 5 to 10 minutes longer. Season with salt and pepper. Set aside.

In a saucepan, bring the meat broth to a boil. Add the *stroncatelli* and simmer for 20 minutes. Add the celery mixture and cook for 15 to 20 minutes. Ladle into shallow soup bowls to serve.

Quadrucci in Brodo con Spinaci o Piselli
Pasta Squares in Broth with Spinach

Use packaged egg-pasta squares, or make them by rolling out fresh pasta, cutting it into strips, and then cutting the strips into squares. Simmer the squares in broth along with cooked onions and cooked chopped spinach or peas. This is a traditional fast breaker for Yom Kippur.

Note: One of the best-known Italian soups, *stracciatella*, calls for beating together eggs and grated Parmesan and dropping the mixture into hot broth, where it forms raglike shapes (*stracciatelle* means "little rags"). In this kosher version, the cheese is omitted because of the use of chicken broth. Matzoh meal adds body that would normally come from cheese. To make, in a saucepan, bring 8 cups chicken or meat broth to a boil. In a bowl, beat 4 eggs and the juice of one lemon until frothy. Then beat in ¹/₄ teaspoon cinnamon and 4 tablespoons matzoh meal. Pour the egg mixture into the boiling broth while stirring constantly. Simmer for 1 to 2 minutes, then serve at once in shallow soup bowls. Serves 6.

 Quadrucci in Brodo con Spinaci

PASTA SQUARES IN BROTH WITH SPINACH

Brodo con Polpette e Uova per Pesach
PASSOVER SOUP WITH CHICKEN DUMPLINGS AND EGGS

When I was a little girl, my family lived near a kosher poultry market. We would select the chicken and the butcher would clean it while we waited. If we were lucky, inside there was a treasure of unborn eggs. I loved those tiny egg yolks, which we poached in chicken soup, because when I bit into them, they popped in my mouth. I remember them with great nostalgia, for today they are nowhere to be found. To approximate their texture, boil eggs in the shell for about 6 minutes, discard the whites, and use the yolks in the soup. They are, sadly, a poor substitute for this long-ago delicacy. When I am feeling nostalgic, I separate eggs, slide the yolks onto a saucer, slip them into the broth, and poach them gently until barely set, all the while hoping they don't break.

In days gone by, Italian Jews added these immature eggs to the chicken soup they served at Passover. Rice and little "meatballs" made of chicken and matzoh meal went into the soup as well.

SERVES 8

1 large boneless whole chicken breast, ground (about ⅔ pound)

1 egg, lightly beaten

⅓ cup matzoh meal

Salt and freshly ground black pepper to taste

Pinch of ground cinnamon

8 to 10 cups chicken broth

½ to 1 cup white rice

8 hard-boiled egg yolks, chopped

In a bowl, combine the ground chicken, beaten egg, matzoh meal, salt, pepper, and cinnamon.

Form into walnut-sized balls. Refrigerate until ready to cook.

In a large saucepan, bring the chicken broth to a boil. Add the rice and the chicken balls, cover, reduce the heat to medium-low, and simmer until the rice and chicken balls are cooked, about 20 minutes.

Ladle into shallow soup bowls and garnish with the hard-boiled egg yolks. Or, if you like, just before serving separate raw eggs, reserving the whites for a Passover cake, and very carefully poach the yolks in the broth until semifirm.

Note: Some cooks prepare the easier *minestra dayenu*. *Dayenu* in Hebrew translates as "that would have been enough." Stir 4 broken matzohs and 4 egg yolks into hot chicken broth that has been highly flavored with cinnamon.

Zuppa di Azzime
PASSOVER MATZOH SOUP

This is a cross between a *panada* (a layered bread soup) and a *scacchi*, a layered matzoh pie (see page 150). In Sephardic cooking, the layered matzoh pie is called *mina*, *ma'ina*, or *megina*. In Turkey, it is *mina di karne* if made with meat, or *pita de pesah* in Izmir.

SERVES 6

2 to 3 tablespoons rendered chicken or goose fat or margarine

1 onion, chopped

2 celery stalks, chopped

3 carrots, peeled and chopped

2 or 3 cloves garlic, minced

3 tablespoons chopped fresh flat-leaf parsley

2 tablespoons chopped fresh basil

1 cup Tomato Sauce (page 163)

2 cups chopped leftover cooked meat

1 cup cooked English peas

2 cups chopped cooked spinach (about 1 pound uncooked)

6 to 8 cups meat broth, or as needed

Lots of freshly grated nutmeg

2 teaspoons salt

½ teaspoon freshly ground black pepper, or to taste

6 matzohs

Melt the poultry fat or margarine in a saucepan over medium heat. Add the onion, celery, carrots, garlic, parsley, and basil (the mixture is known as the *battuto*) and sauté until softened, about 10 minutes. Add the tomato sauce and cooked meat and simmer for a few minutes. Add the cooked peas and spinach and, if the mixture seems dry, pour in a bit of the broth. Mix well and remove from the heat. Season with nutmeg, salt, and pepper.

Preheat an oven to 350 degrees F.

In a bowl, soak the matzohs in some of the broth to cover until softened. Drain the matzohs and arrange a layer of half of them in a deep baking pan. Cover with the vegetable-and-meat mixture, then the rest of the matzohs. Alternatively, make the soup with 3 layers of matzohs: matzohs, meat, matzohs, meat, matzohs. Pour in the broth to cover the layers. Bring to a boil over medium-high heat on the stove top, then cover and place in the oven. Bake until the broth is absorbed, 30 to 45 minutes.

To serve, scoop out with a spoon into warmed soup bowls. If you like, you may heat up additional broth to spoon over each serving.

Indivia Rehamina
Curly Endive Soup

In style, this Roman recipe resembles a *panada*, or layered bread soup. Broth, vegetables, and bread are stacked in a heavy pan and baked in the oven until the bread absorbs most of the broth. The cakey mixture is then eaten with a spoon. The pleasantly bitter curly endive (sometimes known as chicory) can be replaced by escarole.

Serves 4 to 6

4 cups meat or vegetable broth

2 large heads curly endive, well rinsed and chopped

Stale slices of coarse country bread as needed

Salt and freshly ground black pepper to taste

*Grated Parmesan cheese for serving,
if using vegetable broth*

Preheat an oven to 325 degrees F.

In a wide, heavy saucepan with a tight-fitting lid, bring the broth to a boil. Add the chopped greens and wilt them quickly, then cover the greens with the bread slices in a single layer. Remove from the heat, cover the pan, and place in the oven.

Bake until almost all of the broth is absorbed, 45 to 60 minutes. Season with salt and pepper. To serve, scoop out into shallow soup bowls. If you have used vegetable broth, you may sprinkle with grated Parmesan. If you have used a meat broth, serve as is.

Note: The soup can also be cooked on the stove top over very low heat for about 1 hour.

Ceci
con Pennerelli
CHICKPEA AND VEAL SHANK SOUP

The Jews in the Roman ghetto traditionally made this soup, a quintessential example of how thriftiness can blend with culinary ingenuity. Along with the very filling chickpeas (which must soak overnight), they used *nervetti*, an inexpensive cartilaginous cut left after the trimming of shank bones. *Nervetti* make a rich, very gelatinous broth. To get the desired effect, use veal shanks, also known as osso buco, or beef shanks. They must be meaty, as you will want to be able to remove about 1/2 pound meat from the bones. This is a very homey, thick and filling, comforting soup. Mama food at its best.

SERVES 6 TO 8

2 cups (about 1 pound) dried chickpeas,
picked over and rinsed

3 pounds meaty veal or beef shanks

Meat broth (for an extra-rich soup) or water

2 large onions, chopped

4 celery stalks, chopped

6 carrots, peeled and chopped

1 1/2 cups tomato puree

Salt and freshly ground black pepper to taste

Chopped fresh flat-leaf parsley for garnish

Place the chickpeas in a bowl with water to cover generously; let soak overnight.

The next day, place shanks in a large pot with ample water to cover. Bring to a boil, skimming off any foam. Add the onions, celery, and carrots, reduce the heat to low, and simmer for 1 hour. Drain the chickpeas and add to the shanks along with the tomato puree. Continue to cook until the chickpeas and shanks are tender, about 1 hour longer.

Remove the shanks from the soup. When they are cool enough to handle, cut away any meat still clinging to the bone, and return it to the pot. Bring back to a simmer and season with salt and pepper. Serve at once in shallow soup bowls, garnished with the parsley. You may also chill the soup, skim off the fat, and reheat to serve.

Rape e Riso
BROTH WITH BROCCOLI RABE AND RICE

Rice takes the place of bread in this soup of broth and greens. It is based on a simple and delicious Roman recipe from Donatella Limentani Pavoncello, author of the charming cookbook *Dal 1880 ad oggi: la cucina ebraica della mia famiglia*.

SERVES 4 TO 6

2 heads broccoli rabe

6 cups rich beef broth

2 cups Arborio rice

Salt and freshly ground black pepper to taste

Trim the broccoli rabe, removing any discolored leaves, then thinly slice. To reduce the bitterness, place the greens in a bowl with cold water to cover and change the water a few times over the course of 2 hours.

In a saucepan, bring the broth to a boil. Add the rice and greens, cover, reduce the heat to medium-low, and simmer until the rice is tender, about 20 minutes. Season with salt and pepper. Ladle into shallow soup bowls and serve at once.

Note: This soup could be enriched by adding *boccette*, little beef meatballs made by seasoning ground beef with salt and pepper and binding the meat with an egg and either bread crumbs or matzoh meal.

Crema di Carciofi Ester

ARTICHOKE SOUP

In the Jewish Italian kitchen the repertoire of dishes made with artichokes is particularly large. When I asked a woman at the ghetto market why this was the case she said, "Well, artichokes are bitter, and that's part of our heritage." This artichoke soup is named after Esther, Queen of Persia, and is served at Purim, a joyful holiday that commemorates her triumph over the evil minister Haman and her rescue of the Jews. While it is traditionally thickened with a *besciamella*, you can make a less rich version by using rice or potato as a thickening agent and adding only broth, or perhaps a little milk or cream in addition to broth for thinning. This recipe was inspired by one from the dairy section of *La cucina nella tradizione ebraica*.

SERVES 6 TO 8

Juice of 1 lemon

12 artichokes

3 tablespoons butter

2 cloves garlic, minced

¾ pound potatoes, peeled and diced, or ½ cup white rice

3 cups vegetable broth

Milk or heavy cream for thinning

Salt and freshly ground black pepper to taste

Chopped peeled toasted hazelnuts or pine nuts or chopped flat-leaf fresh parsley or mint for garnish

Have ready a large bowl of water to which you have added the lemon juice. Working with 1 artichoke at a time, cut off the stem flush with the bottom. Remove all the leaves until you reach the pale green heart. Pare away the dark green area from the base. Cut the artichoke in half lengthwise and scoop out and discard the choke from each half. Then cut each half lengthwise into ¼-inch-thick slices and drop into the lemon water.

Melt the butter in a large saucepan over medium heat. Drain the artichokes and add to the pan. Sauté for a few minutes, then add the garlic, the potatoes or rice, and about 1½ cups of the broth, or enough to just cover the artichokes. Cover the pan and simmer over medium heat until the artichokes are very tender and almost falling apart, 25 to 30 minutes.

Remove from the heat and transfer to a food processor. Puree until smooth, then return the puree to the saucepan. Add the remaining 1½ cups broth. Reheat, adding more broth and/or a little milk or cream to achieve the consistency you prefer. Season with salt and pepper. The artichoke flavor intensifies as the soup sits, so it's best to make it a few hours ahead of time or even the day before and reheat it at serving time.

Serve in shallow soup bowls. Sprinkle with chopped hazelnuts, pine nuts, parsley, or mint.

VARIATIONS:

To make the rich version of this soup, make a *besciamella* (see page 162) with 2 tablespoons each butter and flour and 1 cup milk and use it in place of the 1½ cups broth added to the puree. You may find that you will still need to thin the soup with a little broth.

Although not a Purim specialty, you can make a wonderful asparagus soup by substituting 2 pounds trimmed asparagus (3½ to 4 pounds untrimmed) for the artichokes. Season it with a hint of saffron and garnish with chopped pistachios or pine nuts.

Pasta e Fagioli
alla Veneta
VENETIAN WHITE BEAN SOUP WITH
PASTA AND BEEF SAUSAGE

Here's a Venetian version of *pasta e fagioli*, called *fasoi co la luganega* in dialect, that calls for fresh pasta and homemade beef sausage. It is my version of a recipe in *La cucina nella tradizione ebraica*, and is a wonderfully homey and filling bean soup that can be a meal-in-a-bowl. If you like, add 2 cups chopped cooked Swiss chard or curly endive during the last 10 minutes of cooking.

SERVES 6

*1 ³/₄ cups (about 14 ounces) dried white or borlotti beans,
picked over and rinsed*

7 tablespoons extra-virgin olive oil

2 onions, finely chopped

2 celery stalks, finely chopped

2 carrots, peeled and finely chopped

*³/₄ pound freshly made or purchased fresh fettuccine, cut
into* maltagliati *(irregular 1 ¹/₂-inch pieces)*

About 2 cups meat broth

*¹/₂ pound meat mixture for Beef Sausage (page 141)
rolled into tiny meatballs*

Salt and freshly ground black pepper to taste

Place the beans in a saucepan with cold water to cover generously and bring to a boil. Boil for 2 minutes. Remove from the heat, cover, and let stand for 1 hour. Drain well, add fresh water to cover, and again bring to a boil.

Meanwhile, warm 4 tablespoons of the olive oil in a sauté pan over medium heat. Add the onions, celery, and carrots and sauté until softened, about 10 minutes. Add to the beans and return to a boil. Cover, reduce the heat to low, and simmer until the beans are tender, about 1 ¹/₂ hours.

Remove the bean mixture from the heat. Scoop out and reserve about 2 cups of the beans. Puree the remaining beans in batches in a blender or food processor, and place the puree, the reserved beans, and any cooking liquid in a large saucepan. Bring to a boil; if the mixture is too thick, thin with hot water.

While the soup is reheating, cook the pasta in boiling water until al dente, then drain. Add to the bean soup. At the same time, bring the meat broth to a gentle boil, add the meatballs, and poach until cooked through, about 5 minutes, depending on their size. Add the meatballs and the broth to the bean soup and simmer for 10 minutes to blend the flavors. Stir often with a wooden spoon so the beans don't scorch and stick to the bottom of the pan. If the soup begins to thicken too much, you may need to add a little hot water.

Just before serving, season the soup with salt and pepper. Ladle into warmed bowls and drizzle with the remaining 3 tablespoons olive oil. Grind a little pepper over the top and serve.

Note: Mira Sacerdoti, author of *Italian Jewish Cooking*, uses dried *tubetti* pasta instead of fresh noodles for this soup.

 Pasta e Fagioli alla Veneta

Venetian White Bean Soup with Pasta and Beef Sausage

Minestra di Esau
LENTIL SOUP WITH MEATBALLS

Here, Esau's biblical "mess of pottage" is a delicious lentil soup enriched with little meatballs. In tracing this recipe, I found one version that called for 8 cups water and 1 cup lentils, another that specified 1 cup water and 2 cups lentils. Let common sense and experience be your guides. One recipe also suggested adding rosemary and a few cloves of garlic. This is my interpretation of a recipe that appears in Aldo Santini's *La cucina maremmana.* You may use brown or green lentils. The brown are more readily available and cook and break down more quickly. Not all green lentils are from Le Puy in France. Green lentils are also a specialty of Umbria.

SERVES 6

2 cups (about 1 pound) dried green or brown lentils

3 large or 6 small onions, finely chopped

2 carrots, peeled and finely chopped

2 celery stalks, finely chopped

1 cup tomato puree or sauce

⅓ cup chopped fresh flat-leaf parsley

About 4 cups water, or as needed

1 pound ground beef

Salt and freshly ground black pepper to taste

5 tablespoons rendered chicken or goose fat or margarine

Place the lentils in a bowl with water to cover generously; let soak for a few hours.

Drain the lentils and place in a saucepan with the onions, carrots, celery, tomato puree or sauce, parsley, and enough water to cover the lentils and vegetables by about 2 inches. Bring to a boil, cover, reduce the heat to medium-low, and cook until the lentils are tender yet still firm, 15 to 20 minutes.

Meanwhile, season the ground beef with salt and pepper and form into marble-sized meatballs. Melt the poultry fat or margarine in a large sauté pan over medium-high heat. Add the meatballs and brown on all sides. Remove from the heat.

Add the meatballs and the fat from the pan to the lentil soup and simmer until the lentils are tender and the meatballs are cooked through, about 30 minutes. Season with salt and pepper. Ladle into shallow soup bowls to serve.

Quadrettini di Patate in Brodo
POTATO DUMPLINGS IN BROTH

I love to make potato *gnocchi,* but to make them well I need to set aside a few hours so I can fully enjoy this meditative task. When the *gnocchi* craving hits me, I don't always have the time to spare. So I was delighted to find an interesting recipe in *La cucina nella tradizione ebraica* for a potato dumpling often served at the Friday night Sabbath meal. A dough similar to that for potato *gnocchi* is made, but instead of forming it into individual small dumplings—a very time-consuming practice—the potato mixture is patted into a roll, wrapped in cheesecloth, and simmered in broth for an hour until firm. Then it is cooled, weighted, cut into cubes as needed, and reheated in broth. What could be better or easier? The potato mixture keeps for about 4 days in the refrigerator, but it should be removed from the cheesecloth when cold and stored in plastic wrap.

SERVES 8

2 ¼ pounds russet, Yukon Gold, or Yellow Finn potatoes, peeled and cut into chunks

5 eggs, lightly beaten

5 tablespoons fine dried bread crumbs

*4 tablespoons chopped fresh flat-leaf parsley,
plus extra for garnish*

Salt and freshly ground black pepper to taste

1 teaspoon freshly grated nutmeg

8 to 10 cups meat or chicken broth

Place the potatoes in a saucepan with water to cover, bring to a boil, and cook until tender, about 30 minutes. Drain well, place in a bowl, and mash with a potato masher. Add the eggs, bread crumbs, and 4 tablespoons parsley, and season to taste with salt, pepper, and nutmeg.

Shape the potato mixture into a cylinder 3 to 4 inches in diameter. Wrap in cheesecloth and tie the ends securely with kitchen string.

In a wide saucepan, bring the broth to a simmer. Carefully lower the wrapped potato mixture into the broth. Cover and simmer for 1 hour. Remove from the broth and let cool. Place on a shallow plate. Top with a second plate or tray, and then with a weight such as a brick. Refrigerate until all the liquid drains away, about 2 hours. Add any broth that is captured on the plate back to the soup pot.

Unwrap the potato "cake" and cut into small squares. Reheat them in the simmering broth at serving time. Ladle into shallow soup bowls and sprinkle with parsley.

Zuppa di Pesce
Passato
PUREE OF FISH AND POTATO SOUP

This rich puree of fish and fish stock thickened with potato is often flavored with a pinch of saffron. Although the recipe is adapted from one that appears in *La cucina nella tradizione ebraica*, it resembles the Provençal *soupe de poisson*, minus the *rouille*.

SERVES 6

2 pounds assorted mild white fish fillets

1 large potato, peeled and cut into large dice

3 tablespoons olive oil

1 carrot, peeled and finely diced

2 celery stalks, finely diced

2 onions, finely diced

*4 tablespoons chopped fresh flat-leaf parsley,
plus extra for garnish*

1/8 to 1/4 teaspoon saffron threads (optional)

Salt and freshly ground black pepper to taste

Grilled bread or broken pieces of matzoh

Put the fish and potato into a saucepan with water to cover. Bring to a boil, reduce the heat to medium-low, and simmer until both of them are tender, about 20 minutes.

Remove the pan from the heat. Using a slotted spoon, transfer the fish and potato to a food processor and puree, or pass them through a food mill placed over a bowl. Then pass the puree through a fine-mesh sieve placed over a bowl. Reserve the puree and cooking liquid.

Warm the olive oil in a heavy pot over medium heat. Add the carrot, celery, and onions and sauté until softened, about 10 minutes. Add the parsley, the fish puree, the reserved cooking liquid, and the saffron (if using). Stir well and bring just to a boil. Cover, reduce the heat to low, and simmer for 30 minutes to blend the flavors. Season with salt and pepper.

Ladle into shallow soup bowls and garnish with croutons of grilled bread or pieces of matzoh and additional chopped parsley.

Pasta e Riso
PASTA AND RICE

Pasta all'Uovo   *Fresh Egg Pasta*

Ravioli con la Zucca Barucca   *Pumpkin-Filled Ravioli*

Hamin per Sabato   *Sabbath Pasta Dish from Emilia-Romagna*

Rotoli di Pasta   *Stuffed Pasta Rolls*

Rotolo di Carne al Forno   *Baked Meat-Filled Pasta Roll*

Bigoli con Salsa alla Veneziana   *Whole-Wheat Pasta with Anchovies and Garlic*

Spaghetti al Tonno   *Pasta with Tuna Sauce*

Penne al Sugo Verde   *Penne with Green Tomato Sauce*

Fettuccine Fredde   *Cold Fresh Noodles*

Pasticcio di Maccheroni con Funghi e Piselli   *Deep-Dish Pasta Pie with Mushrooms and Peas*

Bomba di Riso   *Baked Rice Casserole*

Risotto con le Melanzane   *Rice with Eggplant*

Risotto alla Zucca Gialla   *Butternut Squash Risotto*

Risotto Marzolino   *Springtime Risotto*

Risotto con Regagli   *Rice with Giblets*

Risotto al Cedro   *Rice with Citron*

Riso con Brodo di Piselli   *Rice in Pea Pod Broth with Peas*

Riso del Sabato   *Sabbath Rice*

Polenta

Pasta e Riso

Pasta and rice, along with vegetables, were—and still are—the basis of the Italian Jewish meal. In the past, the Italian Jewish diet was largely vegetarian, with meat and fish playing the role of flavor accents to grain and vegetable dishes. Dried commercial pasta was used, but the making of *pasta all'uovo*, fresh egg noodles, was part of every cook's training. Sheets of pasta were cut into *tagliarini* or *fettuccine*, into wide strips for *pappardelle* and *lasagne*, into squares for *cannelloni*, and rectangles for *rotoli* (pasta rolls), or they were formed into *ravioli* filled with meat, brains, pumpkin, or greens and cheese.

Pasta dishes that were prepared before sundown on Friday evening evolved into room-temperature main courses for Saturday lunch, the unintentional forerunners of the now ubiquitous pasta salad we see present at every deli counter.

Rice has long been central to the Italian Jewish table. Traditionally, it was made into a simple but elegant *riso per sabato*, rice colored with a pinch of expensive saffron, served on Friday night. Today, the same dish is the well-known *risotto alla milanese*. Risotto was also made with artichokes, asparagus, eggplant, squash, or peas and, like pasta, was an ideal dish to serve for dairy meals. Any leftover cooked risotto could be formed into a *bomba* stuffed with cheese and baked or fried. Leftover rice pilaf was dressed with oil and lemon juice or vinegar and turned into rice salad, simple or adorned with tuna and roasted peppers.

Pasta all'Uovo
Fresh Egg Pasta

Fresh egg pasta is an essential part of the Italian Jewish culinary repertoire. It is easy to make at home with a small, hand-cranked pasta machine, not an extruder that produces an elastic and often rather tough dough. For a tender noodle, use unbleached all-purpose flour, not the coarser semolina flour that is meant for commercially made extruded pasta. The following recipe makes a rather stiff and dry-feeling dough, but ultimately will yield a lighter pasta. It is essential to let the dough rest before rolling it out, giving the gluten in the flour time to relax. A drier dough produces a pasta that will not be gummy when cooked. So take the time to knead it well and you will be rewarded with a silky, light, and tender noodle. Measure flour by spooning it into a measuring cup and leveling it with a knife. Weather affects pasta, so if the day is damp you may need a bit less flour. For the richest pasta, use more egg yolks than whole eggs. Three large egg yolks are the equivalent of a single large egg in moisture content.

Of course, you may buy fresh pasta, but it is rarely as delicate and tender as the pasta you make fresh at home. Most pasta shops roll the dough too thick, and the dough is often damp, causing the noodles to stick together. Finding an acceptable fresh pasta is not impossible, however. Shop around until you locate the brand or store that produces the lightest, finest noodle.

For a Scant 1½ Pounds (Serves 6):

3 to 3 ¼ cups unbleached all-purpose flour

1 teaspoon salt

4 large eggs or 3 large eggs and 3 egg yolks, lightly beaten

3 to 4 tablespoons water, or as needed

For 1 Pound (Serves 4):

2 ¼ to 2 ½ cups unbleached all-purpose flour

¾ teaspoon salt

3 large eggs

2 to 3 tablespoons water, or as needed

For ½ Pound (Serves 2):

1 ¼ to 1 ½ cups unbleached all-purpose flour

½ teaspoon salt

2 large eggs

1 to 2 tablespoons water, or as needed

Note: If you use extra-large eggs you will not need any water. But since most of us have large eggs on hand, I have used them in the basic recipe.

In a large bowl, stir together the flour and salt. Make a well in the center and add the eggs. Beat the eggs and flour together lightly with a fork, then gradually pull the flour into the well until all of it is incorporated and a supple dough has formed. If it seems too dry, add a bit of water. If it is too wet, add a bit more flour. Turn out the dough onto a lightly floured surface and knead until smooth, 10 to 15 minutes. Pat into a flattened disk and slip into a plastic bag. Allow to rest at room temperature for 30 to 60 minutes.

You may also assemble the pasta dough in a food processor. Put in the flour and salt. Pulse in the eggs, and then the water if needed. (Resist the temptation to add too much water or the dough will be too soft and sticky to roll out after it rests.) Gather the dough into a rough ball. The dough will be crumbly, so you will need to knead it on a lightly floured surface until it is smooth, 10 to 15 minutes. Pat into a flattened disk, slip into a plastic bag, and let rest at room temperature for 30 to 60 minutes.

When ready to roll out the pasta, divide it into 2 pieces for a ½-pound batch, 4 pieces for a 1-pound batch, and 6 pieces for a 1½-pound batch. With a rolling pin, flatten each piece into a rectangle about the width of the rollers of a hand-cranked pasta machine. It should be thin enough to get through the widest setting of the machine.

Roll the dough through the thickest setting of the machine. Fold it in thirds and roll it through 2 times. Fold it in thirds again and roll it through one more time. Now proceed to roll it through all the settings of the machine, making it thinner and thinner until you've rolled it through the thinnest setting. (If you want the dough to be even thinner for the most delicate fettuccine, cover it with plastic wrap, let it rest for 15 minutes so the gluten relaxes, and then roll it through the thinnest setting again. Do not do this for lasagne, cannelloni, or ravioli. If they are rolled too thin they may tear in the stuffing process.)

For Fettuccine or *Tagliarini*:

After the dough has been rolled through the thinnest setting on the machine, cut into lengths of 9 to 10 inches. Let dry on a rack for 15 to 20 minutes. You may roll up the dough like a jelly roll and cut it by hand with a sharp knife, or use the cutter blades on the pasta machine. To prevent it from sticking, toss the pasta with granular flour like Wondra, fine semolina flour, or fine cornmeal, and place on baking sheets. You may cook the pasta immediately or cover the baking sheets with large plastic bags to prevent the pasta from drying out and refrigerate for up to 24 hours.

For Lasagne or *Pappardelle*:

After the dough has been rolled through the thinnest setting on the machine, cut into 9-inch lengths for *pappardelle* or into lengths to match the dimensions of your lasagne pan, with some overlap. With a pastry wheel, cut into 1-inch-wide strips for *pappardelle* and 2- to 3-inch-wide strips for lasagne. To prevent sticking, toss the noodles with granular flour like Wondra, fine semolina, or fine cornmeal, and store on baking sheets until you are ready to cook. Cover loosely with plastic wrap or a large plastic bag.

For Cannelloni:

Roll out the dough on the thinnest setting or the next-to-thinnest setting on the pasta machine. Cut with a pastry wheel at 4-inch intervals. You want squares that measure about 4 inches or 3½ by 4 inches.

For Ravioli:

Using a pasta machine set on the next-to-thinnest setting, roll the dough into lengths 15 to 18 inches long. Fold in half lengthwise, to mark it, and unfold. Place mounds of filling along the bottom half of the dough at 2-inch intervals. Spray lightly with water from a mister, then fold the top half of the dough over the lower half, covering the mounds. Press between each mound of filling to seal, but do not seal the bottom edge. Using a pastry wheel, cut between the mounds, pressing the air out of each ravioli from the top and letting it escape through the bottom opening. Finally, press the bottom edge to seal. Trim the bottom edge with the pastry wheel. Place the ravioli, not touching one another, on baking sheets that have been lined with parchment paper. Lightly sprinkle them with granular flour like Wondra, fine semolina flour, or fine cornmeal. These may be refrigerated, uncovered, for a few hours. Do not cover them with plastic, or they will get gummy and stick to the paper and to one another.

 Ravioli con la Zucca Barucca
PUMPKIN-FILLED RAVIOLI

Ravioli con la Zucca Barucca
PUMPKIN-FILLED RAVIOLI

Pumpkin arrived in Italy via the Spanish and Portuguese Jews after the Inquisition. Although popular in Ancona and Ferrara, these much-loved ravioli are a specialty of Mantua, where a sizable Jewish community thrived during the reign of the Gonzaga family. The pumpkin filling may include the addition of crunchy *amaretti* (almond macaroons), ground toasted almonds, chopped raisins, or *mostarda di frutta*, a condiment of candied fruit in a mustard-flavored syrup that is a specialty of Cremona. Although not essential, such additions bring an interesting sweetness to the filling.

SERVES 6

*1 sugar pumpkin, kabocha, or butternut squash,
2 1/2 pounds*

1 cup grated Parmesan cheese

Freshly grated nutmeg to taste

1 cup crushed amaretti *or ground toasted almonds
(optional)*

1 cup chopped mostarda di frutta *(optional)*

1/2 cup chopped raisins (optional)

Dried bread crumbs, if needed

1 1/2 pounds dough for Fresh Egg Pasta (page 52)

6 tablespoons unsalted butter, melted and kept hot

1 tablespoon chopped fresh sage

1/2 cup chopped toasted hazelnuts or almonds (optional)

Preheat an oven to 400 degrees F. Place the pumpkin or other squash in a baking pan and bake until soft when pierced, about 1 hour. Remove from the oven and, when cool enough to handle, cut in half and scoop out and discard the seeds and fibers. Scoop the flesh from the halves into a food mill placed over a bowl and pass it through the mill. (Alternatively, mash the flesh in a bowl with a potato masher.) Transfer the pureed flesh to a sieve placed over a bowl, cover, and refrigerate overnight to drain off excess moisture.

The next day, squeeze the squash flesh with your hands to remove any additional moisture. Place in a bowl and add the cheese, a generous amount of nutmeg, and the *amaretti* or almonds, *mostarda di frutta*, or raisins, if using. If the mixture still seems too moist, add bread crumbs as needed to absorb the moisture.

Roll out the pasta dough and use the squash mixture to form ravioli as directed on page 53. Alternatively, cut the rolled-out dough into 3- to 4-inch rounds, place a heaping tablespoonful of filling in the center of each round, dampen the edges of the round with water, fold in half, and press the edges to seal. The ravioli can be assembled up to 6 hours ahead and placed on well-floured baking sheets lined with parchment. However, they do not keep for a long time, as the squash continues to give off moisture, causing the dough to break down.

Bring a large pot of salted water to a boil. Add the ravioli and cook until al dente. Using a slotted skimmer, scoop out the ravioli and place in a warmed serving dish. Drizzle with the melted butter and sprinkle on the sage. If you have not put almonds or *amaretti* in the filling, top with the hazelnuts or almonds.

Hamin per Sabato
SABBATH PASTA DISH
FROM EMILIA-ROMAGNA

Hamin means "oven" but also is the name for this incredibly rich dish served on *sabato bescialach*, a sabbath that is special to Italy. (See page 18 for holidays.) The crispy noodle pancake with a tender middle is also known as *ruota di faraone*, or "pharaoh's wheel," or *frisinsal* in Venetian dialect. Originally it was made with goose salami and a fine mince of rosemary and sage. Today it's easy to purchase chicken or turkey sausage, which work well in place of the salami.

SERVES 6

*2 to 3 tablespoons rendered goose or chicken fat,
plus fat for greasing dish*

*2 cups coarsely chopped cooked Beef Sausage
(page 141), poultry sausage, or roast chicken*

⅔ cup pine nuts, lightly toasted

*½ cup raisins, plumped in hot water for 30 minutes
and drained*

1 cup meat juices from a roast or stew or rich meat stock

*1 pound freshly made Tagliarini (page 53)
or purchased fresh fettucine*

Preheat an oven to 350 degrees F. Grease a 9-by-12-inch gratin dish or other baking dish.

Warm the goose or chicken fat in a sauté pan over medium heat. Add the sausage or chicken, pine nuts, and raisins and toss with a little of the meat juices or rich broth to moisten. Remove from the heat.

Meanwhile, bring a large pot of salted water to a boil. Drop in the pasta, stir well, and cook until al dente, only a minute or two. Drain well and, while the noodles are warm, toss them with the remaining meat juices or broth.

Make a layer of half the noodles in the pre-pared baking dish. Top with all the meat mixture, and then the remaining noodles. Bake until golden, about 30 minutes. The noodle pancake should be crispy on the outside and still tender in the middle. Remove from the oven, let cool completely, and serve at room temperature.

Rotoli di Pasta
STUFFED PASTA ROLLS

Pasta rolls are a specialty of Emilia-Romagna, but they are also found in the *cucina ebraica* of Padua. I imagine you can buy commercial pasta sheets and roll them out a bit thinner, as most store-bought ones are too thick. But it's better if you make the pasta dough at home and roll it out yourself. The dough is then spread with the filling, rolled, wrapped, and simmered in salted water. (A fish poacher or large roasting pan with a rack is ideal.) Once removed and unwrapped, the roll can be sliced and served warm as is with a light sauce, or sliced and placed in a baking dish, topped with melted butter and Parmesan or a light sauce, and warmed in the oven.

A variety of fillings are used, with a mixture of spinach and ricotta the most common. The following recipes are interpretations of those found in Giuseppe Maffioli's *La cucina padovana*, as well as some from other Italian cookbooks.

To shape, cook, and serve the pasta rolls make a ½-pound batch of fresh pasta (see page 52). On a lightly floured board, roll out 1 disk of dough into a 10-by-20-inch rectangle. Spread with half the filling. Starting on a short side, roll up the pasta sheet to enclose the filling fully. Wrap in cheesecloth or plastic wrap and tie both ends and once in the middle with kitchen string. Repeat with the remaining dough and filling. (You may refrigerate the filled dough at this time for up to 2 hours.)

To cook the rolls, carefully lower them into a pan of simmering salted water. Cover and simmer for 20 minutes. Remove carefully and drain well.

Allow the pasta rolls to cool a bit, unwrap, and then slice them crosswise ½ to 1 inch thick. Serve as is or with a sauce. Alternatively, place the warm slices (or let the rolls cool completely and then slice) in a buttered baking dish. Drizzle with melted butter and sprinkle with grated Parmesan cheese. Place in a preheated 350 degree F oven for 10 minutes if the pasta roll was warm when you sliced it. If not, cover the pan with foil or plastic wrap, place in a bain marie (water bath), and heat for 30 minutes. Serve with Tomato Sauce (page 163), if desired.

Rotoli di Spinaci e Ricotta
SPINACH AND RICOTTA FILLING
FOR PASTA ROLLS

1 ½ cups (¾ pound) ricotta cheese

*2 pounds fresh spinach, well rinsed,
or 2 packages frozen chopped spinach, thawed*

4 tablespoons unsalted butter

2 eggs, lightly beaten

½ teaspoon salt

½ teaspoon freshly ground black pepper

¼ teaspoon freshly grated nutmeg, or to taste

Spoon the ricotta cheese into a sieve placed over a bowl and refrigerate for 2 hours to drain off the liquid. If using fresh spinach, cook it in the rinsing water clinging to the leaves until wilted, 3 to 5 minutes. Drain well and chop finely. If using thawed, frozen spinach, squeeze dry.

Melt the butter in a large sauté pan over medium heat and let it color just slightly. Add the spinach and toss it in the butter for a few minutes. Transfer to a bowl. Add the ricotta and eggs to the spinach, and then season with the salt, pepper, and nutmeg. Mix well and let cool.

Shape, cook, and serve the pasta rolls as directed on page 56. This same filling can be used to make ravioli.

Rotoli di Tonno e Ricotta
ROMAN TUNA AND RICOTTA FILLING

*2 cans (7 ounces each) olive oil–packed tuna,
preferably Italian (see recipe introduction, page 24),
drained (9 ounces drained)*

1 ⅓ cups (11 ounces) ricotta cheese

2 tablespoons grated Parmesan cheese

3 tablespoons chopped fresh basil

2 cloves garlic, finely minced

½ teaspoon salt

¼ teaspoon freshly ground black pepper

In a bowl, combine all the ingredients and mix well. Shape, cook, and bake the pasta rolls as directed on page 56, then serve with Tomato Sauce (page 163).

Rotolo di Carne al Forno

BAKED MEAT-FILLED PASTA ROLL

Some rotoli, such as this one, call for baking the roll rather than poaching it. This was inspired by a description in *La cucina padovana* by Giuseppe Maffioli, but Mira Sacerdoti, in her book *Italian Jewish Cooking*, offers a similar recipe called "Meat Loaf in a Dressing Gown." It includes the classic additions of pine nuts and raisins.

SERVES 6

1 ½ pounds dough for Fresh Egg Pasta (page 52)

3 tablespoons olive oil

2 onions, chopped

3 cloves garlic, minced

4 tablespoons chopped fresh flat-leaf parsley

1 pound ground beef or veal

1 ½ teaspoons salt

¼ teaspoon freshly ground black pepper

¼ teaspoon freshly grated nutmeg

½ teaspoon ground cinnamon

1 cup Madeira, Marsala, or sherry wine

Grated zest of 1 lemon (optional)

Fine dried bread crumbs to bind

1 egg, lightly beaten, plus beaten egg for coating

2 cups Tomato Sauce (page 163), optional

Make the pasta dough as directed, divide it in half, flatten each half into a disk, slip into a plastic bag and let rest for 30 to 60 minutes.

Heat the olive oil in a large sauté pan over medium heat. Add the onions and sauté until tender and translucent, about 8 minutes. Add the garlic and parsley and cook for a few minutes longer. Add the beef or veal, salt, pepper, nutmeg, and cinnamon, and cook until the meat loses its color, about 8 minutes. Add the wine and the lemon zest (if using). Let the wine bubble up and continue to cook until it has evaporated. Remove from the heat. Bind the mixture with the bread crumbs and the 1 egg. Let cool for 30 minutes.

Preheat an oven to 350 degrees F. Lightly oil a baking sheet or line it with parchment paper.

On a lightly floured work surface, roll out 1 disk of pasta dough into a rectangle measuring 20 by 10 inches. Spread half the filling on the rectangle and roll up into a cylinder, enclosing the filling fully. Place seam side down on the prepared baking sheet. Make a second roll with the remaining pasta dough and filling and place on the baking sheet. Brush both rolls with the beaten egg.

Bake until golden, about 30 minutes. Slice and serve warm with Tomato Sauce, if desired.

Bigoli con Salsa alla Veneziana

WHOLE-WHEAT PASTA WITH ANCHOVIES AND GARLIC

Bigoli are a whole-wheat spaghetti, somewhat thicker and longer than the regular packaged spaghetti. They are made with eggs and, instead of being rolled, are pushed through a press called a *bigolaro*. It is very likely that you will be using packaged whole-wheat pasta rather than homemade, but keep in mind that it cooks very quickly and does not hold well. In other words, it starts to break down after a while in the bowl. You can, of course, make this dish with a regular durum-wheat packaged pasta. Long, thin shapes are best.

This classic Venetian pasta is dressed simply with anchovy, garlic, and olive oil. Salt-packed anchovies are preferred, but olive oil-packed anchovies can be substituted. Don't omit the parsley. It's more than just a note of color. It also must not be chopped too fine, as it is essential for balance of flavor. A little grated lemon zest or a handful of toasted bread crumbs will lighten the fish flavor.

SERVES 6

1 pound whole-wheat spaghetti

4 to 6 tablespoons extra-virgin olive oil

12 salt-packed anchovies, filleted, rinsed, and finely chopped, or 24 olive oil-packed fillets (about a 3-ounce jar), drained and finely chopped

3 or 4 cloves garlic, finely minced

6 tablespoons chopped fresh flat-leaf parsley

Freshly ground black pepper to taste

Grated zest of 1 large lemon (optional)

¹/₂ cup toasted bread crumbs (optional)

Bring a large pot of salted water to a boil. Drop in the pasta, stir well, and cook until al dente.

Meanwhile, warm the olive oil in a large sauté pan over medium heat. Add the anchovies and cook, stirring, for 1 minute, then add the *battuto* of chopped garlic and parsley. Cook briskly for 1 minute.

Drain the pasta and add to the sauce in the pan over medium heat. Toss well to coat, then stir for a minute or two to flavor the pasta with the sauce. Sprinkle with pepper and the lemon zest and/or toasted bread crumbs, if using. Serve immediately.

Note: In her excellent book *The Splendid Table*, Lynn Rossetto Kasper has a Ferrarese version of this sauce, which is called *bagnabrusca* by one cook. It includes the addition of tomatoes and a bit of lemon juice to the anchovy, garlic, and parsley sauce, and instead of whole-wheat pasta, fresh *tagliarini* are used. In this instance, *bagnabrusca* is a misnomer, as the classic Jewish name, *bagna brusca*, refers to a variation on *avgolemono*, a close relative of the Sephardic *agristada*. In that recipe, meat juices are thickened with the egg-and-lemon mixture and the sauce is tossed with fresh egg pasta (see page 52).

Spaghetti
al Tonno
Pasta with Tuna Sauce

This takes the previous recipe one step further. It's a bit more filling, as chopped onion is sautéed in the olive oil, and canned tuna and capers are tossed in to the basic anchovy-garlic sauce at the last minute. In Italy, the tuna is usually canned, but you could use fresh tuna, broiled or baked. Sometimes tomato is added, sometimes not.

Serves 4 or 5

1 pound long pasta such as spaghetti

5 tablespoons extra-virgin olive oil

1 large onion, finely chopped (about 2 cups)

12 salt-packed anchovies, filleted, rinsed and very finely chopped, or 24 olive oil-packed fillets (about one 3-ounce jar), drained and very finely chopped

3 cloves garlic, finely minced

6 tablespoons chopped fresh flat-leaf parsley

1 can (6 ounces) olive oil-packed tuna, preferably Italian (see recipe introduction, page 24), drained and broken up

2 tablespoons capers, rinsed and chopped

1 to 2 cups chopped canned plum tomatoes (optional)

Grated zest of 1 lemon (optional)

Freshly ground black pepper to taste

Bring a large pot of salted water to a boil. Drop in the pasta, stir well, and cook until al dente.

Meanwhile, warm the olive oil in a large sauté pan over medium heat. Add the onion and sauté until tender and translucent, 5 to 6 minutes. Add the anchovies, garlic, and parsley and cook for 1 minute. Add the tuna and capers and the tomatoes and lemon zest, if using, and cook until warm, about 2 minutes.

Drain the pasta and add to the sauce in the pan. Toss well to coat, then stir for a minute or two to flavor the pasta with the sauce. Sprinkle with pepper and serve immediately.

 Spaghetti al Tonno

Pasta with Tuna Sauce

Penne al Sugo Verde

PENNE WITH GREEN TOMATO SAUCE

This refreshing summer pasta sauce is my adaptation of one that appears in *Le ricette di casa mia* by Milka Belgrado Passigli. Green tomatoes don't give off much liquid when they are cooked and they also may be difficult to peel. If you can peel them, the sauce will be more tender. Green tomatoes need the addition of olive oil and a little water to help them soften and become a sauce that will coat the noodles. The original recipe called for grated Parmesan, but after tasting this a few times I found that saltier pecorino cheese is a better balance for the tart green tomatoes.

SERVES 3 OR 4 AS A FIRST COURSE

6 tablespoons extra-virgin olive oil

1 tablespoon finely minced garlic

½ cup finely chopped fresh flat-leaf parsley

1 teaspoon red pepper flakes, or 1 small dried red pepper

2 pounds green (unripened) tomatoes, peeled, if possible, and coarsely chopped

¼ cup water or vegetable broth

Salt and freshly ground black pepper to taste

½ pound penne

Grated pecorino cheese

Warm 3 tablespoons of the olive oil in a large sauté pan over medium heat. Add the garlic, half of the parsley, and the red pepper flakes or whole pepper and sauté for 3 to 4 minutes. Add the tomatoes and the water or broth and cook over medium heat until the tomatoes have broken down and the sauce is slightly thickened, about 20 minutes. Season with salt and pepper.

Meanwhile, bring a large pot of salted water to a boil. Drop in the penne, stir well, and cook until al dente. Drain, add to the sauté pan, and toss with the sauce, adding a generous sprinkling of pecorino cheese and remaining parsley. Season with salt and pepper and swirl in the remaining extra-virgin olive oil. Serve immediately. Pass more grated cheese, if desired.

Note: You can eat this cold, but it will require more olive oil and more salt (see Cold Fresh Noodles, page 63).

Fettuccine
Fredde
Cold Fresh Noodles

In keeping with the Jewish laws not to work on the Sabbath, this dish was traditionally prepared on Friday to be served Saturday at midday. It is made with fresh egg noodles, and the sauce is cold when the noodles are dressed. This particular version includes a meat-enriched tomato sauce, but other recipes call for dressing the pasta with garlic, olive oil, and a pinch of red pepper flakes; with meat juices; with Bagna Brusca (page 166), a savory mixture of meat juices, egg, and lemon; or with a spicy tomato sauce seasoned with garlic and hot pepper. In summer, an uncooked tomato sauce would be good. For the lightest dish, use a thin noodle, rather than fettuccine or any heavier dried pasta.

Serves 6

1 pound freshly made Tagliarini (page 53)
or purchased fresh tagliarini

Olive oil for tossing with pasta, plus 4 tablespoons

1 large onion, chopped

1 large celery stalk, chopped

1 large carrot, peeled and chopped

1 teaspoon salt

½ teaspoon freshly ground black pepper

10 ounces ground beef

1 cup dry white wine

4 cups peeled, seeded, and chopped tomatoes
(fresh or canned)

4 tablespoons chopped fresh basil

Bring a large pot of salted water to a boil. Drop in the noodles, stir well and cook until al dente, just a minute or two. Drain well and place in a bowl.

Toss with a bit of olive oil to prevent sticking.

Warm the 4 tablespoons olive oil in a large sauté pan over medium heat. Add the onion, celery, and carrot and sprinkle with the salt and pepper. Sauté until softened, about 8 minutes. Add the beef and cook, stirring often, until it loses its color, about 10 minutes. Add the wine and simmer for 3 minutes to cook off the alcohol. Add the tomatoes and simmer until reduced, about 15 minutes. Remove from the heat and let cool completely.

Adjust the seasonings in the sauce and add the basil, mixing well. Add to the noodles and toss well. In keeping with the laws of the Sabbath, chill overnight, then bring to room temperature the next day before serving.

Note: Of course, you can eat this hot or warm at any other time.

Pasticcio
di Maccheroni con Funghi e Piselli
Deep-Dish Pasta Pie
with Mushrooms and Peas

Anyone who has seen the film *Big Night* will find this dish somewhat reminiscent of the famed *timpano*, or *timballo* as it is more commonly known, that is prepared in the film. This recipe is my interpretation from a description in *La cucina veneziana* by Giuseppe Maffioli. Maffioli provides two variations: one is meatless, filled with vegetables and lots of grated cheese, and the other mixes the pasta with sautéed chicken livers, little meatballs, cut-up pieces of cooked veal, beef, or chicken, and (as if that's not already rich enough) beef marrow.

Serves 8 to 10

For the pastry:

3 ½ to 4 cups all-purpose flour

Pinch of salt

1 ¼ cups (10 ounces) unsalted butter

2 eggs, lightly beaten

½ cup sweet white wine or Marsala

For the filling:

1 pound dried pasta such as ziti, maccheroni, or penne

Olive oil for tossing with pasta,
plus 4 tablespoons olive oil or unsalted butter

2 onions, chopped

3 cloves garlic, minced

1 tablespoon chopped fresh rosemary

½ cup dried porcini, soaked in hot water
to cover for 30 minutes, drained with soaking liquid
reserved and strained, and mushrooms chopped

1 ½ pounds assorted fresh mushrooms,
sliced ¼ inch thick

1 ½ to 2 cups cooked English peas or a
mixture of cooked peas and chopped cooked carrots

2 teaspoons salt

½ teaspoon freshly ground black pepper

Freshly grated nutmeg to taste (optional)

1 ½ cups grated Parmesan cheese, or a bit more

1 egg yolk mixed with a little milk or water

To make the pastry, stir together 3 ½ cups of the flour and the salt in a large bowl. Cut in the butter with a pastry blender until the mixture resembles coarse meal. Add the eggs and wine and mix until the dough comes together in a rough mass, adding more flour if needed. Alternatively, place the flour and salt in a food processor and pulse briefly to mix. Add the butter and process until the mixture resembles coarse meal. Add the eggs and wine and pulse to incorporate. Divide the dough into 2 balls, one slightly larger than the other. Place in a plastic bag and refrigerate until firm, about 1 hour.

On a lightly floured work surface, roll out the larger ball of dough into a round about 15 inches in diameter. Ease it into a deep 10-inch springform pan. Refrigerate. Roll out the remaining ball of dough into a 12-inch round and refrigerate.

To make the filling, bring a large pot of salted water to a boil. Drop in the pasta, stir well, cook until almost tender, and drain. Place in a bowl and toss with a little olive oil. Set aside.

Warm the 4 tablespoons olive oil or melt the butter in a sauté pan over medium heat. Add the onions and sauté until softened, about 8 minutes. Add the garlic, rosemary, and chopped rehydrated mushrooms and cook, stirring, for 3

recipe continues on page 66

 Pasticcio di Maccheroni con Funghi e Piselli
Deep-Dish Pasta Pie with Mushrooms and Peas

to 4 minutes longer. Add the fresh mushrooms and continue to cook over medium heat until the mushrooms give off their liquid, about 8 minutes.

Add the reserved mushroom liquid to the sauté pan along with the peas or peas and carrots. Stir in the salt and pepper and season with the nutmeg (if using). Add to the cooked pasta, toss well, and fold in the grated cheese.

Preheat an oven to 375 degrees F.

Spoon the pasta mixture into the pastry-lined pan. Top with the pastry round, turn under the edges and seal well, pinching the edges together. Cut a few slits in the top crust, then brush with the egg mixture.

Bake until golden, 35 to 40 minutes. Let rest for 10 minutes before cutting. Serve hot.

Pasticcio di Maccheroni con Polpettine
Deep-Dish Pasta Pie
with Little Meatballs

Make the pastry as directed, using olive oil, or chicken or goose fat in place of the butter. Season 1 1/2 pounds ground beef with salt, freshly ground black pepper, and freshly grated nutmeg. Form into little meatballs and fry them in olive oil until cooked through. Add to the cooked pasta along with 2 onions, chopped, and 1/2 pound chicken livers, both sautéed in olive oil. Omit the cheese and brush the pastry with egg yolk mixed with water, not milk. Fill and bake as directed. Let rest for 10 minutes before cutting. Serve hot.

Bomba di Riso
Baked Rice Casserole

Risotto saltato is a homey dish of refried risotto. Instead of frying the cooked rice in the classic pancake manner, here it is baked. What you want is a crispy golden exterior and melting cheese inside. Rich—and a great way to use up leftover risotto.

Serves 6

2 1/2 cups Arborio rice

4 eggs, lightly beaten

1/3 cup grated Parmesan cheese

Salt and freshly ground black pepper to taste

Freshly grated nutmeg to taste

1 1/2 cups (3/4 pound) ricotta cheese

3/4 pound fresh mozzarella cheese, cut into 1/2-inch cubes

Preheat an oven to 350 degrees F. Oil a 9-inch ring mold or 1 1/2- to 2-quart soufflé dish.

Bring a saucepan of salted water to a boil. Add the rice and cook until al dente, 15 to 18 minutes. Drain and place in a bowl. Add the eggs and Parmesan cheese and mix well. Season with salt, pepper, and nutmeg.

Pack half of the rice mixture into the prepared mold or dish. Top with the ricotta and mozzarella cheeses, and then the remaining rice mixture.

Bake until golden, about 25 minutes. Serve hot.

Notes: Edda Servi Machlin's recipe omits the ricotta and adds raisins and grated lemon zest to the rice mixture. The rice has a layer of mozzarella in the center, and is baked or sautéed (*al salto*) in a pan on the stove top.

The mixture of rice, eggs, and Parmesan cheese can be formed into small rice balls with a tiny cube of mozzarella tucked into the center of each one. Coat the balls in fine dried bread crumbs and deep-fry them until golden and the cheese is melted. The balls are like the Roman *suppli al telefono*, rice croquettes stuffed with mozzarella cheese, tomato sauce, and sometimes porcini (and in nonkosher versions with chopped prosciutto as well). The *al telefono* comes from the mozzarella, which resembles telephone cords when it melts. Serve as an antipasto.

Risotto con le Melanzane
RICE WITH EGGPLANT

Rice, eggplant, and artichokes were brought to Sicily by the Arabs in the tenth century, and first adopted by Jewish cooks. Without them, we would not have this delicious dish or many others. Some cooks prepare this as a pilaf, adding all the broth at once and letting the rice absorb it, covered, over very low heat with no stirring.

SERVES 4 TO 6

1 pound firm eggplants, peeled and cut into ½-inch dice

Salt

6 cups vegetable broth

¼ cup olive oil, or as needed

3 cloves garlic, finely minced

4 tablespoons chopped fresh flat-leaf parsley

2 cups Arborio rice

Grated Parmesan cheese for serving

Place the diced eggplant in a colander, sprinkle generously with salt, and let drain for 30 min-

utes. Rinse the eggplant and wipe dry. Pour the broth into a saucepan and bring to a simmer; adjust the heat to maintain a gentle simmer.

Warm the olive oil in a large, wide nonstick sauté pan over medium heat. Add the eggplant and cook until softened, about 8 minutes. Add the garlic and parsley and cook, stirring often, until the eggplant is soft, about 5 minutes. Add the rice and stir until opaque, about 3 minutes. Add a ladleful (about 1 cup) of the simmering broth and stir for 3 to 4 minutes until the broth is absorbed. Reduce the heat and continue to add the broth a ladleful at a time, waiting until each addition is absorbed before adding the next, until the rice kernels are al dente at the center and creamy on the outside, 18 to 20 minutes in all. Remove from the heat and transfer to a warmed serving dish. Pass a bowl of Parmesan cheese at the table. Serve immediately.

Risotto alla Zucca Gialla

Butternut Squash Risotto

Here is Aunt Zita's recipe from Milka Passigli's *Le ricette di casa mia* for a risotto made with the beloved *zucca barucca*, the "blessed" pumpkin of the Veneto. Our butternut squash is the closest to the Italian *zucca*, so it's best to use it instead of pumpkin. For the history of its name, see page 91.

Serves 6

6 cups vegetable broth

3 tablespoons olive oil, or part oil and part unsalted butter

2 tablespoons chopped garlic

2 tablespoons chopped fresh sage

2 $\frac{1}{2}$ to 3 cups peeled, cubed butternut squash ($\frac{1}{2}$-inch cubes)

Salt to taste

2 cups Arborio rice

$\frac{1}{2}$ cup dry white wine (optional)

6 to 8 tablespoons grated Parmesan cheese

Freshly ground black pepper to taste

Chopped fresh flat-leaf parsley or sage for garnish

Pour the broth into a saucepan and bring to a simmer; adjust the heat to maintain a gentle simmer.

Warm the olive oil and/or butter in a large deep sauté pan over medium heat. Add the garlic and sage and sauté for a few minutes. Add the squash, sprinkle it with salt, and cook, stirring, for 1 minute. Add the rice and stir until opaque, about 3 minutes. Add the white wine (if using) and cook until it evaporates, just a few minutes. Add a ladleful (about 1 cup) of the simmering broth, and stir for 3 to 4 minutes until the liq-

uid is absorbed. Reduce the heat and continue to add the broth a ladleful at a time, waiting until each addition is absorbed before adding the next, until the rice kernels are al dente in the center and creamy on the outside, 18 to 20 minutes in all. Stir in 4 tablespoons of the Parmesan cheese. Season to taste with salt and pepper.

Remove from the heat and transfer to a warmed serving dish. Sprinkle with the remaining grated cheese and the parsley and serve immediately.

Notes: If you don't want to take a chance of overcooking the squash with the rice and having it break down, which is the old-fashioned Jewish Italian way, you can cook it separately in the vegetable broth and add it to the rice along with the last addition of broth.

I like to add 1 cup peeled, cooked, and coarsely chopped chestnuts along with the last addition of broth.

For a slightly lighter-tasting dish, make a classic *gremolata* of 2 tablespoons grated lemon zest, 6 tablespoons chopped fresh flat-leaf parsley, and 1 tablespoon minced garlic, and stir it into the risotto during the last few minutes of cooking.

Risotto Marzolino
Springtime Risotto

March (*Marzo*) is the month when asparagus and artichokes appear at the market. Inspired by a recipe in Milka Passigli's *Le ricette di casa mia*, this festive saffron-tinged risotto uses both vegetables. Again, this dish might profit from a little grated lemon zest and chopped fresh parsley, basil, or mint.

Serves 6

1 pound asparagus

Juice of 1 lemon

3 large artichokes

6 cups vegetable broth

$^{1}/_{2}$ teaspoon saffron threads, chopped

2 to 3 tablespoons unsalted butter

1 small onion, chopped

2 cups Arborio rice

1 cup heavy cream

$^{1}/_{2}$ cup grated Parmesan cheese

Cut away all the tough ends from the asparagus, leaving only the tips and tender parts. Blanch in salted boiling water for 5 minutes, then refresh in cold water. Drain, pat dry, and cut into 1 $^{1}/_{2}$-inch pieces and set aside.

Have ready a large bowl of water to which you have added the lemon juice. Working with 1 artichoke at a time, cut off the stem flush to the bottoms. Remove all the leaves, and cut the tender heart in half lengthwise. Cut away the choke, then slice the halves lengthwise into $^{1}/_{4}$-inch-thick slices. Drop into the lemon water. When all the artichokes are trimmed, bring a saucepan of salted water to a boil. Drain the artichokes, add to the saucepan, and blanch for 2 minutes. Drain and set aside.

Pour the broth into a saucepan and bring to a simmer; adjust the heat to maintain a gentle simmer.

Ladle out 1 cup of the hot broth, place in a bowl, and add the saffron; set aside.

Melt the butter in a large, deep sauté pan over medium heat. Add the onion and sauté until softened, 5 to 8 minutes. Add the rice and stir until opaque, about 3 minutes. Add a ladleful of the simmering broth and stir for 3 to 4 minutes until the broth is absorbed. Reduce the heat and continue to add the broth a ladleful at a time, waiting until each addition is absorbed before adding the next. For the final cup, add the saffron and its broth along with the asparagus and artichokes. Stir until the broth is absorbed and the rice kernels are al dente at the center and creamy on the outside, 18 to 20 minutes in all. Stir in the cream and Parmesan cheese and heat through, about 2 minutes. Remove from the heat and transfer to a warmed serving dish. Serve immediately.

Risotto con
Regagli
RICE WITH GIBLETS

The thrifty Italian Jewish cook wasted no part of the chicken. And it's easy for us to buy inexpensive giblets for this rich and delectable risotto. Donatella Pavoncello, in her delightful *Dal 1880 ad oggi: la cucina della mia famiglia*, cooks the rice in the giblet sauce and spoons some reserved sauce on top. I find it's easier to make the sauce, cook the rice, and then combine the two. That way you don't run the risk of gummy overcooked rice. Incidentally, this sauce is also wonderful tossed with *pappardelle*.

SERVES 6

*3/4 pound assorted chicken giblets
(gizzards, hearts, and livers)*

*5 tablespoons olive oil,
plus oil for sautéing livers (optional)*

2 onions, diced

2 carrots, peeled and diced

2 celery stalks, diced

2 cloves garlic, minced

2 cups dry red or white wine

7 cups chicken broth

2 cups Arborio rice

Salt and freshly ground black pepper to taste

*1 cup peeled, seeded, and diced plum tomatoes
(fresh or canned)*

Trim the livers, cutting away any connective pieces and any dark spots. Cut into large bite-sized pieces, keeping the lobes intact as much as possible. Refrigerate until needed. Trim the chicken hearts of fat.

Trim all the fat, connective tissue, and gristle from the gizzards, leaving just the meaty parts.

Warm 3 tablespoons of the olive oil in a large sauté pan over medium heat. Add 1 of the onions, the carrots, and the celery and sauté until softened, 5 to 8 minutes. Add the garlic and the gizzards and hearts and sauté for 5 minutes. Add the wine and let it bubble up in the pan. When it is reduced by half, add enough of the broth to barely cover the gizzards and hearts (about 2 cups). Simmer over low heat until tender, about 1 hour or so. Remove the giblets from the pan with a slotted spoon, transfer to a cutting board, and chop coarsely. Set the giblets aside.

Pour the remaining broth (about 5 cups) into a saucepan and bring to a simmer; adjust the heat to maintain a gentle simmer. Heat the remaining 2 tablespoons olive oil in a saucepan over medium heat. Add the remaining diced onion and sauté until softened, about 8 minutes. Add the rice and stir until opaque, about 3 minutes. Add a ladleful (about 1 cup) of the simmering broth and stir for 3 to 4 minutes until the broth is absorbed. Reduce the heat and continue to add the broth a ladleful at a time, waiting until each addition is absorbed before adding the next, until the rice kernels are al dente at the center and creamy on the outside, 18 to 20 minutes in all.

Meanwhile, cook the chicken livers: If you want to keep this kosher, broil the livers until cooked through. If not, you may sauté them in a separate pan in olive oil until golden on the outside and still pink at the center. Season with salt and pepper and set aside; keep warm.

Just before the rice is ready, stir in the giblets and tomatoes and warm through. Transfer to a warmed serving dish and garnish with the chicken livers. Serve immediately.

Risotto al Cedro
Rice with Citron

Citron (*etrog*) is carried along with a wand of willow leaves and palm fronds as part of the Sukkot holiday. The ceremonial citron is not edible, however, but other varieties of citron were traditionally used in cooking. Although we usually think of citron as a candied fruit to be added to pastry, grated fresh citron has long been used as a favorite flavor accent of Italian Jewish cooks. I am happy to report that some fresh citron is appearing at my market, although ironically it is a cultivated variety called Buddha's Hand. (And it does resemble a hand, with the long, tapered fingers we associate with statues of Buddha.) Citron adds lightness and fragrance to this risotto, which is inspired by a recipe from Milka Passigli's book. If you cannot find citron, use grated lemon zest or, even better, Meyer lemon zest, which is sweeter and more perfumed.

Serves 4 to 6

6 cups vegetable broth

3 tablespoons olive oil or unsalted butter

1 onion, chopped

2 cups Arborio rice

½ cup dry white wine

5 tablespoons grated or finely minced fresh citron or grated zest of 2 to 3 large lemons (3 to 4 tablespoons)

½ cup grated Emmenthaler cheese

4 tablespoons grated Parmesan cheese

½ cup heavy cream

Salt and freshly ground black pepper to taste

Pour the vegetable broth into a pan and bring to a simmer; adjust the heat to maintain a gentle simmer. Warm the olive oil in a large, deep sauté pan over medium heat. Add the onion and sauté until softened, about 8 minutes. Add the rice and stir until the rice is opaque, about 3 minutes. Add the white wine and stir until it evaporates, just a few minutes. Add a ladleful (about 1 cup) of the simmering broth and stir for 3 to 4 minutes until the broth is absorbed. Reduce the heat and continue to add the broth a ladleful at a time, waiting until each addition is absorbed before adding the next, until the rice kernels are al dente at the center and creamy on the outside, 18 to 20 minutes in all. Add the citron or lemon zest and simmer for a minute or two. Then stir in the grated cheeses and the cream and cook for 1 minute. Season with salt and pepper. Remove from the heat and transfer to a warmed serving dish. Serve immediately.

Variation:

If you like, add 1 ½ cups cooked asparagus cut into 1-inch pieces or whole English peas after the last addition of broth.

Riso con Brodo di Piselli

Rice in Pea Pod Broth with Peas

Unlike the Venetian classic *risi e bisi* that it resembles, this Jewish version of pea risotto uses a broth made from pea pods rather than chicken or meat broth. The result is a lovely pale green risotto. In the original recipe from *La cucina nella tradizione ebraica*, the peas and onions were sautéed, then rice was added, and the rice and peas were cooked nearly a half hour. Most peas are tender after 10 to 15 minutes, so if you like you can add the peas midway during the cooking time of the risotto. A shorter time over the heat will help them retain their color as well.

Serves 6

3 pounds English peas

2 onions, chopped

2 large carrots, peeled and chopped

2 celery stalks, chopped

2 tablespoons olive oil

⅔ cup chopped fresh flat-leaf parsley

2 cups Arborio rice

Salt and freshly ground black pepper to taste

Grated Parmesan cheese (optional)

Remove the peas from their pods. Set the peas aside (you should have 3 to 3½ cups) and put the pods, 1 of the chopped onions, the carrots, and the celery in a large saucepan. Add water to cover and bring to a boil. Reduce the heat to low and simmer, uncovered, until the pea pods are very tender, 30 to 40 minutes. Remove from the heat.

Working in batches, puree the vegetables, pea pods, and the cooking water in a blender. If the puree is too fibrous, pass it through a food mill or a sieve. You will need 6 cups broth for the risotto, so add additional vegetable broth or water to the puree to total this amount and so it is thin enough to be easily absorbed by the rice. Pour the broth into a saucepan and bring to a simmer. Adjust the heat to maintain a gentle simmer.

Warm the olive oil over medium heat. Add the remaining chopped onion and half of the parsley and sauté until softened, about 8 minutes. Add the rice and stir until opaque, about 3 minutes. Add a ladleful (about 1 cup) of the simmering broth and stir for 3 to 4 minutes until the liquid is absorbed. Reduce the heat and continue to add the broth a ladleful at a time, waiting until each addition is absorbed before adding the next, until the rice kernels are al dente at the center and creamy on the outside, 18 to 20 minutes in all. Add the peas midway during the cooking (just before the last 2 additions of broth). Season with salt and pepper.

Remove from the heat and transfer to a warmed serving dish. Sprinkle with the remaining parsley and a little Parmesan cheese, if using. Serve immediately.

Notes: If English peas are not in season, use snow peas or sugar snap peas for the broth. If you don't want to use frozen peas in the risotto, use sugar snap peas cut in half and blanched. Just remember that most vegetables in the Italian Jewish tradition are not al dente but are cooked all the way through.

Mira Sacerdoti's family uses less rice in this recipe and thins the dish with lots of pea broth. The result is a pea soup with rice rather than rice made with pea broth.

 Riso con Brodo di Piselli

RICE IN PEA POD BROTH WITH PEAS

Riso del Sabato
SABBATH RICE

The classic Italian Jewish Friday night rice dish is a simple saffron-flavored rice that recalls the classic *risotto alla milanese*. Some cooks make it in the manner of a risotto, adding broth in increments. Others prepare it as a pilaf, adding all the liquid at once and cooking it, covered, on top of the stove. In *La cucina nella tradizione ebraica*, the rice is sautéed in oil and the hot broth and saffron are added all at once. It is covered and put in the oven for 18 minutes. Once out of the oven it rests, covered, for 10 minutes and then is served with mushrooms, peas, or other seasonal vegetables. This version might also be served at room temperature. For Hanukkah, raisins are added and the dish becomes *riso con l'uvette*.

SERVES 4 TO 6

*5 to 6 cups chicken or beef broth,
or part water and part broth*

2 tablespoons olive oil or rendered chicken fat

2 cloves garlic, minced

3 tablespoons chopped fresh flat-leaf parsley

1 ½ cups Arborio rice

*¼ teaspoon chopped saffron threads,
infused in 2 tablespoons hot broth*

*¾ cup grapes, or golden raisins plumped
in white wine for 30 minutes (optional)*

Salt and freshly ground black pepper to taste

Pour the broth (or water and broth) into a saucepan and bring to a simmer; adjust the heat to maintain a gentle simmer.

Warm the olive oil or chicken fat in a large deep sauté pan over medium heat. Add the garlic and parsley and sauté for a few minutes until softened. Add the rice and stir until opaque, about 3 minutes. Add a ladleful

(about 1 cup) of the simmering broth and stir for 3 to 4 minutes until the liquid is absorbed. Reduce the heat and continue to add broth a ladleful at a time, waiting until each addition is absorbed before adding the next, until the rice kernels are al dente in the center and creamy on the outside, 18 to 20 minutes in all. Add the saffron and its broth about halfway through, and add the grapes or raisins during the last addition of broth, if using. Season with salt and pepper. Remove from the heat and transfer to a warmed serving dish. Serve immediately.

Polenta

Polenta is a basic accompaniment for many Italian Jewish dishes. It can be served warm, soft and comforting as porridge, unadorned or enriched with butter or cheese. Or it can be allowed to firm up and then cut into slices to be baked, fried, or grilled.

SERVES 3 TO 4

1 cup polenta (not instant)

1 teaspoon salt, plus salt to taste

4 cups water or as needed

3 to 4 tablespoons unsalted butter (optional)

⅓ cup grated Parmesan cheese (optional)

Combine the polenta, 1 teaspoon salt, and water in a heavy-bottomed saucepan and place over medium heat. Bring to a gentle boil, whisking occasionally. Adjust the heat to maintain a gentle simmer and cook, stirring often, until very thick and no longer grainy on the tongue, about 30 minutes. If the polenta thickens too quickly but still feels undercooked and grainy, stir in some hot water and continue to cook until it is cooked through and soft. Season to taste with salt and add the butter or cheese, if desired.

Serve warm right out of the pot. You may hold it over hot water in a double boiler for a half hour or so, adding hot water as needed to keep it soft and spoonable. Or pour the polenta out onto a buttered or oiled 9-by-12-inch baking pan or baking sheet, let cool, cover and refrigerate until fully set. Cut the polenta into strips or triangles while it is still in the pan.

To sauté, cook the polenta strips or triangles over high heat in clarified butter or olive oil in a nonstick or cast-iron frying pan until golden on both sides.

To bake, preheat an oven to 400 degrees F. Place the polenta strips or triangles in buttered gratin dishes and sprinkle with grated Parmesan cheese. Bake until golden and crusty, 20 to 30 minutes.

To deep-fry, coat the strips or triangles with flour, then beaten egg, then bread crumbs. Deep-fry a few pieces at a time in olive oil heated to 350 degrees F. Drain on paper towels. Serve hot.

Verdure
VEGETABLES

Carciofata di Trieste   *Spring Vegetable Stew*

Fagioli Cotti sotto la Bietola   *White Beans under Greens*

Stufato di Fave, Carciofi, e Lattuga Romana   *Braised Favas, Artichokes, and Lettuce*

Verze Sofegae   *Suffocated Cabbage*

Guscetti   *Braised Pea Pods*

Piselli in Tegame   *Braised Peas*

Carote alla Giudia   *Braised Carrots, Jewish Style*

Testine di Spinaci   *Braised Spinach Stems*

Sformato di Spinaci   *Spinach Pudding*

Polpettine di Spinaci   *Spinach Croquettes*

Spinaci con Pinoli e Passerine   *Spinach with Pine Nuts and Raisins*

Lattughe Farcite   *Stuffed Lettuce*

Torzelli   *Deep-fried Curly Endive*

Cipolle Ripieni   *Stuffed Baked Onions*

Zucca Disfatta   *Melted Golden Squash*

Zucca Gialla in Agrodolce   *Sweet-and-Sour Squash*

Budino di Zucca Gialla   *Squash Pudding from the Veneto*

Carciofi alla Romana   *Artichokes with Mint and Garlic, Roman Style*

Carciofi alla Giudia   *Crispy Fried Artichokes, Jewish Style*

Concia *Zucchini with Mint and Vinegar*

Melanzane in Insalata *Grilled Eggplant*

Cardi Gratinati *Cardoon Gratin*

Finocchi Gratinati *Fennel Gratin*

Finocchi alla Giudia *Braised Fennel, Jewish Style*

Peperoni Ripieni *Peppers Stuffed with Eggplant*

Roba Fritta *Mixed Fry*

Crochette di Patate *Potato Croquettes*

Patate e Pomodori *Potato and Tomato Gratin*

Pomodori a Mezzo *Baked Tomatoes with Tomato Sauce*

Pomodori con l'Uva *Tomatoes with Grape Juice*

Verdure

In the old days, most Italian Jewish meals were based around grains and vegetables, so it is not surprising that vegetables make up the largest chapter of this book and that it falls here in the middle rather than after the meats, as is the convention in most Italian cookbooks. Because vegetables were readily available and generally inexpensive, an extensive repertoire of vegetable recipes evolved. Cooks loved to take these humble ingredients and make them festive and filling. They were combined with bread crumbs and cheese or *besciamella* in gratins, or pureed and enriched with eggs for *sformate*, baked savory puddings. Such dishes were often the centerpiece of the meal, and rivaled the huge roster of vegetable-based pastas, risotti, and savory pies that the Italian Jews also favored.

Conventional leafy salads are a recent development in the history of Italian Jewish cooking, however. Greens tossed in a vinaigrette are rare in older Italian cookbooks, and composed salads of leafy greens and proteins are part of Italy's *nuova cucina*, which has been influenced by French cuisine.

In keeping with the Jewish laws of not working on the Sabbath, vegetables that were served hot on Friday were set out at room temperature on Saturday. Many such dishes are versatile in that they are equally good hot and cold. Other vegetable dishes like sweet-and-sour squashes and peppers dressed with olive oil that are left to marinate and later served at room temperature are generally thought of as part of an antipasto assortment.

Even though vegetables were plentiful and not costly, there was a constant pre-occupation with thrift. Nothing was wasted. Vegetable trimmings became part of a broth. Peas were used in a festive dish one day, but the reserved pods were used, too, turned into a special braised dish called *guscetti*, or simmered and pureed for a pea broth for cooking risotto. Even the stems of spinach and Swiss chard leaves were made into their own dishes.

Italian Jewish cooks also commonly used a style of preparation called *sofegae*, in which vegetables were cooked in olive oil with very little water so that they caramelized and thus developed an intense flavor. It's a wonderful cooking technique, one I find useful in getting the last bit of sweetness out of vegetables, but also one that may seem odd to those of us who dwell in the land of al dente. Give it a try, nonetheless. Fennel, carrots, cauliflower, artichokes, cabbage, eggplant, and peppers will take on a sweetness you've not tasted before. Many of these *sofegae* dishes, and other vegetable dishes as well, were treated to the classic Arab Sicilian addition of pine nuts and raisins.

 Carciofata di Trieste

SPRING VEGETABLE STEW

Carciofata di
Trieste
Spring Vegetable Stew

In *carciofata*, a spring vegetable stew from Trieste, all of the vegetables are cooked separately to maintain their texture and color, then combined and heated through at serving time.

Serves 6

Juice of 1 lemon

3 medium artichokes or 6 small (½ pound trimmed)

3 tablespoons olive oil

2 teaspoons minced garlic, or to taste

4 tablespoons chopped fresh flat-leaf parsley

1 cup shelled English peas, blanched for 1 minute

*½ pound baby carrots,
peeled and parboiled for 5 to 7 minutes*

*½ pound mushrooms, sliced,
and sautéed in olive oil for 5 minutes*

½ pound asparagus tips, blanched for 2 minutes

*½ pound little new potatoes, parboiled for 7 to 10
minutes, depending on size, drained*

*½ pound tiny pearl onions,
parboiled for 4 to 5 minutes, drained, and peeled*

2 cups vegetable broth, or as needed

Salt and freshly ground black pepper to taste

Pinch of sugar, if needed

*Chopped fresh mint, flat-leaf parsley, or basil for garnish
(optional)*

Fill a medium saucepan with lightly salted water and bring to a boil. Meanwhile, have ready a bowl of water to which you have added the lemon juice. Working with 1 artichoke at a time, cut off the stem even with the base. Remove all the leaves until you reach the pale green heart. Pare away the dark green area from the base. Cut the artichoke in half and scoop out and discard the choke. Then cut the tender heart lengthwise, into quarters. Drop into the lemon water. When all the artichokes are trimmed, drain and add to the boiling water. Parboil for 5 minutes and drain.

Warm the olive oil in a large sauté pan over medium heat. Add the garlic and parsley and stir for a minute or two. Add the artichokes, peas, carrots, mushrooms, asparagus, potatoes, pearl onions, and enough vegetable broth to moisten. Bring to a simmer and cook, uncovered, until all the vegetables are tender, about 10 minutes.

Taste and adjust the seasonings with salt and pepper, and add the sugar, if needed, for flavor balance. Transfer to a warmed serving dish. A little chopped parsley, basil, or mint would make a nice garnish. Serve hot.

Variation:
When the vegetables are tender, beat 1 egg with ¼ cup fresh lemon juice until frothy. Add a bit of the vegetable cooking liquid to the egg-and-lemon mixture (*bagna brusca*) to temper it, then whisk it into the vegetables. Stir well and remove from the heat. Sprinkle with chopped fresh parsley, basil, or mint. Serve at once.

Fagioli Cotti sotto la Bietola
WHITE BEANS UNDER GREENS

Emma Belforte, in a recipe described in *La cucina livornese*, recommends cooking the white beans and greens for three (!) hours, and then serving them with couscous for a full meal. I have cut the cooking time in half. For a fuller flavor, use broth instead of water. While most versions of this recipe ignore garlic, you would not be remiss in adding some. A Roman version includes lettuce and omits the onions. It is called *fagioli con la lattuga*.

SERVES 6

1 ¼ cups dried white or borlotti beans, picked over and rinsed

3 tablespoons virgin olive oil

2 red onions, chopped or thinly sliced

3 cloves garlic, minced (optional)

2 pounds beet greens or Swiss chard, well rinsed and finely chopped (about 10 cups)

3 cups diced canned plum tomatoes and their juices

Salt and freshly ground black pepper to taste

2 to 3 cups vegetable broth or water, or as needed

In a saucepan, combine the beans with lightly salted water to cover, bring to a boil, and boil for 2 minutes. Cover, remove from the heat, and let stand for 1 hour. Drain.

Warm the olive oil in a large, heavy pot over medium heat. Add the onions and garlic (if using) and sauté until softened, 5 to 8 minutes. Remove from the heat and turn into a large bowl. Add the greens and mix well. Spread half of the mixture over the bottom of the pot. Add half of the drained beans. Spread the remaining onion-greens mixture over the beans, then top with the remaining beans. Layer the chopped tomatoes and their juices on top. Add salt and pepper and enough vegetable broth or water to cover the beans amply.

Place over low heat and bring slowly to a boil. Cover, reduce the heat to low, and simmer very slowly until the beans are tender, 1 to 1 ½ hours. Taste and adjust the seasonings before serving.

VARIATION:

To speed up the cooking process, simmer the beans in water to cover for 30 minutes, and blanch the greens before mixing with the onion mixture. Layer the half-cooked beans and the greens in the pot as directed, then simmer, covered, for only 45 minutes.

Stufato di Fave, Carciofi, e Lattuga Romana
BRAISED FAVAS, ARTICHOKES, AND LETTUCE

This classic spring vegetable ragout is from *La cucina livornese*. It is another gem from the repertoire of Emma Belforte, whose palate I obviously share, although we may differ on cooking times. The dish is often served at Passover, the ultimate Jewish rite of spring. I've suggested the contemporary garnish of *gremolata*, a mixture of lemon zest, garlic, parsley, or, in this case, basil, to bring lightness and sparkle.

SERVES 6

Juice of 1 lemon

6 large artichokes

2 pounds fava beans, shelled (about 1 generous cup)

2 small heads romaine or butter lettuce

4 tablespoons extra-virgin olive oil, or as needed

4 tablespoons chopped fresh flat-leaf parsley

4 tablespoons chopped fresh basil

Salt and freshly ground black pepper to taste

½ cup water or vegetable broth, or as needed

Gremolata:

Grated zest of 2 lemons

6 tablespoons chopped fresh flat-leaf parsley or basil

1 tablespoon finely minced garlic

Have ready a large bowl of water to which you have added the lemon juice. Working with 1 artichoke at a time, cut off the stem even with the base. Remove all the tough outer leaves until you reach the pale green heart. Pare away the dark green area from the base. Cut the artichoke in half lengthwise and scoop out and discard the choke from each half. Drop the heart into the lemon water to prevent discoloration.

Bring a small saucepan of water to a boil, add the favas, and blanch for 30 seconds. Drain and, when cool enough to handle, slip off the thin skin covering each bean. Core the lettuces and slice the leaves crosswise into ½-inch-wide strips. Drain the artichoke hearts, pat dry, and cut into quarters, eighths, or thick slices.

Warm the 4 tablespoons of olive oil in a large, deep sauté pan over low heat. Add the artichokes and sauté, stirring often, for about 5 minutes. Add the favas, lettuces, parsley, basil, salt, pepper, and enough water or vegetable broth to cover barely. Raise the heat to medium and cook, stirring occasionally, until the artichokes are cooked through and most of the water has evaporated, 10 to 15 minutes. In the meantime, combine the *gremolata* ingredients.

Remove the artichoke mixture from the heat, sprinkle with the *gremolata*, and stir well. Let rest for 5 minutes—enough time for the garlic in the gremolata to soften—then serve.

Verze Sofegae
SUFFOCATED CABBAGE

A classic Italian Jewish style for cooking vegetables is *sofegae*, which means "suffocated." The vegetables are very slowly cooked over the lowest heat in olive oil or goose or chicken fat and the minimum amount of water. *La cucina nella tradizione ebraica* suggests two or three hours! Here's a typical *sofegae* recipe for cabbage, although I have cut the traditional cooking time considerably.

SERVES 4 TO 6

1 head cabbage

3 to 4 tablespoons rendered goose or chicken fat or olive oil

1 onion, chopped

2 cloves garlic, minced

1 to 2 teaspoons chopped fresh rosemary (optional)

Salt and freshly ground black pepper to taste

Dash of wine vinegar

Pinch of sugar (optional)

Cut the cabbage into quarters through the stem end. Cut away the tough core, then cut the quarters crosswise into narrow strips.

Warm the goose or chicken fat or olive oil in a sauté pan over low heat. Add the onion, garlic, and the rosemary, if using, and sauté until tender, about 8 minutes. Add the cabbage, salt, pepper, vinegar, and the sugar, if using, and cover the pan. Cook until the cabbage is very tender, about 30 minutes, then serve.

Guscetti
BRAISED PEA PODS

Many traditional Italian Jewish recipes demonstrate the creative use of "leftovers," using parts of foods that might normally be discarded. This dish is from Ferrara, in the region of Emilia-Romagna, and one version is described in *La cucina nella tradizione ebraica*. Today the Italian Jewish cook could use sugar snap peas or snow peas (a pound of either would work for this recipe), but this dish was designed to use every part of the familiar English pea.

SERVES 4

2 pounds young English peas

4 tablespoons olive oil

2 cloves garlic, finely minced

3 tablespoons chopped fresh flat-leaf parsley

¼ cup water or vegetable broth

Salt and freshly ground black pepper to taste

A few tablespoons white wine vinegar (optional)

Chopped fresh mint (optional)

Shell the peas and use them for another dish such as a risotto or *carciofata* (see page 81). Blanch the pea pods in boiling water for 2 minutes, refresh in cold water, and peel off the thin membranes from each pod.

Warm the olive oil in a sauté pan over medium heat. Add the garlic and parsley and sauté until softened, about 3 minutes. Add the peeled pea pods and the water or vegetable broth, cover, lower the heat, and braise until tender, 15 to 20 minutes. Season with salt and pepper.

If you like, sprinkle the pea pods with a bit of vinegar, although the vinegar, while tasting good, will turn the pea pods a bit yellow-brown. For a contemporary touch, sprinkle them with a little chopped mint at the end of cooking. Serve warm or at room temperature.

Piselli in Tegame
BRAISED PEAS

Also called *pisellini alle cegole*, or "peas with onions," in Venetian dialect, this simple braise of sweet spring peas uses wine instead of water. Some versions add the kosher chopped goose prosciutto while sautéing the onion.

SERVES 4

2 pounds English peas, shelled (about 2 cups)

2 small onions, finely chopped

6 tablespoons olive oil

¼ cup pine nuts, chopped

¼ cup dry white wine or water

Chopped fresh flat-leaf parsley, for garnish

Combine the peas, onions, and olive oil in a small saucepan. Place over low heat and cook slowly for 10 minutes. Add the pine nuts and wine or water and cook until very tender, 10 to 15 minutes. Sprinkle with a little parsley just before serving.

Carote alla Giudia
Braised Carrots, Jewish Style

A dish of cooked carrots, *sofegae* style, from the Veneto. The presence of pine nuts and raisins and the dash of vinegar to balance the sweetness of the raisins are give-aways of the Arabic or Levantine origins. Some cooks add a tablespoon of sugar as well, making this *carote in agrodolce*.

Serves 4

1/4 to 1/3 cup rendered goose or chicken fat, or olive oil

1 1/2 pounds carrots, peeled and thinly sliced

1/4 cup water

6 tablespoons raisins, plumped in water or sweet wine

3 tablespoons pine nuts, toasted

Salt and freshly ground pepper to taste

Dash of vinegar or sugar to taste (optional)

Warm the goose or chicken fat or olive oil in a sauté pan over medium heat. Add the carrots and sauté until well coated with fat, 5 to 8 minutes. Add the water and cover the pan. Reduce the heat to very low and simmer until the carrots are tender, about 20 minutes.

Add the raisins with their liquid, and the pine nuts. Season with salt and pepper. Add a little vinegar or sugar, or both if you like. Serve warm or at room temperature.

Testine di Spinaci
Braised Spinach Stems

Testine means "little heads." An old Venetian recipe for these spinach stems calls the dish *gambetti de spinasse* in dialect, or "little legs." How thrifty to use the spinach leaves for one dish and then use the stems and inner tiny leaves to make this antipasto or side dish. You will need to start with almost 4 pounds of spinach to yield about 1 pound of the stems.

Serves 3 or 4

1 pound spinach stems and inner tiny leaves

1/2 cup olive oil

Dash of red wine vinegar

Salt and freshly ground black pepper to taste

Wash the stems well in several changes of water, then trim off the roots. Place the stems in a saucepan with the olive oil and enough water to barely cover. Bring to a boil over high heat and cook quickly until the water evaporates and the stems are tender, 8 to 10 minutes.

Add the vinegar and cook over high heat until the vinegar evaporates and the roots turn red, just a few minutes. Season with salt and pepper.

Remove from the heat, let cool, and chill before serving.

Note: The Italians are not the only thrifty cooks. Turkish Jews also cook spinach stems and call the dish *ravikos*.

Sformato di
Spinaci
SPINACH PUDDING

A *sformato* is a classic steamed pudding much beloved by Italian Jewish cooks as it makes a festive and elegant dish out of a few simple and inexpensive ingredients. This recipe is from *La cucina nella tradizione ebraica.* You can serve it from the baking dish in the manner of a soufflé or, more traditionally, unmold (*sformare*) it and accompany with sautéed mushrooms or with a light Tomato Sauce (page 163).

SERVES 6

7 tablespoons unsalted butter

3 tablespoons fine dried bread crumbs

3 pounds fresh spinach, stems removed or 3 packages (10 ounces each) frozen spinach, thawed and squeezed dry

1 small onion, finely minced

Salt and freshly ground black pepper to taste

Freshly grated nutmeg to taste

3 tablespoons all-purpose flour

1 ½ cups milk, heated

6 eggs, separated

4 tablespoons grated Parmesan cheese

Preheat an oven to 400 degrees F. Spread 1 tablespoon of the butter in an 8 ½-inch tube pan, large casserole, or soufflé dish and sprinkle with the bread crumbs, coating evenly. (For more foolproof unmolding, line the pan with buttered parchment paper or use a springform pan.)

Rinse the fresh spinach and remove the stems (reserve for Braised Spinach Stems, page 85). Place in a large saucepan or sauté pan with only the rinsing water clinging to the leaves. Cook over medium heat, turning as necessary until wilted, just a few minutes. Drain, rinse in cold water, and drain again. Chop, then squeeze dry. If using frozen spinach, omit this step.

Melt 3 tablespoons of the butter in a sauté pan over medium heat. Add the onion and sauté until softened, about 8 minutes. Stir in the cooked spinach and season with salt, pepper, and nutmeg. Transfer to a large bowl and set aside.

Melt the remaining 3 tablespoons butter in a small saucepan over medium heat. Add the flour and cook, stirring, until well blended and bubbly, 3 to 5 minutes. Gradually add the hot milk, whisking continuously. Cook, stirring, until the sauce coats the back of a spoon, 3 to 5 minutes.

Add the sauce to the spinach and stir in the egg yolks and Parmesan cheese, mixing well. Beat the egg whites until stiff peaks form, then fold them into the spinach mixture just until no white streaks remain. Pour into the prepared pan.

Bake until golden and set, about 30 minutes. (You can also put the pudding mold in a bain-marie to bake, unless you're using a springform pan. It will be slightly moister than the one baked dry. It may be a little harder to unmold, but it will have a more delicate texture.) Remove from the oven and let rest for 10 minutes. Run a knife around the edge of the pudding. Invert a warmed platter on top. Holding the mold and platter together, shake once, then invert together and lift off the mold. The *sformato* should unmold easily. Serve warm or hot.

 Sformato di Spinaci

SPINACH PUDDING

Polpettine di Spinaci

SPINACH CROQUETTES

From a description in Maffioli's *La cucina veneziana* comes this interpretation of little spinach dumplings. The finely chopped spinach is cooked in butter or oil and bound with bread crumbs, eggs, raisins, pine nuts, and garlic. The mixture is then formed into little cakes, and fried in oil. In more elaborate versions of the recipe, the cooked croquettes are simmered in broth for a few minutes and transferred to a heated platter. The broth is then thickened with a *bagna brusca* (see page 166), and spooned over the spinach cakes, much like Greek dolmas coated in an *avgolemono* sauce.

SERVES 4

6 tablespoons unsalted butter or olive oil

1 pound spinach, finely chopped

2 cups fresh bread crumbs, soaked in milk or water and squeezed dry

2 whole eggs, lightly beaten, plus 1 egg yolk

½ cup pine nuts, toasted

⅓ cup raisins, plumped in sweet white wine

2 cloves garlic, finely minced

Salt and freshly ground black pepper to taste

1 cup vegetable broth if using butter, or chicken broth if using oil

Juice of 1 large lemon

Melt 3 tablespoons of the butter or oil in a large sauté pan over medium heat. Add the spinach and turn in the pan until wilted, just a few minutes. Transfer to a bowl and add the soaked bread crumbs, the whole eggs, the pine nuts, the raisins, and the garlic. Season with salt and pepper. Form into little cakes about 2 ½ to 3 inches in diameter.

Rinse the pan and place over medium heat. Warm the remaining 3 tablespoons of the butter or olive oil. Add the cakes and sauté, turning once, until golden, about 5 minutes total. Add the broth, reduce the heat and simmer for 5 minutes. Remove the spinach cakes to a warmed platter. (Or for cakes with a firmer texture, remove the croquettes from the pan when golden and place on a warmed serving platter. Deglaze the pan with the broth, and simmer the broth for 5 minutes.)

Whisk the yolk with the lemon juice until frothy, then whisk in a little of the hot broth. Stir the egg yolk mixture into the sauté pan and cook gently, stirring often, until thickened. Spoon over the spinach croquettes and serve at once.

Spinaci con Pinoli e Passerine
SPINACH WITH PINE NUTS AND RAISINS

Spinach with pine nuts and raisins is a classic Sephardic dish that appears on tables in Greece, Spain, Turkey, and in Italy, where it is a staple on Venetian and Genoese menus. It is a perfect accompaniment to delicate fish or poultry dishes and is often served at room temperature.

SERVES 6

2 ½ pounds spinach

2 to 3 tablespoons olive oil

2 small yellow onions or 6 green onions, minced

4 tablespoons raisins, plumped in hot water and drained

4 tablespoons pine nuts, toasted

Salt and freshly ground black pepper to taste

Rinse the spinach well and remove the stems (reserve the stems for Braised Spinach Stems on page 85). Place in a large sauté pan with only the rinsing water clinging to the leaves. Cook over medium heat, turning as needed, until wilted, just a few minutes. Drain well and set aside. Add the olive oil to the now-empty pan and place over medium heat. Add the onions and sauté until tender, about 8 minutes. Add the spinach, raisins, and pine nuts and sauté briefly to warm through. Season with salt and pepper and serve warm or at room temperature.

Lattughe Farcite
STUFFED LETTUCE

The ancient Romans believed that lettuce was an aid to digestion, and this recipe, based on one that appears in Mira Sacerdoti's book *Italian Jewish Cooking*, is actually a very old Roman dish. Don't worry that the lettuces are braised on top of the stove without any liquid except olive oil. The finished dish will be moist enough because lettuce gives off quite a bit of liquid as it cooks.

SERVES 4

4 small heads lettuce, preferably butter

½ to ⅓ cup pitted Mediterranean-style black olives

1 can (2 ounces) olive oil–packed anchovy fillets, drained

1 heaping tablespoon capers, rinsed

5 tablespoons extra-virgin olive oil

Salt and freshly ground black pepper to taste

Remove any bruised outer leaves from the lettuce heads. Rinse, drain, and dry the heads well. Chop the olives, anchovies, and capers coarsely. Add 2 tablespoons of the olive oil and mix well.

Carefully open the leaves of each head of lettuce and spread the olive paste between the leaves and into the core. Gently reform the heads.

Place the lettuces close together in a saucepan. Drizzle with the remaining 3 tablespoons olive oil and cover the pan tightly. Braise over low heat until tender, about 25 minutes. Serve warm or at room temperature.

Torzelli
DEEP-FRIED CURLY ENDIVE

A Roman specialty, crispy curly endive (also known as chicory, and similar to *frisée*, which can be substituted) is usually served as a side dish to roasts. If you can't find perfect heads of *indivia*, radicchio or even Belgian endive can be used in their place. Because the original recipes don't advise dipping the chicory in a batter or flour, I first tried it unadorned. It was good, but quite greasy. Dipping the greens in an egg wash and flour before frying eliminates the problem.

SERVES 6

6 small heads curly endive

Olive, peanut, or safflower oil for deep-frying

2 eggs

4 tablespoons water

All-purpose flour for coating

Salt and freshly ground black pepper to taste

Lemon wedges for serving (optional)

Pick off any limp or unsightly outer leaves but keep each head intact. Drop the heads into a large pot of boiling salted water and simmer for about 5 minutes. Drain, squeeze out excess moisture gently with a clean dish towel, then spread to dry well on another towel. (This pre-cooking can be done a few hours ahead of time.)

To serve, pour oil to a depth of 2 inches in a saucepan and heat to 375 degrees F. Meanwhile, prepare an egg wash by lightly beating the eggs with the water in a bowl large enough for dipping a head of endive. Spread the flour on a plate or in a shallow soup bowl. When the oil is ready, one at a time, dip the endives into the egg wash and then in the flour, coating lightly. Slip into the oil in batches and deep-fry, turning with tongs as necessary, until golden, 3 to 4 minutes. Transfer to paper towels to drain; keep hot until all the heads are cooked. Sprinkle with salt and pepper and serve at once with lemon wedges, if desired.

Cipolle Ripieni
STUFFED BAKED ONIONS

The dolma theme that runs through Sephardic cooking is present in this recipe for stuffed onions. Turkish Jews call these *reynadas de sevoya*, so we know these onions came to Italy via the Spanish Jews.

SERVES 6

*Meat mixture filling for Meatballs, Jewish Style
(page 140)*

6 large onions

Salt and freshly ground black pepper to taste

Olive oil

Make the meat filling as directed. Preheat an oven to 350 degrees F.

Bring a large saucepan filled with water to a boil, add the onions, and boil until they are tender but not soft, about 10 minutes. Drain and, when cool enough to handle, cut in half crosswise. Scoop out part of the centers and chop, then combine with the meat filling. Season with salt and pepper to taste. Spoon this mixture into onion cavities and place them in a baking dish. Drizzle liberally with olive oil.

Bake until golden and tender when pierced, about 20 minutes. Serve warm.

Zucca Disfatta
Melted Golden Squash

The yellow-orange squash of the Veneto is commonly called *zucca barucca*. For Jews, *barucca* is related to *baruch*, the Hebrew word for "blessed." Non-Jewish Italians say this name is dialect for *verruca*, meaning bumpy and wartlike, describing the outer peel of the squash. What we do know for sure is that there are many Italian Jewish (as well as Spanish and Moroccan Jewish) recipes that call for the *zucca barucca*, the pumpkin squash that was brought to Italy by the Sephardim from Spain and Portugal.

Disfatta means "defeated" or "decomposed" squash, in other words, melted and quite soft. Baking the squash provides a richer taste than boiling it. This recipe is from the Veneto, Ferrara to be exact, and traditionally was served to break the fast at the end of Yom Kippur. It calls for fresh citron, which is sweeter and more aromatic than grated lemon zest. You'll find, however, that the sweetness of the squash will help balance any slight bitterness of the lemon zest. Some versions of this dish add a pinch of cinnamon; others add chopped parsley and rosemary.

Serves 6

1 or 2 hard-skinned yellow squashes such as butternut, banana, or acorn, 3 pounds total weight

3 tablespoons olive oil or unsalted butter

1 onion, finely chopped (about 1 ¼ cups)

Salt and freshly ground black pepper, to taste

3 tablespoons finely minced citron, or 2 tablespoons grated lemon zest

½ teaspoon ground cinnamon (optional)

Chopped fresh mint, flat-leaf parsley, or rosemary for garnish (optional)

Preheat an oven to 375 degrees F. Prick the squash or squashes with the tip of a knife and place in a pan in the oven. Bake until tender when pierced, 45 to 60 minutes, depending on size. Remove from the oven and, when cool enough to handle, cut in half. Scoop out the seeds and fibers and discard. Scoop out the flesh and pass it through a food mill placed over a bowl, or mash it with a potato masher. You should have about 3 cups puree.

Warm the olive oil or butter in a sauté pan over low heat. Add the onion and sauté until very soft and sweet, about 15 minutes. Add the pureed squash, season with salt and pepper, and add the citron or lemon zest and cinnamon, if using. Cook over very low heat, stirring often, until dry, about 10 minutes. Transfer to a warmed serving dish and sprinkle with mint, parsley, or rosemary, if you like.

Notes: Edda Servi Machlin has a version of this recipe called *zucca sfranta*, using zucchini or yellow summer squash. It is seasoned very simply with basil and parsley. You might also try substituting yams or sweet potatoes for the hard-skinned squashes.

Zucca Gialla in Agrodolce
SWEET-AND-SOUR SQUASH

Sicily is probably the origin of this recipe, adapted from Cia Eramo's *La cucina mantovana*. It is identical to the classic *fegato ai sette cannoli*, named after a fountain in Palermo with seven spouts. Few people in the surrounding poverty-stricken neighborhood could afford meat. Pumpkin is meaty, however, and when cooked has so much body that they likened it to liver (*fegato*). Use pumpkin, Hubbard, butternut, or another large yellow hard-skinned winter squash for this dish.

SERVES 6 TO 8

2-pound piece butternut squash or pumpkin

⅓ cup olive oil, or as needed

½ cup coarsely chopped fresh mint

2 or 3 large cloves garlic, sliced paper-thin

½ cup red wine vinegar

½ cup sugar

Pinch of ground cinnamon (optional)

Salt and freshly ground black pepper to taste

Halve the squash, discard the seeds and fibers, peel the halves, and cut the pulp into ⅓-inch-thick slices.

Warm half the olive oil in a large sauté pan over medium heat. In batches, add the squash slices and sauté, adding oil as needed and turning to brown both sides, until tender, 6 to 8 minutes. Using a slotted spatula, transfer to a serving platter. Cover with the mint and garlic.

To the oil remaining in the pan, add the vinegar, sugar, and the cinnamon, if using, and cook until the sugar dissolves and the sauce thickens, about 5 minutes. Season with salt and pepper.

Pour the sauce over the squash. Serve at room temperature.

Notes: Some versions of this dish call for cooking the garlic in the oil, discarding it, and then cooking the squash. Some omit both the vinegar and cinnamon.

 Zucca Gialla in Agrodolce
SWEET-AND-SOUR SQUASH

Budino di Zucca
Gialla
SQUASH PUDDING FROM THE VENETO

From the dairy section of *La cucina nella tradizione ebraica* comes the inspiration for this recipe for a rich and irresistible pumpkin squash pudding. It is served warm as a side dish and would be great as part of a Thanksgiving meal. I know it sounds funny, given the salt, pepper, and Parmesan, but in the old days it occasionally was served cold as dessert, topped with a fruit sauce. Our butternut squash is closest in flavor to the Italian *zucca*.

SERVES 6

*1 ½ pounds peeled, seeded, and diced butternut
or kabocha squash (5 to 6 cups)*

Salt and freshly ground black pepper to taste

Sugar to taste, if needed

1 teaspoon ground cinnamon, or to taste (optional)

5 tablespoons unsalted butter

3 tablespoons all-purpose flour

1 cup milk, heated

3 egg yolks, lightly beaten

4 tablespoons grated Parmesan cheese

Freshly grated nutmeg to taste (optional)

Place the squash in a saucepan with salted water to cover, bring to a boil, and cook until tender, about 25 minutes. Drain and pass through a ricer or food mill placed over a saucepan, or mash with a potato masher. Place the pan over low heat to evaporate any excess liquid. Season with salt and pepper. Add a bit of sugar or the cinnamon if the flavor is too flat. Remove from the heat.

Preheat an oven to 350 degrees F. Butter a 1- to 1 ½-quart mold, soufflé dish, or baking dish with 3-inch sides.

Melt the butter in a small saucepan over medium heat. Add the flour and cook, stirring, until well blended and bubbly, about 3 minutes. Gradually whisk in the hot milk and cook, stirring, until thick enough to coat the back of a spoon, about 5 minutes.

Fold the sauce into the pureed squash, then let cool a bit. Add the egg yolks and Parmesan cheese. Season to taste with more salt and pepper, and some nutmeg, if you like. Spoon into the prepared dish. Place the dish in a baking pan and add hot water to reach halfway up the sides of the dish. (The bain-marie will keep the pudding moist and velvety as it cooks.)

Bake until set and golden, about 40 minutes. Remove from the oven and let rest for 10 minutes. Run a knife around the edge of the pudding. Invert a warmed platter on top. Holding the mold and platter together, shake once, then invert together and lift off the mold. Serve hot.

Note: For a more caramelized flavor, bake 1 or 2 whole squashes in an oven preheated to 375 degrees F. When tender, after about 1 hour, remove from the oven, halve, remove the seeds and fibers, and mash or puree. Then proceed as directed.

Carciofi alla Romana

ARTICHOKES WITH MINT AND GARLIC, ROMAN STYLE

In Italian cooking, artichokes were originally a Jewish specialty, and artichokes stuffed with a mixture of mint, parsley, and garlic and braised in olive oil are a Roman specialty. Sometimes bread crumbs or minced anchovies are added to the stuffing mixture. It is unlikely that the stems on the artichokes you purchase will be tender enough to leave intact. In that case, cut the stems off flat at the base and cook the artichokes bottom side down, as opposed to the Roman style of cooking with the stems up.

SERVES 4

2 lemons

4 artichokes

2 or 3 cloves garlic, minced

4 tablespoons chopped fresh flat-leaf parsley

4 tablespoons chopped fresh mint

1 cup fine dried bread crumbs (optional)

2 tablespoons minced olive oil–packed anchovy fillets

Salt and freshly ground black pepper to taste

Olive oil, as needed

Lemon wedges for serving

Fill a large bowl with cold water and squeeze the juice of one of the lemons into it. Halve the other lemon. If the artichoke stems are tender, trim them to 1 1/2 inches and peel. If not, cut the stems off close to the base. Rub the cut areas with the lemon. Remove all of the tough outer leaves until you reach a pale green, pointy core about 1 1/4 to 1 1/2 inches in diameter at its base. Carefully open the leaves by rapping the artichoke very gently on a tabletop or pok-

ing it open with your fingers. Be careful not to crack the leaves at their base. Carefully scoop out the choke with a melon baller, or a small pointed spoon. Rub the artichoke with the cut lemon. As each artichoke is trimmed, drop it into the lemon water.

In a small bowl, combine the garlic, parsley, mint, the bread crumbs, if using, and the anchovies. Season with salt and pepper and drizzle with olive oil. Drain the artichokes and pat dry. Stuff the bread-crumb mixture into the artichokes, into the cavity left by the choke and in between the leaves. Tightly close the leaves over the filling.

If you have artichokes without stems, place them close together in a dutch oven or saucepan. Drizzle liberally with 1 part water and 2 parts olive oil, to a depth of about 2 inches. Cover the pan and place over very low heat. Cook gently until tender when a thin skewer is inserted into the base, 45 to 60 minutes.

If you have artichokes with stems, preheat an oven to 350 degrees F. Tie the leaves closed with kitchen string, and put the artichokes stems up in a baking dish or ovenproof pan in which they fit snugly. Season with salt and add 1 part water to 2 parts olive oil to cover completely. Cover the baking dish or pan and place in the oven. Cook until tender when tested with a thin skewer, about 1 hour.

These artichokes can be eaten warm or at room temperature. Serve with lemon wedges.

Note: You can also use artichoke hearts for this dish. Fill the centers with the stuffing, place them side by side in a baking dish, drizzle with olive oil, and add 1 cup water to the dish. Cover and bake in a preheated 350 degree F oven until tender, about 25 minutes. (They can also be cooked in a heavy-bottomed saucepan on the stove top for about the same amount of time.) Serve cold with lemon wedges.

Carciofi alla Giudia

CRISPY FRIED ARTICHOKES, JEWISH STYLE

The first time you eat one of these artichokes, it is so delicious, you will want to cry. It's also beautiful—like a crispy chrysanthemum. You vow that you are going to make these Roman deep-fried artichokes the minute you get home, so you can enjoy them again and again. Oh, would that it were so simple. *Carciofi alla giudia* is easier to write about than to cook. American artichokes are not like Roman artichokes. Ours have tough, fibrous chokes and prickly spines at the ends of the outer leaves. Most of theirs do not. When we get artichokes at the market, the stems are no longer moist and tender, if they are attached at all. Roman artichokes come to the market with their long stems intact—tender and flexible.

I know you've seen recipes for *carciofi alla giudia* in cook-books. They all look easy: just pound the chokes open and fry. But if you have tried to make them, you were probably as frustrated as I was. The stems are tough! The leaves fall off! I experimented with these for over a year. My chances for complete success are now about eighty to twenty. I'd like to share the process with you.

First, working with 1 artichoke at a time, remove the tough outer leaves with their prickly spines. You must keep enough of the inner leaves to form a large, pointy, pale green core. The next step, opening the leaves, seems simple enough. Some cooks suggest tapping one artichoke against the other, others call for pushing a lemon into the center. Once done, very gently scoop out the choke with a melon baller or spoon. Now flatten the artichoke on a tabletop, again gently. Herein lies the potential for disaster: if the artichokes are not flexible and tender, more often than not the leaves crack in the opening process and then break off in the final frying, leaving you with a choke but no flower.

To get around this, I have used baby artichokes that have soft, tender chokes, but they are really too small to make a flower. They taste great, but they aren't chrysanthemums—more like dandelions after the wind. The small ones will, however, give you the crispy texture of the *classic carciofi alla giudia* and are easy to work with. In other words, they're a good start.

I have tried jumbo artichokes, but the chokes are really tough and hard to remove without major leaf loss. I have finally resorted to the medium size variety. (In the Bay Area, where I live, I have found one farmer who is growing chokeless, spineless artichokes. They work well for the classic Roman recipe, but these are hard to find, as supply is limited.) To keep your sanity, make this for 2 to 4 people the first few times—good friends who will enjoy them and appreciate your efforts even if the artichokes are not perfect.

SERVES 4

2 lemons

4 medium-sized artichokes, with stems intact

Olive oil

Salt to taste

Fill a large bowl with water and squeeze the juice of 1 of the lemons into it. Halve the remaining lemon. Working with one artichoke at a time, cut off all but 1½ inches of the stem. Pare the stems and the base, removing the dark green areas, then rub with the cut lemon. Remove all of the tough outer leaves, until you reach a pale green, pointy core about 1¼ to 1½ inches in diameter at its base. Carefully open the leaves by rapping the artichoke very gently on a tabletop or poking it open with your fingers. Be careful not to crack the leaves at their base. Carefully scoop out the choke with a melon baller or a small pointed spoon. Rub the artichoke with the cut lemon. As each artichoke is trimmed, drop it into the lemon water. When all of them have been trimmed, drain well, dry with a kitchen towel, and place, stem up, on another towel.

recipe continues on page 98

 Carciofi alla Giudia

CRISPY FRIED ARTICHOKES, JEWISH STYLE

For the first cooking, select a pot that is large enough to hold all of the artichokes, stem up. Place them in the pot, fill halfway with olive oil, and then add water to cover. Bring to a simmer and cook gently, uncovered, until just cooked through but not soft, 15 to 17 minutes. Test the base with a thin wooden skewer. If they are undercooked, the second frying will take at least 10 to 12 minutes and is riskier, as more leaves may fall off. Despite that, it is better that they are undercooked than overcooked.

Using tongs or a skimmer, remove from the pot and place on a platter, stem up, pressing down gently to keep an open flower shape. You can prepare the artichokes up to this point 2 to 3 hours in advance.

For the second cooking, select a deep cast-iron frying pan. Pour in olive oil to a depth of 2 ½ inches and heat to about 350 degrees F (a low boil). Add 2 artichokes, stem up. Using tongs, hold them down, pressing on them to keep the open flower shape. Fry them until golden and crisp, about 8 minutes. Transfer to paper towels to drain, then sprinkle with salt. Keep warm in a low oven. Fry the remaining artichokes the same way. It is just about impossible to fry 4 artichokes at a time, as you can't hold them down and flat unless two of you are cooking them at the same time or you are an octopus.

Eat at once. Swear not to be discouraged if many of the leaves fall off. They are still scrumptious, aren't they?

Concia
Zucchini with Mint and Vinegar

Concia is served as part of an assorted antipasto or as an accompaniment for meat dishes, especially *bollito* (boiled beef). It can also be made into a wonderful snack by layering it between two pieces of bread, or using it as a topping for *crostini*. Although this dish is popular in the Roman Jewish community, it is of Sicilian origin. It is called *zuchete in aseo* in the Veneto, and *zucchini all'aceto* or *zucchini all'agro* elsewhere. Eggplant is prepared the same way and called *concia di malignane* or *melanzane all'aceto*.

Serves 4

4 to 6 small zucchini, about 1 ½ pounds total weight

Salt

3 tablespoons chopped fresh mint or basil

2 tablespoons chopped fresh flat-leaf parsley

2 large cloves garlic, minced

6 tablespoons olive oil

4 tablespoons red or white wine vinegar

Cut the zucchini into ¼-inch-thick slices, or to prepare it Veneto fashion, cut the zucchini lengthwise into ¼-inch-thick slices. Sprinkle with salt and let stand in a colander for 30 minutes to drain off any bitter juices. Rinse and pat dry.

In a small bowl, combine the mint or basil, parsley, and garlic.

Warm the olive oil in a frying pan over medium-high heat. In batches, add the zucchini and cook, turning as needed, until golden on both sides, 4 to 5 minutes.

Transfer to a shallow serving dish and sprinkle with some of the mint mixture and some of the vinegar. Repeat with the rest of the zucchini, mint mixture, and vinegar. Leave at room temperature for 1 or 2 hours, basting occasionally with vinegar in the dish, before serving.

Melanzane
Eggplants

Eggplants were brought to Spain and Italy by the Arabs. The Jews took to this new food readily. In his famous 1891 cookbook, *La scienza in cucina e l'arte di mangiare bene*, Pellegrino Artusi observed, "Forty years ago you could hardly find eggplant or fennel in the markets of Florence, because they were considered Jewish food and were abhorred." When the Inquisition banned the Jews from Spain and Spanish settlements in southern Italy, the Italian Jews fled north, bringing with them a repertoire of eggplant dishes. It's not surprising that many of the best eggplant recipes are of Sicilian origin, as that is where the Sephardic and Arabic influence was the greatest. Incidentally, many of the eggplant dishes are served at room temperature, in other words, prepared on late Friday to be served at Saturday lunch.

Melanzane in Insalata
Grilled Eggplant

This is a variation on *concia* made with eggplant (see recipe introduction, page 98); but here the eggplant slices are grilled or broiled instead of sautéed. If grilling, cut the slices a little thicker than for frying, as eggplant shrinks in cooking and these need to be substantial enough to turn easily on the grill.

Serves 6

2 eggplants, peeled and cut lengthwise into
½-inch-thick slices

½ cup olive oil, or as needed

Salt and freshly ground black pepper to taste

2 cloves garlic, minced

¼ cup red wine vinegar

Chopped fresh mint or flat-leaf parsley for garnish

Prepare a charcoal fire. Brush the eggplant slices with the olive oil and sprinkle with salt, pepper, and the garlic. Place over the hot coals and grill, turning once, until golden and tender, 4 to 5 minutes.

Transfer to 1 or 2 platters and sprinkle with the vinegar. Sprinkle with the mint or parsley. Serve at room temperature.

Melanzane Roste
Venetian Eggplant Salad

Slice the eggplant very thin. Marinate for 30 minutes in olive oil, salt, freshly ground black pepper, chopped garlic, and chopped fresh flat-leaf parsley. Place on a baking sheet and cook in an oven preheated to 450 degree F or in a broiler. If you should decide to grill these, don't cut them quite so thin, as they will be difficult to turn. Transfer to a platter and garnish with strips of anchovy, a drizzle of extra-virgin olive oil, and additional chopped fresh parsley.

Cardi Gratinati
CARDOON GRATIN

Cardoons look like giant prickly celery, but taste like artichokes, and are often served in gratins. Fennel would make a good substitute for the cardoons.

SERVES 6 TO 8

Juice of 1 lemon

2 pounds cardoons

4 tablespoons unsalted butter

4 tablespoons all-purpose flour

1 cup milk, heated

1 cup heavy cream, heated

2 egg yolks

½ cup grated Parmesan cheese

Salt and freshly ground black pepper to taste

Preheat an oven to 350 degrees F. Butter a 2-quart baking dish.

Have ready a large bowl of water to which you have added the lemon juice. Trim the prickly leaves from the cardoons and pull off the strings. Cut the stalks crosswise into 3-inch pieces and drop into the lemon water until ready to cook. Drain the cardoons and place in a large saucepan of salted water. Bring to a boil and cook until tender, 25 to 30 minutes. Drain well and set aside.

Melt the butter in a small saucepan over low heat. Add the flour and cook, stirring until well blended and bubbly, about 5 minutes. Whisk in the hot milk and cream and continue to whisk until thickened enough to coat the back of a spoon thickly, 8 to 10 minutes. Remove from the heat, whisk in the egg yolks and Parmesan, and season with salt and pepper.

Place the cardoons in the prepared baking dish. Spoon the cream sauce evenly over the top. Bake until golden, about 30 minutes. Serve hot.

Finocchi Gratinati
FENNEL GRATIN

For salad lovers, raw fennel drizzled with olive oil and a squeeze of lemon juice is ideal. Cooking fennel subdues the anise taste but brings up a different kind of sweetness. Donatella Pavoncello, in her book *Dal 1880 ad oggi: la cucina ebraica della mia famiglia*, boils fennel and then fries it in olive oil. It can also be baked simply or, if you like some crunch as I do, you can add a topping of bread crumbs, garlic, and parsley. For a dairy meal, mix grated Parmesan cheese with the crumb topping.

SERVES 6

3 large or 6 small fennel bulbs

4 tablespoons olive oil

4 cloves garlic, finely minced

4 tablespoons finely minced fresh flat-leaf parsley

Salt and freshly ground black pepper to taste

6 to 8 tablespoons toasted bread crumbs

4 tablespoons grated Parmesan cheese (optional)

Cut off the stalks and feathery tops of the fennel bulbs and reserve for another use. Trim off the rough outside leaves. Cut the bulbs in halves or quarters lengthwise. Remove the tough central core. Bring a saucepan filled with water to a boil, add the fennel pieces, and boil until tender, 10 to 15 minutes, depending upon the size of the bulbs. Drain well.

Preheat an oven to 375 degrees F.

Warm the olive oil in a large sauté pan over medium-high heat. Add the fennel, garlic, and parsley and sauté until golden, 5 to 8 minutes. Transfer to a baking dish and sprinkle with salt, pepper, bread crumbs, and Parmesan, if using.

Bake until the crumbs are golden, 15 to 20 minutes. Serve hot.

heat. Add the garlic and sauté until pale gold. Discard the garlic and place the fennel in the pan. Sauté, turning often, until the fennel pieces take on a golden color, about 10 minutes. Add ½ cup water or vegetable broth and salt and cover the pan. Braise until tender, about 20 minutes longer. Add additional water or broth if needed until the fennel is tender and golden. Do not be afraid to let it get rather brown and the sauces syrupy. Serve hot or at room temperature.

Notes: You can make this without the garlic.

Grated Parmesan or a mixture of Parmesan and toasted bread crumbs can be sprinkled over the top just before serving.

Finocchi
alla Giudia
BRAISED FENNEL, JEWISH STYLE

Fennel is braised here, resulting in another typically Jewish *sofegae*, or "suffocated," dish.

SERVES 6 TO 8

6 small or 3 large fennel bulbs

¼ cup olive oil

3 cloves garlic

½ cup water or vegetable broth, or as needed

Salt to taste

Cut off the stalks and feathery tops of the fennel bulbs and reserve for another use. Trim off the rough outside leaves from the bulbs. Cut the bulbs in halves or quarters lengthwise. Remove the tough central core.

In a pan large enough to hold all the fennel in a single layer, warm the olive oil over medium

Peperoni Ripieni
PEPPERS STUFFED WITH EGGPLANT

The dairy section of *La cucina nella tradizione ebraica* is the source of this delicious adaptation of eggplant-stuffed peppers. It is basically a Sephardo-Italian dolma or a chopped version of eggplant Parmesan slipped inside a pepper.

SERVES 4

3 eggplants, about 1 pound each, peeled and diced

Salt

Olive oil, as needed

1 egg

5 tablespoons chopped fresh basil

3 to 4 tablespoons fine dried bread crumbs

Freshly ground black pepper to taste

4 large bell peppers, halved lengthwise and stems, seeds, and thick ribs removed

1/2 to 3/4 pound fresh mozzarella cheese, sliced

3 to 4 tablespoons water

Sprinkle the diced eggplant with salt, place in a colander, and let stand for about 1 hour to drain off any bitter juices. Rinse and pat dry.

Warm 1/4 cup olive oil in a sauté pan over low heat. Add the eggplant in batches and sauté until tender, about 10 minutes, adding more oil as needed. Transfer to a bowl and mash with a fork, or pulse in a food processor. (A 1-pound eggplant yields about 1 3/4 cups puree.) Add the egg, basil, bread crumbs, and salt and pepper to taste.

Preheat an oven to 350 degrees F.

Arrange the peppers hollow ends up in a baking dish. Stuff the eggplant mixture into the peppers, dividing it evenly. Top each pepper half with a slice of mozzarella. Drizzle a little olive oil into the baking dish and add the water. Cover with aluminum foil.

Bake until the peppers are tender and cheese is melted, 35 to 40 minutes. Serve warm.

Notes: Although not traditional, the eggplant mixture could be seasoned with a few tablespoons pesto instead of chopped basil. A few tablespoons of chopped sun-dried tomatoes could also be added to the filling.

To reduce the amount of oil in this dish, the whole eggplants can be baked in an oven preheated to 350 or 400 degrees F until tender. Let cool, then peel and remove the seeds if they are numerous. Drain the pulp in a colander for 15 minutes, then chop coarsely and proceed with the recipe. I tried this both ways and I must report that the eggplant sautéed in oil tasted a lot better.

 Peperoni Ripieni

PEPPERS STUFFED WITH EGGPLANT

Roba Fritta
Mixed Fry

Deep-frying is an old Roman Jewish tradition. In the past cooks known as *friggitori* sold crisp, piping-hot vegetables from street stands. Today, most of the restaurants in the ghetto offer some form of *fritto misto*. Rice croquettes and little deep-fried *ovolini* of fresh mozzarella, apples, even pieces of soaked salt cod, are sometimes added to this vegetable mélange. Serve with lemon wedges to cut the richness.

Serves 6

For the vegetables:

3 zucchini, sliced or cut into batons, salted, drained for 30 minutes, rinsed, and dried

3 artichokes, pared to the heart, sliced or quartered, and placed in lemon water until needed

1 eggplant, peeled, sliced, salted, drained for 30 minutes, rinsed and dried

1 or 2 parsnips, peeled and sliced

2 potatoes, peeled and sliced

1 small head broccoli, trimmed into florets

1 small cauliflower, trimmed into florets

1 small butternut squash, peeled, seeded, and sliced

2 onions, sliced and soaked in cold water for 30 minutes to sweeten

For the batter:

3 ½ cups all-purpose flour

1 teaspoon salt

Pinch of baking soda

3 tablespoons olive oil

2 tablespoons red wine vinegar

About 3 cups water

Vegetable or olive oil for deep-frying

Prepare all the vegetables as directed and set aside.

To make the batter, in a bowl, combine the flour, salt, baking soda, olive oil, vinegar, and enough water to make a smooth, dense batter.

In a deep-fat fryer, deep frying pan, wok, or saucepan, pour in oil to a depth of 3 inches. Heat the oil to 375 degrees F. In batches, dip the vegetables (reserve the onions) into the batter and slip into the oil. Do not crowd the pan or the oil temperature will drop and the vegetables will absorb the oil. Fry, turning as needed, until golden brown, about 5 minutes. Using tongs or a slotted spoon, transfer to paper towels to drain, then keep warm on a warmed platter in an oven preheated to 200 degrees F. Fry the onions last and scatter the slices over the top. Serve hot with the lemon wedges.

Notes: Paper-thin lemon slices, halved mushrooms, and pieces of cardoon and fennel can also be dipped in batter and fried. Cook the cardoon in boiling salted water for 20 minutes and the fennel for 10 minutes before coating with batter and deep-frying.

Crochette di
Patate
POTATO CROQUETTES

This recipe is inspired by Giuseppe Maffioli's *La cucina padovana*, but Donatella Pavoncello also includes a version in *Dal 1880 ad oggi: la cucina ebraica della mia famiglia* that she calls *frittura di patate*, in which chicken fat is used instead of butter. These delicious potato croquettes could be added to an elaborate *fritto misto*, but traditionally they are served as an appetizer or as an accompaniment to cooked fish.

SERVES 4 TO 6

1 ¹/₂ pounds boiling potatoes, peeled and cut into quarters

2 whole eggs, separated, plus 2 eggs

4 tablespoons unsalted butter, at room temperature

³/₄ cup grated Parmesan cheese

Salt and freshly ground black pepper to taste

Freshly grated nutmeg or ground mace to taste

Vegetable or olive oil for deep-frying

Fine dried bread crumbs for coating

Place the potatoes in a saucepan with salted water to cover. Bring to a boil and cook until tender, about 20 minutes. Drain and, while still warm, pass them through a potato ricer placed over a bowl, or mash well with a potato masher.

Add the 4 egg yolks, butter, and Parmesan cheese to the warm potatoes. Stir to mix and season well with salt, pepper, and nutmeg or mace. Form into oval croquettes the length of your thumb (about 3 inches long).

Pour oil to a depth of 2 inches in a deep frying pan. Heat the oil to 375 degrees F. Meanwhile, in a bowl, beat the egg whites until soft peaks form. Spread the bread crumbs on a plate. Dip the croquettes first into the beaten egg whites and then into the crumbs, coating evenly. Place on racks or parchment paper–lined baking sheets until time to fry. (Or refrigerate for up to 6 hours before frying.)

When the oil is hot, working in batches, slip the croquettes into the oil and deep-fry until golden, about 5 minutes. Using tongs or a slotted spoon, transfer to paper towels to drain, then keep warm on a warmed platter in an oven preheated to 200 degrees F. Serve hot.

Patate e Pomodori
POTATO AND TOMATO GRATIN

Although this recipe is from Ferrara, it is of Spanish Sephardic origin. This gratin can be cooked slowly on top of the stove in a heavy pan or in a baking dish in the oven. If the tomatoes give off too much liquid, reduce the juices over high heat or bake uncovered for the last 10 minutes to evaporate them. If the tomatoes don't give off enough liquid and the potatoes are still undercooked, add a little stock or water to the pan. The gratin is usually served at room temperature.

SERVES 6

4 or 5 cloves garlic, finely minced

1 cup chopped fresh flat-leaf parsley

1 ½ to 2 pounds large, ripe tomatoes,
sliced ¼- to ⅓-inch thick

Salt and freshly ground black pepper to taste

Olive oil, as needed

2 pounds waxy potatoes, peeled and sliced ¼ inch thick

1 cup water or broth, or as needed (optional)

If baking in an oven, preheat to 350 degrees F. Oil a large gratin dish.

In a small dish, stir together the garlic and parsley to form a *battuto*. Place a layer of one-third of the tomato slices in the bottom of the prepared dish or in an oiled large, heavy, deep frying pan, preferably cast iron, if cooking on the stove top. Sprinkle with salt and pepper and add a sprinkling of about one-fourth of the battuto and a spritz of olive oil. Top with a layer of half of the potato slices. Sprinkle with another spritz of olive oil. Layer with half of the remaining tomatoes, some salt and pepper, half of the remaining *battuto*, and a drizzle of olive oil. Top with all the remaining potato slices, then the remaining tomatoes, the remaining *battuto*, salt, pepper, and a spritz of olive oil. Cover the gratin dish or frying pan.

Place the dish in the oven or the pan on the stove top over medium-low heat. Cook until the potatoes are tender but not falling apart, about 30 minutes. If the potatoes are still undercooked at that point and there is not enough liquid in the pan to cook them, add water or broth as needed. If, in contrast, the tomatoes have given off too much liquid, uncover the dish or pan, and cook until the liquids are absorbed. Serve warm.

Pomodori a
Mezzo
Baked Tomatoes with Tomato Sauce

In this simple and delicious Roman recipe for oven-braised tomatoes, the peeled, seeded tomatoes break down and make a sauce for the unpeeled halves. The idea comes from Donatella Pavoncello's book *Dal 1880 ad oggi: la cucina ebraica della mia famiglia.*

SERVES 6

6 ripe but firm tomatoes

Extra-virgin olive oil, as needed

Salt and freshly ground black pepper to taste

1 to 2 tablespoons finely minced garlic

4 tablespoons chopped fresh flat-leaf parsley

Preheat an oven to 400 degrees F.

Bring a small saucepan of hot water to a boil. Dip 3 of the tomatoes briefly into the water to loosen the skins. Drain and peel, then cut in half cross-wise and gently squeeze out the seeds. Set aside.

Cut the 3 remaining tomatoes in half crosswise. Squeeze to remove most of the seeds.

Pour enough olive oil into a frying pan to create a film on the bottom. Sear the unpeeled tomato halves, cut side down, in the hot oil until golden. Transfer to a heavy ovenproof pot with a lid, placing them cut side up and arranging them closely. Sprinkle with salt and pepper. In a small bowl, stir together the garlic and parsley and spread over the top.

Place the peeled tomato halves on top. Drizzle with olive oil and sprinkle with salt and pepper. Cover and place on the stove top over medium heat. Cook for 5 minutes, then spoon out excess liquid. Recover and place in the oven.

Bake until the top layer of tomatoes breaks down to form a soft sauce atop the bottom halves, 20 to 30 minutes. Sprinkle lightly with salt and serve at once.

Pomodori con l'Uva
Tomatoes with Grape Juice

I found a reference to this dish, in which fresh grape juice is poured over fried tomatoes while they are still warm, in Milka Belgrado Passigli's book of Jewish recipes. It was originally made with tart red wine grapes. But, as most of us do not have easy access to a vineyard, supermarket table grapes are what we'll have to use. They tend to be sweeter rather than tart, so to approximate the acidity, it's best to add a bit of balsamic vinegar to the juices to accentuate the tartness. Look for Zante grapes, dark wine grapes, or any black or red seedless grapes. If grapes are not in season, use bottled grape must (*verjus*) mixed with a bit of balsamic vinegar.

I added the cornmeal to the flour for a crunchier texture. The original recipe fried finely chopped garlic and rosemary along with the tomatoes, but they burned too quickly and tasted acrid. So I added the rosemary to the flour and smashed the garlic to flavor the oil.

Serves 6

1 small bunch dark grapes (about 1 cup)

1 to 2 tablespoons balsamic vinegar, if needed

All-purpose flour and yellow cornmeal, in equal parts

Salt and freshly ground black pepper to taste

1 tablespoon finely chopped fresh rosemary

6 firm but almost ripe tomatoes, sliced ½ inch thick

Olive oil, as needed

2 cloves garlic, smashed

Puree the grapes in a blender, then strain the juices into a bowl. Season with balsamic vinegar if the grapes are too sweet. Combine the flour, cornmeal, salt, pepper, and rosemary on a plate, mixing well. Dip the tomato slices in the mixture, coating on both sides.

Pour a little olive oil into a large nonstick frying pan, just enough to create a film on the bottom. Add the garlic and place over medium heat. When the oil is hot, add the tomato slices and cook, turning once, until golden on both sides, about 6 minutes total. Sprinkle with salt and pepper and, using a spatula, transfer to a serving plate. Pour the grape juices over the hot tomatoes. Serve at once.

Note: You can make this with unripened tomatoes, too.

 Pomodori con l'Uva

Tomatoes with Grape Juice

Pesce
Fish

Pesce in Saor   *Marinated Fish*

Pesce Freddo alla Salsa di Noce   *Fish with Walnut Sauce*

Triglie alla Mosaica   *Red Mullet, Jewish Style*

Triglie con Pinoli e Passerine   *Mullet with Pine Nuts and Raisins*

Indivia e Alici   *Curly Endive with Anchovies*

Pesce e Indivia   *Fish and Bitter Greens*

Sopa di Pesce Spina all'Ebraica   *Venetian Fish Soup*

Polpettine di Pesce   *Fish Cakes*

Pesce al Sugo di Carciofi   *Fish with a Sauce of Artichokes*

Tonno Fresco con Piselli   *Fresh Tuna with Peas*

Baccalà Mantecato alla Veneziana   *Whipped Salt Cod in the Style of Venice*

Baccalà al Pomodoro   *Salt Cod with Tomato Sauce*

Pasticcio di Baccalà e Spinaci all'Uso Fiorentina   *Florentine Gratin of Salt Cod and Spinach*

Pesce

According to kosher law, Jews are forbidden to eat any fish that does not have scales—most swordfish, monkfish, ray, skate, turbot, shark, eel—as well as all shell-fish. Despite this proscription, fish was always an important part of the Italian Jewish culinary repertoire. Because it is pareve, it could be served as a course in a meat-based meal and was often the centerpiece of a dairy meal. Many of the dishes used inexpensive fish like anchovies and sardines. Fish cakes and fish balls were thrifty ways to stretch the budget, and often the fish were combined with greens and other vegetables, with the fish acting as the flavor accent and the vegetables forming the bulk of the dish. Sole and mullet were used for special dinners. Tuna, when used, was mostly canned, but I did find a wonderful recipe for fresh tuna with peas.

The traditional Italian Jewish kitchen boasted quite a large repertoire of salt cod recipes. Pieces of soaked *baccalà* were cooked with tomato sauce, in a sweet-and-sour sauce, or pureed for *baccalà mantecato*. Because fish is an important part of the dairy repertoire, many salt cod dishes (and other fish dishes as well) include simmering in milk or topping with Parmesan cheese in a gratin. The dishes are then paired with polenta or potatoes, making the meals even more substantial.

Again, because of the laws of the Sabbath, many of the fish dishes were cooked ahead of time and served at room temperature. Marinated dishes like the Venetian classic sole or sardines in *saor*, in a sweet-and-sour onion sauce, were cooked and left to marinate for a day or two. Fish was also poached and then served cold with a rich nut sauce or *salsa verde*—a bright mixture of chopped parsley, capers, hard-boiled egg yolks, and vinegar—or with a great homemade mayonnaise.

Pesce in Saor
Marinated Fish

This typical Venetian Sabbath dish for marinated fish resembles a Spanish *escabèche*, or as it's called in Italian, *a scapece*. The wealthy Jews used sole, while the poorer ones relied on sardines. *Saor* is dialect for *sapore*, or "flavor." The fish is cooked ahead of time and allowed to marinate and mellow for a day or two in a cool place. Given the American fear of foods sitting out of the refrigerator for more than a few minutes, and the American absence of "cool places," it's likely that you'll put this in the refrigerator. No crime, but remember to bring the dish to room temperature at serving time. As it is difficult to find fresh sardines at most fish markets, you'll probably use fillets of sole. Incidentally, this technique for cooking and marinating fish is also used for vegetables such as eggplants and peppers.

Serves 4 to 6

2 pounds whole fresh sardines or 1 ½ pounds sole fillets

All-purpose flour for coating

Pure olive oil for frying

Salt to taste

2 pounds white onions, thinly sliced

1 ½ cups red or white wine vinegar

If using whole sardines, clean them and remove their heads. Remove their backbones as well, leaving the fillets attached. Rinse well and open them flat like a book. Dry thoroughly with paper towels.

Spread flour on a plate and dip the sardines or fillets in it, coating both sides lightly.

Pour enough olive oil into a large sauté pan to film the bottom and place over medium-high heat. When hot, add the fish and fry in batches, turning once until golden on both sides and cooked through, 5 to 6 minutes. Using a slotted spatula, transfer to paper towels to drain. Sprinkle with salt.

Add a bit more oil to the pan and add the onions. Sauté them over low heat, being careful not to let them take on any color, until soft, 15 to 20 minutes. Add salt and 1 cup of the vinegar, raise the heat to medium, and cook until the vinegar is absorbed, 5 to 10 minutes.

Layer half of the fish on a platter. Top with half of the onions, then the remaining fish, and finally the remaining onions. Sprinkle with the remaining ½ cup vinegar. Let marinate for 1 or 2 days before serving, either in a cool place or in the refrigerator.

Note: Some versions of this dish add raisins and pine nuts to the onions, and a sprinkling of ground cinnamon and freshly ground black pepper.

 Pesce in Saor

MARINATED FISH

Pesce Freddo alla Salsa di Noce

FISH WITH WALNUT SAUCE

One of my childhood nightmares was having to face a plate of boiled fish—dry, overcooked, not at all appealing. But here is a recipe for simple poached fish, moist and delicate, served with a lively nut sauce. This was often served at room temperature on the Sabbath or Passover.

SERVES 4 TO 6

For the fish broth:

6 to 8 pounds fish frames (bones, heads, tails, with gills removed) from mild fish such as snapper, rock fish, halibut, or sea bass

3 cups dry white wine

3 to 4 onions, chopped

5 celery stalks, chopped

1 large bay leaf

4 lemon zest strips

10 black peppercorns

4 coriander seeds

3 whole allspice

5 fresh flat-leaf parsley sprigs

2 fresh thyme sprigs

dried chili pepper (optional)

1 teaspoon fennel seeds (optional)

About 8 cups water

2 pounds mild white fish fillets such as sea bass, flounder, rock cod, halibut, or sole

Walnut Sauce (page 164)

To make the fish broth, rinse the fish frames well and set aside. In a deep saucepan combine the wine, all the vegetables, the bay leaf, lemon zest, spices, and herbs. Add water to cover all the ingredients generously and bring to a boil. Add the fish frames and return to a boil. Reduce the heat to maintain a steady simmer. Cook, skimming off foam as needed, for 20 minutes. Strain through a colander lined with wet cheesecloth. You should have about 2 ½ quarts broth. Chill, uncovered, until cold, then cover and refrigerate for up to 4 days or freeze for up to 4 months.

Measure out enough fish broth to fill a wide saucepan to a depth of 1 ½ inches. Reserve the rest for another use. Bring the fish broth to a boil. Slip in the fish, cover the pan, adjust the heat to maintain a gentle simmer, and poach gently until the fish tests done, 8 to 10 minutes per inch of thickness. Using a slotted spatula, transfer to a platter. Serve with Walnut Sauce.

Note: You may also reduce the pan juices so that when they are chilled they will form a jelly, which is then spooned over the fish. Alternatively, Green Sauce (page 164) or Egg-and-Lemon Sauce (page 166) can replace the walnut sauce.

Triglie alla Mosaica
Rᴇᴅ Mᴜʟʟᴇᴛ, Jᴇᴡɪsʜ Sᴛʏʟᴇ

You've probably seen this classic Jewish recipe for red mullet, more commonly known as *triglie alla livornese,* on many restaurant menus in Italy. It has long been a part of the cuisine of Livorno, where there was a sizable Jewish community largely established by Spanish and Portuguese Jews after the Inquisition—the same Sephardic Jews who brought tomatoes to Italy. The name of the dish is derived from Moses, and refers to the Mosaic laws of Judaism. The tomato sauce is symbolic of the Red Sea.

In some versions, the fish is first sautéed, then braised with a rich tomato sauce seasoned with parsley, garlic, and sometimes celery. In other versions, one from Tullia Zevi, doyenne of the Roman Jewish community, and one from Pia Bedarida, in *La cucina livornese,* the fish is simply braised in the tomato sauce. Despite its many bones, red mullet is highly prized for its sweetness and bright color. As we are unable to get mullet at most supermarkets in the United States, you can try this recipe with small whole fish like sand dabs. If you are phobic about bones, you may use fillets of sole, rockfish, or other mild, sweet fish.

Sᴇʀᴠᴇs 6

6 tablespoons olive oil

4 cloves garlic, finely minced

½ cup chopped fresh flat-leaf parsley

¼ cup chopped celery (optional)

1 pound tomatoes, peeled, seeded, and chopped

Salt and freshly ground black pepper to taste

All-purpose flour for coating

*2 pounds small whole fish, cleaned, or 1 ½ pounds
fish fillets (see recipe introduction)*

Warm 2 tablespoons of the olive oil in a small sauté pan or saucepan over medium heat. Add the garlic, half of the parsley, and the celery, if using, and sauté until soft, 3 to 4 minutes. Do not let the garlic turn dark brown. Add the tomatoes, salt, and pepper and simmer until the vegetables are tender, about 10 minutes. Remove from the heat and puree in a blender or food processor. If the tomato sauce is not rich and slightly thick, return it to the pan and reduce over medium heat.

Heat the remaining 4 tablespoons olive oil in a large sauté pan over high heat. Meanwhile, spread the flour on a plate and season with salt and pepper. Dip the fish or fish fillets in flour, coating both sides lightly. Add to the hot oil and sauté quickly, turning once, until golden on both sides. Add the tomato sauce, reduce the heat to low, and simmer until the fish tests done, 5 to 10 minutes, depending upon the thickness. Baste the fish with the sauce from time to time. Using 1 or 2 slotted spatulas, carefully transfer the fish to a warmed serving platter or individual plates. Spoon the sauce on top and sprinkle with the remaining parsley.

Triglie con Pinoli e Passerine
MULLET WITH PINE NUTS AND RAISINS

Edda Servi Machlin calls this *triglie all'ebraica*. It is closely related to the *in saor* dishes of the Veneto, and in Rome is often served to break the Yom Kippur fast. Raisins and pine nuts reveal the Sicilian—and thus Arabic—roots of this classic sweet-and-sour fish dish. It is usually prepared with the wonderful red mullet of the Mediterranean. You may use a whole rockfish or snapper or even fillets of a mild, firm-fleshed white fish.

SERVES 6

½ cup red wine vinegar

3 tablespoons sugar

½ cup pine nuts, toasted

½ cup raisins, plumped in hot water

4 tablespoons extra-virgin olive oil

*1 whole fish, about 2 pounds, cleaned,
or 1½ pounds fish fillets (see recipe introduction)*

Salt to taste

In a small bowl, stir together the vinegar, sugar, pine nuts, raisins, and a little of the raisin plumping water. Set aside.

Warm the olive oil in a large sauté pan over medium heat. Add the fish and sauté briefly on one side until pale gold. Turn and sprinkle with salt. Add the vinegar mixture, cover, and cook over medium heat until the fish tests done, 10 minutes for whole fish, 5 minutes for fillets. Transfer to a platter and serve warm or at room temperature.

Indivia e Alici
CURLY ENDIVE WITH ANCHOVIES

With its sharp flavors of bitter greens and strong-tasting fish, this Roman dish is not for sissies. *La cucina nella tradizione ebraica* recommends two parts greens to one part fish, but according to a recipe from Donatella Pavoncello, it should be prepared with equal parts fresh anchovies and curly endive (also known as chicory), and baked with lots of olive oil. It is served hot or at room temperature.

If you can find fresh anchovies, use 2 pounds of them and follow the instructions for preparing the sardines on page 112. If you can't find them, you can use canned salted anchovies. Escarole or radicchio might be used in place of chicory.

SERVES 6

Olive oil for oiling baking dish, plus ½ cup

2 pounds curly endive

16 salt-packed anchovies, filleted and rinsed

Freshly ground black pepper to taste

½ cup dry white wine

Lemon wedges for serving

If baking, preheat an oven to 350 degrees F. Oil a 9-by-12-inch baking dish. If cooking on the stove top, select a wide, heavy saucepan and oil the bottom.

Trim away the core from the heads of curly endive, and cut the leaves crosswise into strips 2 inches wide. Bring a large saucepan filled with salted water to a boil, add the greens, and cook until almost tender, about 3 minutes. Drain in a colander. Refresh in cold water and drain again.

Layer half of the drained endive in the bottom of the prepared dish or pan. Top with all of the anchovies, arranging them in a single layer. Spread the remaining endive over the fish. Sprinkle with pepper. Pour the ½ cup olive oil and the wine over the top. Cover the dish or pan.

Bake in the oven or braise over low heat until tender, 25 to 30 minutes. Serve at room temperature with lemon wedges.

Pesce e Indivia
Fish and Bitter Greens

As in Curly Endive with Anchovies (see page 116), the fish and greens in this classic Jewish dish traditionally hold equal weight in flavor intensity. To stay closer to this original concept, opt for a stronger fish such as tuna or mackerel. If you should decide to use a mild fish like flounder, cod, or sea bass, the bitter endive will predominate. To enliven the staid fish-and-bitter-greens theme, I like to add sautéed onions, capers, and olives to the cooked greens. Although this makes the dish less authentic, it does make it more interesting. Serve with rice or potatoes.

Serves 4 to 6

Olive oil for oiling baking dish, plus ½ cup

2 pounds curly endive, or part escarole, Belgian endive, and frisée

2 onions, chopped or thinly sliced

3 tablespoons capers, rinsed and coarsely chopped

½ cup pitted Mediterranean-style black olives, halved or coarsely chopped

Salt and freshly ground pepper to taste

1 ½ pounds flounder, rock cod, sea bass, tuna, or mackerel fillets (see recipe introduction)

½ cup dry white wine

Lemon wedges for serving

If baking, preheat an oven to 350 degrees F. Oil a 9-by-12-inch baking dish. If cooking on the stove top, select a wide, heavy saucepan and oil the bottom. Trim and boil the endive as directed in the previous recipe.

Warm 2 or 3 tablespoons of the olive oil in a sauté pan over medium heat. Add the onions and sauté until tender, 5 to 8 minutes. Add the greens to the pan and sauté until tender, about 5 minutes. Stir in the capers and olives and season with pepper. You probably won't need any salt, but taste for it anyway. Remove from the heat.

Layer half of the greens in the prepared pan. Top with the fish fillets. Sprinkle with salt and pepper and cover with the remaining greens. Pour the remaining olive oil and the wine over the top. Cover the dish or pan. Bake in the oven or braise on the stove top over low heat until the fish is cooked through, about 25 minutes. Serve warm with lemon wedges.

Sopa di Pesce Spina all'Ebraica
Venetian Fish Soup

Despite the name, this is more of a fish ragout than a soup. In keeping with kosher laws, it is to be made only with fish with scales, and the fish should be on the bone—*con spina*. This Jewish-style *zuppa di pesce* from the Veneto resembles the famed *cacciucco alla livornese*, but here chopped tomatoes replace the tomato paste. In an interesting North African–inspired Livornese touch, Mira Sacerdoti suggests adding a bit of ginger to the *battuto* of garlic, parsley, and chili pepper. For a change of pace, in place of chopped basil or parsley, add a generous dollop of pesto for garnish.

Serves 6

2 celery stalks, chopped

2 carrots, peeled and chopped

1 large onion, chopped

2 cloves garlic, left whole,
plus 1 tablespoon finely minced garlic

2 teaspoons salt

About 8 cups water

2 ½ to 3 pounds assorted firm whole white fish,
cleaned and heads removed and reserved

3 tablespoons olive oil

3 tablespoons finely minced fresh flat-leaf parsley

1 tablespoon finely minced garlic

1 teaspoon hot red pepper flakes (optional)

2 teaspoons peeled and grated fresh ginger (optional)

1 to 2 cups dry white wine

Pinch of saffron threads (optional)

3 tablespoons tomato paste or
2 cups diced seeded peeled tomatoes (optional)

4 tablespoons finely minced fresh flat-leaf parsley

4 tablespoons finely minced fresh basil

Small, coarse country bread slices fried
in olive oil or matzohs for serving

In a large stockpot, combine the celery, carrots, onion, whole garlic cloves, salt, and water. Bring to a boil and cook for 10 minutes. Add the fish, reduce the heat to medium-low, and simmer for about 12 minutes. Using 1 or 2 slotted spatulas, gently remove the fish from the liquid. Carefully remove the skin and bones from the fish and set the fillets aside. Return the skin and bones to the pot along with the reserved heads. Simmer until the liquid is infused with flavor, about 30 minutes. Strain the liquid through a colander lined with wet cheesecloth and set aside.

Warm the olive oil in a deep sauté pan over medium heat. Add the *battuto* of parsley and minced garlic and sauté until the garlic is pale gold, about 5 minutes. Add the hot pepper flakes, if using, and the ginger, if you want that North African-inspired Livornese touch. Add the white wine and saffron, if using, and let it bubble for a minute or two, then the reserved fish fillets and the strained broth. Bring to a simmer. If desired, add a few tablespoons of tomato paste for color, or diced tomatoes if you want a Livorno-style dish. Warm the fish until heated through. Adjust the seasonings. Stir in the parsley and basil. Serve topped with fried bread or crumbled matzoh.

Note: In the Marches, a similar fish soup is made. It calls for sautéing onions first and then adding the fish and the water, wine, or broth along with tomatoes. All the ingredients are then simmered together. It is called *brodetto di pesce ad uso marchigiano*.

Polpettine di Pesce
Fish Cakes.

My recipe for fish cakes was created from a description in Giuseppe Maffioli's *La cucina veneziana*. These *polpettine* are not to be confused with classic Ashkenazic gefilte fish balls. They are more like fish croquettes and can be bound with bread crumbs or, during Passover, matzoh meal. You can tell these are from the Veneto from the use of aromatic sweet spices. Your fishmonger may be willing to grind the fish for you. If not, cut it into small pieces and pulse it in a food processor.

To soften the raw onion taste, soak the sliced onion in cold water for an hour, then drain and chop. The seasoned fish mixture can be rolled into small fish balls, poached in fish broth (see page 114), and served with couscous (see page 145) with a *bagna brusca* (page 166) made with the fish broth. Don't forget the lemon wedges. Sautéed spinach makes a delicious side dish.

Serves 6

1 1/2 pounds firm white fish or salmon fillets, ground

1 1/2 cups finely chopped or grated onion

1 cup fresh bread crumbs or matzoh meal, moistened with
fish broth (see page 114), or water

1/2 cup chopped fresh flat-leaf parsley

2 teaspoons salt

1 teaspoon freshly ground black pepper

1 teaspoon ground cinnamon

1/8 teaspoon ground cloves

1/4 teaspoon freshly grated nutmeg

2 or 3 olive oil-packed anchovy fillets, finely minced
(optional)

2 cloves garlic, finely minced

1 cup fine dried bread crumbs or matzoh meal for coating

Olive oil or clarified butter for sautéing

Lemon wedges for serving

In a bowl, combine the ground fish, onion, moistened bread crumbs or matzoh meal, parsley, salt, pepper, cinnamon, cloves, nutmeg, and the anchovies, if using, and garlic. Mix well. To be sure you like the seasoning, fry a small piece of the mixture in a little olive oil or butter, taste, and adjust the seasonings. When you are happy with the flavors, form into cakes about 3 inches in diameter. Spread the bread crumbs or matzoh meal on a plate and coat the cakes on both sides. (You can shape these up to a day in advance; place them on baking sheets lined with parchment paper, cover, and refrigerate until ready to fry.)

Warm 4 tablespoons olive oil or clarified butter in a large sauté pan over medium-high heat. In batches, add the fish cakes and fry, turning once, until golden brown. Add more oil or butter with each batch. Transfer to a warmed platter and serve with lemon wedges.

 Pesce al Sugo di Carciofi

Fish with a Sauce of Artichokes

Pesce al Sugo di Carciofi

Fish with a Sauce of Artichokes

You would be surprised at how many different versions of this dish appear not only in the Italian Jewish cooking repertoire, but in Sephardic and Moroccan Jewish cooking as well. In the Moroccan version, ample garlic is used and the onions are seasoned with coriander, sweet paprika, and cayenne. In Greek and Turkish versions, the artichokes are made sweet and sour with lemon juice and a pinch of sugar, and a little saffron is added, too.

The Italian Jewish version is a bit more subdued. The onions are sautéed in olive oil, then sliced artichokes are added, some diced tomatoes, and, occasionally, a little chopped mint or parsley. Since Passover is a spring holiday, it is not unusual to find this classic pairing of fish and springtime's tender artichokes on the celebratory table. Sometimes fennel and cardoons are used in place of artichokes. Serve with roasted potatoes or rice.

Serves 4

*4 fish fillets such as salmon or sea bass,
about 6 ounces each*

Kosher salt to taste

Juice of 1 lemon

4 large or 8 medium-sized artichokes

About 8 tablespoons olive oil, or as needed

2 onions, sliced

1 cup peeled, seeded, and diced tomatoes

Salt and freshly ground black pepper to taste

*Chopped fresh mint or flat-leaf parsley for garnish
(optional)*

Sprinkle the fish fillets with kosher salt and refrigerate until needed.

Have ready a large bowl or water to which you have added the lemon juice. Working with 1 artichoke at a time, remove all the leaves until you reach the pale green heart. Pare away the dark green area from the base and any tender stem. Cut in half lengthwise and scoop out and discard the choke from each half. Then cut each half lengthwise into 1/4-inch-thick slices. Drop into the lemon water.

Warm 3 tablespoons of the olive oil in a large sauté pan over medium heat. Drain the artichokes, reserving some of the lemon water. Add the artichoke slices to the pan and sauté until beginning to soften, about 5 minutes. Add a little of the lemon water and cook the artichokes, uncovered, until almost completely tender, about 5 minutes longer. Transfer to a plate.

Add 3 tablespoons olive oil to the same pan and return to medium heat. Add the onions and sauté until tender and translucent, about 8 minutes. Add the tomatoes and return the artichokes to the pan. Stir well and season with salt and pepper. Remove from the heat.

In a large, wide saucepan over medium heat, warm the remaining 2 tablespoons olive oil. Add the fish fillets and sauté, turning once, for a minute or two on each side. Top with the artichoke mixture, cover the pan, and braise until the fish is tender, 8 to 10 minutes. Sprinkle generously with parsley or mint, if desired.

Variations:

Put the fish in a baking dish, top with the artichokes, cover the dish, and bake in an oven preheated to 400 degrees F, until the fillets are tender, about 10 minutes. Or, if you are feeling adventurous, omit the tomatoes, add the grated zest of 1 orange and 1 large lemon to the onions while cooking, and a pinch of red pepper flakes. Garnish the dish with orange segments and chopped fresh mint or parsley.

Tonno Fresco con Piselli
Fresh Tuna with Peas

Most Italian recipes that call for tuna mean canned tuna packed in olive oil. So this dish, which is adapted from *La cucina nella tradizione ebraica* and is also mentioned in Mira Sacerdoti's book, is noteworthy. With the fresh peas of springtime an essential ingredient, we can assume this was served at Passover. Italians cook fish longer than most Americans do—and peas, too. For a happy medium, I suggest cooking the tuna on one side, removing it from the pan, simmering the peas, and then returning the tuna to the pan to complete cooking with the peas and tomatoes. The fish will retain its moisture and tenderness better than if you cook it all the way through and then reheat it.

Serves 3 or 4

1 ¼ pounds tuna fillet, in one piece, about 1 inch thick

Salt and freshly ground black pepper to taste

4 tablespoons olive oil

2 cloves garlic, finely minced

1 small onion, finely chopped

3 tablespoons chopped fresh flat-leaf parsley

1 cup diced canned plum tomatoes

Water or dry white wine, as needed

2 pounds English peas, shelled (about 2 cups)

Sprinkle the tuna with salt and pepper.

Warm the olive oil in a sauté pan over medium heat. Add the garlic, onion, and parsley and sauté for a few minutes; do not allow them to color. Add the tuna and cook it on one side only until half-cooked, about 4 minutes. Remove the tuna from the pan and set aside.

Add the tomatoes, 1 cup water or wine, and the peas. Cover and simmer over medium heat until the peas are tender, 8 to 10 minutes, depending on the starchiness of the peas. Return the tuna to the pan, uncooked side down. Cook until done to taste, about 4 minutes for medium.

Using a slotted spatula, transfer the tuna to a warmed serving platter. Spoon the peas and tomatoes over the tuna. Serve at once.

Note: Edda Servi Machlin uses salmon for her version of this dish, and she omits the tomatoes.

Baccalà Mantecato alla Veneziana
Whipped Salt Cod in the Style of Venice

Baccalà mantecato is whipped salt cod, from the verb *mantecare*, which means to "whip" or "whisk." This puree is usually served atop slices of grilled, fried, or baked polenta. It also can be paired with warm soft polenta for a very voluptuous contrast of hot and cold. In a most unusual pairing, Edda Servi Machlin spoons it atop a bed of sliced raw mushrooms.

Serves 8

2 pounds salt cod fillets

Water or milk, as needed

½ cup extra-virgin olive oil, or as needed

3 or 4 cloves garlic, finely minced

3 tablespoons chopped fresh flat-leaf parsley

Salt and freshly ground black pepper to taste

Fresh lemon juice to taste

Soak the salt cod in water for 2 days, changing the liquid at least 3 times. Drain the salt cod and place in a saucepan. Add water or milk to cover and bring slowly to a gentle simmer. Simmer until the fish is tender, about 10 minutes. Drain the salt cod and when cool enough to handle, break up into 2-inch pieces, removing any errant bones or discolored or tough parts.

Place the salt cod in a food processor and pulse until coarsely chopped. Gradually beat in as much oil as needed for a smooth puree. Pulse in the garlic and parsley and season with salt, pepper, and a bit of lemon juice, if you like. Serve as directed in recipe introduction.

Note: Some cooks simmer the cod in water and then beat 1 cup hot milk into the puree along with the oil, in the French manner of making a *brandade*.

Baccalà al
Pomodoro
SALT COD WITH TOMATO SAUCE

Salt cod cooked in tomato sauce is a culinary classic. This recipe is based on one in Giuseppe Maffioli's *La cucina padovana*. Similar dishes are prepared in Rome, where chopped black olives or pine nuts and raisins are often added.

In most old Italian Jewish recipes, the salt cod is simmered in the tomato sauce for three hours. A recipe sent to me from Tullia Zevi, a leader in the Roman Jewish community, recommends three hours as well, and she adds cut-up potatoes during the last hour. I don't know about the salt cod found in Rome, but after a few days of soaking the salt cod I buy in San Francisco, it is perfectly tender within about fifteen minutes of being placed over the heat. Serve with polenta or potatoes.

SERVES 4

1 ½ pounds salt cod fillet

All-purpose flour for coating

Salt and freshly ground black pepper to taste

Olive oil, as needed

2 onions, chopped

3 cloves garlic, minced

1 cup dry white wine

4 olive oil–packed anchovy fillets, drained and chopped

4 cups Tomato Sauce (page 163)

3 tablespoons chopped fresh flat-leaf parsley

Grated zest of 1 or 2 lemons

Soak the salt cod in water for 2 days, changing the water at least 3 times. Drain the salt cod and break it into 2-inch pieces, removing any errant bones or discolored or tough parts.

Spread the flour on a plate and season with salt and pepper. Dip the cod pieces in the seasoned flour, coating evenly.

Pour olive oil to a depth of 1 ½ inches in a large, deep frying pan and place over medium-high heat. When the oil is hot, in batches, fry the salt cod pieces, turning once, until golden on both sides, 4 to 5 minutes total. Drain on paper towels and set aside.

In another pan, sauté a *battuto* of onions and garlic over medium-high heat in 2 tablespoons olive oil until soft and pale gold, about 8 minutes. Add the white wine and let it bubble up. Then add the anchovies, the tomato sauce, and the cod and simmer until the cod is almost completely cooked and tender, about 15 minutes. Add the parsley and lemon zest and simmer for 5 minutes longer to blend the flavors. Transfer to a warmed serving platter and serve hot.

Pasticcio di
Baccalà e Spinaci all'Uso Fiorentina
FLORENTINE GRATIN OF SALT COD AND SPINACH

Here is an Italian Jewish classic that combines salt cod, *besciamella*—the classic cream sauce—and spinach in a most appealing way. This recipe from *La cucina nella tradizione ebraica* can be assembled ahead of time and baked just before serving. It can also be baked in ramekins; reduce the cooking time to 15 minutes.

SERVES 4

1 pound salt cod fillets

2 cups Salsa Besciamella (page 162)

2 pounds spinach

4 tablespoons unsalted butter

Freshly ground black pepper to taste

Freshly grated nutmeg to taste

²⁄₃ cup fine dried bread crumbs

4 tablespoons grated Parmesan or Gruyère cheese

Soak the salt cod in water for 2 days, changing the water at least 3 times. Drain the salt cod and place in a saucepan. Add water to cover and bring slowly to a gentle simmer. Simmer until the fish is tender, about 10 minutes. Drain the salt cod and, when cool enough to handle, break up into chunks, removing any errant bones or discolored or tough parts. Transfer to a bowl and mash well with fork.

Prepare the sauce and set aside. Preheat an oven to 350 degrees F. Butter an 8-by-11-inch baking dish.

Rinse the spinach well and remove the stems. (Reserve the stems for Braised Spinach Stems, page 85.) Chop the leaves coarsely.

Melt 2 tablespoons of the butter in a large sauté pan over medium heat. Add the spinach gradually, cooking it until it wilts and adding more leaves as each batch cooks down. Stir in the sauce and season with pepper and nutmeg. Stir in the salt cod. Taste and adjust the seasonings. Transfer the cod-spinach mixture to the prepared dish. Top evenly with the bread crumbs, the remaining 2 tablespoons butter, cut into bits, and the grated cheese.

Bake until golden and bubbly, about 25 minutes. Serve hot.

 Pasticcio di Baccalà e Spinaci all'Uso Fiorentina

FLORENTINE GRATIN OF SALT COD AND SPINACH

Pollame
POULTRY

Delizie di Pollo con Peperoni   *Chicken Morsels with Peppers*

Pollo con Polpette e Sedano   *Chicken Fricassee with Chicken Meatballs*

Polpettone di Pollo   *Chicken Loaf*

Pollo Ezechiele   *Ezekiel's Chicken*

Budino di Pollo all'Ebraica   *Jewish-Style Chicken Pudding*

Pollo Fritto di Hanucca   *Fried Chicken for Hanukkah*

Scaloppine di Tacchino Rebecca   *Turkey Scallops with Herbs*

Pollo Arrosto all'Arancia, Limone, e Zenzero   *Roast Chicken with Orange, Lemon, and Ginger*

Pollame

Chicken is so inexpensive today that it has become a staple on the American dining table. But this was not the case in Italy in the past, where chicken was more costly than meat. Thus, the repertoire of recorded Italian Jewish poultry recipes is rather small. The least expensive chicken cuts were used: giblets and odd pieces that were ground and formed into little meatballs, packed into neck skins or stuffed into boned birds to be served for holiday feasts. Roast chicken was served at the special holiday or Sabbath meal, fried chicken was served at Hanukkah, and chicken dumplings on Passover.

The arrival of goose, turkey, and duck recipes in the Veneto has often been attributed to the Ashkenazim. For the Jews, these birds were a surrogate for pork in dishes where fat was required. Goose breast was cured and turned into "prosciutto," while the rest of the bird was ground and spiced and made into sausages and salami. The fat was rendered and turned into cracklings called *grigole*. Every bit of fat and poultry drippings was saved for cooking other dishes, especially vegetables, for dressing pasta, or for preserving cooked meats.

 Delizie di Pollo con Peperoni

CHICKEN MORSELS WITH PEPPERS

Delizie di Pollo con Peperoni
CHICKEN MORSELS WITH PEPPERS

This is my adaptation of a recipe in Donatella Pavoncello's *Dal 1880 ad oggi: la cucina ebraica della mia famiglia.* This simple little stew of chicken morsels, sweet peppers, and tomatoes (and sometimes onions) is suggested as a dish to serve during Passover. It recalls the classic *pollo alla cacciatore*, or "hunters style," except that tiny pieces rather than chicken parts are used here. I like to serve this with soft polenta (see page 75).

SERVES 4

4 large yellow bell peppers

1 ½ pounds chicken breasts, boned, skinned, and cut into bite-sized pieces

Salt and freshly ground black pepper to taste

⅓ cup olive oil

1 onion, chopped (optional)

2 tablespoons finely minced garlic

2 large tomatoes, peeled, seeded, and cut into strips, juices reserved

Preheat a broiler. Arrange the bell peppers on a broiler pan and slip under the broiler. Broil, turning as needed, until blackened and blistered on all sides. Transfer to a work surface, cover loosely with aluminum foil, and let cool for about 10 minutes, then peel off the skins. Halve, remove the stems and seeds, and cut into wide strips or large squares.

Sprinkle the chicken with salt and pepper. Warm the olive oil in a large sauté pan over high heat. Add the chicken pieces and brown on all sides. Reduce the heat to medium-low and add the onion, if using, the garlic, the bell peppers, and the tomato strips and their juices. Simmer until the chicken is tender, 20 to 25 minutes.

Transfer to a warmed serving platter and serve at once.

VARIATIONS:

You can use a mix of red and yellow peppers. You can also sauté the chicken with the tomatoes, but add the roasted peppers at the end. A garnish of pitted Mediterranean-style black olives and chopped fresh flat-leaf parsley or basil is a good addition.

Pollo con Polpette e Sedano

Chicken Fricassee with Chicken Meatballs

When I was growing up in New York, chicken fricassee with little beef meatballs was part of the cooking repertoire of many Jewish families. You can imagine my surprise when I found a recipe for them in Donatella Limentani Pavoncello's charming Roman Jewish cookbook, *Dal 1880 ad oggi: la cucina ebraica della mia famiglia*. It's an Italian fricassee of chicken called *ngozzamodi di pollo con polpette* (the *ngozzamodi* refer to pieces of chicken—*ozza* meaning bones—with the bone in), but the meatballs, or *polpette*, are made with ground chicken. For economy, many versions of this recipe omit the chicken pieces altogether and just use chicken balls. You can even use ground turkey in place of the ground chicken. Celery is a favorite vegetable of the Romans, and I've increased it a bit from the original recipe. Serve the chicken and meatballs with rice or olive oil—mashed potatoes and peas.

Serves 4 to 6

For the meatballs:

1 pound ground chicken breast meat

1/2 to 3/4 cup fresh bread crumbs, or as needed to bind, soaked in 1/2 cup dry white wine

2 eggs, lightly beaten

1 teaspoon ground cinnamon

1 teaspoon salt

1/2 teaspoon freshly ground black pepper

Chicken broth, as needed

6 to 8 tablespoons olive oil, or as needed

1 chicken, 2 1/2 pounds, cut into 8 serving pieces, or 6 thighs

Salt and freshly ground black pepper to taste

2 onions, chopped

3 cloves garlic, minced

1 large head celery, cut into 2-inch lengths

2 to 3 cups peeled, seeded, and diced tomatoes

1/4 cup chopped fresh flat-leaf parsley

To make the meatballs, in a bowl, combine the ground chicken, bread crumbs and wine, eggs, cinnamon, salt, and pepper. Mix gently but thoroughly. Shape a single marble-sized meatball. Bring a small amount of chicken broth to a simmer and poach the meatball to test for seasoning. Adjust the seasonings, then form the mixture into marble-sized balls. Refrigerate until needed.

Pour the olive oil into a wide, deep sauté pan or dutch oven. It should be about 1/4 inch deep. Place over high heat. When hot, add the chicken pieces and brown quickly on all sides, sprinkling with salt and pepper at the same time. Remove the chicken with tongs to a plate.

To the fat remaining in the pan, add the onions and sauté over low heat until tender and translucent, 8 to 10 minutes. Add the garlic, celery, and tomatoes and simmer for 5 minutes. Add the browned chicken and cover the pan. Simmer over low heat for 20 minutes.

Carefully distribute the chicken meatballs among the chicken pieces, pushing them down into the pan juices. Add a little chicken broth if the chicken has not given off enough liquid for poaching the meatballs. Re-cover the pan and poach until the chicken balls are done and the chicken is tender, about 15 minutes. Adjust the seasoning of the pan juices.

Transfer the chicken pieces, meatballs, celery, and pan juices to a warmed deep platter and sprinkle with the parsley. Serve at once.

Note: One version of the recipe omits the

tomatoes, and the dish is finished with a *bagna brusca* (see page 166).

Polpettone di Pollo
CHICKEN LOAF

This is not exactly a meat loaf. It more closely resembles a giant chicken burger, but served chilled. Some recipes add ground veal to the chicken or use turkey instead of chicken. Another variation stuffs the mixture into a turkey-neck skin. In *La cucina nella tradizione ebraica*, there's a version that adds hard-boiled eggs and chopped pistachios to the ground chicken mixture, stuffs it into a boned chicken, and poaches it as if it were a galantine. In yet another version, a turkey is deboned and stuffed in the same manner. These are a lot more work and obviously for festive holidays. Here is my simple everyday version, based on a recipe from Donatella Limentani Pavoncello's book. She doesn't have pistachios in her version, but they really add wonderful texture and another dimension of flavor to what is a rather bland dish. Be sure to test the mixture for seasoning by poaching a little meatball in broth or water. Leftover *polpettone* makes a great sandwich, with a little lemony mayonnaise (see page 162) and lettuce.

SERVES 6 TO 8

1 pound ground chicken breast meat

¹⁄₂ to ³⁄₄ cup fresh bread crumbs, or as needed to bind

2 eggs, lightly beaten

1 teaspoon salt

¹⁄₂ teaspoon white or black pepper, preferably freshly ground

¹⁄₂ teaspoon ground cinnamon or freshly grated nutmeg

¹⁄₄ cup chopped toasted pistachio nuts

Olive oil

¹⁄₂ cup dry white wine or Marsala wine

3 small carrots, peeled and chopped

About 6 cups chicken broth or water, heated

Mayonnaise (page 162) flavored with lemon zest and capers or herbs

In a large bowl, combine the chicken, bread crumbs, eggs, salt, pepper, cinnamon or nutmeg, and the pistachios. Mix gently but thoroughly. Pinch off a small nugget and poach in simmering water or (or broth) to test the seasoning. Adjust the seasoning and form the mixture into a long loaf. Pour enough olive oil into a large nonstick sauté pan to form a film on the bottom and warm over medium-high heat. Add the chicken loaf and brown on all sides, shaking the pan from time to time to prevent sticking. When the chicken is colored on all sides, pour in the wine, and deglaze, scraping up any browned bits on the pan bottom. Add the carrots and the broth or water to cover. Bring to a simmer, cover, adjust the heat to maintain a gentle simmer, and cook until all the liquids are absorbed and the chicken is tender, glazed, and golden, about 30 minutes.

Remove from the heat, transfer to a platter, let cool, then cover and chill the loaf, about 2 hours. To serve, cut the chilled loaf into thin slices. Serve with mayonnaise.

Pollo Ezechiele
Ezekiel's Chicken

The biblical name of this dish is a clue to its Jewish origins. It is an adaptation of a classic recipe that appears in *La cucina nella tradizione ebraica*. Edda Servi Machlin calls a similar recipe *pollo baruch*, named after her father. She adds a sliced onion and tomato paste instead of tomatoes.

Serves 4

*1 small fryer chicken, 2 ½ to 3 pounds,
cut into serving pieces*

Salt and freshly ground black pepper to taste

4 tablespoons olive oil

*⅓ cup pitted Mediterranean-style black olives,
coarsely chopped*

3 cloves garlic, minced

*1 tablespoon chopped fresh sage,
plus extra for garnish (optional)*

*1 tablespoon chopped fresh rosemary,
plus extra for garnish (optional)*

*1 tablespoon chopped fresh basil,
plus extra for garnish (optional)*

*2 large tomatoes, peeled, seeded,
and coarsely chopped*

½ cup dry red wine

Sprinkle the chicken with salt and pepper. Warm the olive oil in a large sauté pan over high heat. Add the chicken pieces and sauté until golden on all sides. Add the olives, garlic, herbs (if using), and tomatoes. Cover, reduce the heat to low, and cook, until the chicken is tender, about 25 minutes.

Uncover the pan and add the red wine. Raise the heat to high and cook rapidly to reduce the pan juices. Adjust the seasonings. Transfer to a warmed platter and sprinkle with more fresh herbs, if desired. Serve at once.

 Pollo Ezechiele

Ezekiel's Chicken

Budino di Pollo all'Ebraica
JEWISH-STYLE CHICKEN PUDDING

Here is a variation on the Chicken Loaf on page 131. In this recipe, a specialty of Lazio, cooked ground chicken is perfumed with dried porcini. Serve warm with a sauce of sautéed mushrooms or a simple Tomato Sauce (page 163).

SERVES 4

1 pound chicken breasts and thighs

2 onions, sliced

2 carrots, peeled and diced

2 celery stalks, diced

1 tablespoon margarine or rendered chicken fat

1 tablespoon all-purpose flour

3 eggs

1/4 cup dried porcini, soaked in 1/2 cup hot water to soften

Salt and freshly ground black pepper to taste

Place the chicken pieces in a saucepan with the onions, carrots, and celery. Add water to cover and bring to a simmer over low heat. Simmer until the chicken pieces are cooked through, about 30 minutes.

Meanwhile, preheat an oven to 300 degrees F. Liberally oil a 3-cup soufflé dish or standard loaf pan with the margarine or chicken fat.

Remove the chicken from the pan (reserve the broth for another use) and, when cool enough to handle, remove the meat from the bones. Put the chicken meat into a food processor. Add the flour and eggs. Drain the mushrooms, reserving the soaking water. Strain the liquid through a sieve lined with cheesecloth and measure out 1/4 cup. Add it to the processor along with the mushrooms. Pulse until pureed. Season with salt and pepper. Transfer to the prepared mold. Cover with oiled aluminum foil, oiled side down. Place in a baking pan. Add hot water to the pan to reach halfway up the sides of the mold.

Bake until golden and firm, about 1 hour. Remove from the oven and let rest 20 minutes in the mold. Run a knife around the edge of the mold. Invert a serving plate on top of the mold. Holding the plate and mold together, invert them and lift off the mold. Slice and serve warm.

Pollo Fritto per Hanucca
FRIED CHICKEN FOR HANUKKAH

Many fried dishes are served at Hanukkah. They are to remind the Jews of the oil lamp that burned for eight days, despite an amount of oil that appeared sufficient for only one day. This recipe for fried chicken, Italian style, is quite bland, so I recommend adding grated lemon and orange zests and a little minced garlic to the marinade, or consider accompanying it with an interesting conserve. The Sabbath Rice with grapes or raisins (page 74) would be a good side dish.

SERVES 4

1 fryer chicken, 2 1/2 pounds, cut into 8 serving pieces

4 tablespoons olive oil, plus oil for frying

4 tablespoons fresh lemon juice

Salt and freshly ground pepper to taste

1 tablespoon grated lemon zest (optional)

2 tablespoons grated orange zest (optional)

1 tablespoon minced garlic (optional)

All-purpose flour for coating

2 eggs, lightly beaten

Lemon wedges for serving

Place the chicken pieces in a shallow nonreactive bowl and add the 4 tablespoons olive oil, lemon juice, salt, and pepper, and the lemon and orange zest and garlic, if using. Turn to coat well, cover, and refrigerate for a few hours.

Pour the olive oil to a depth of 3 inches into a large, deep frying pan and place over high heat. While the oil is heating, remove the chicken pieces from the marinade and pat dry with paper towels. Spread the flour on a plate and season with salt and pepper. Dip the chicken pieces in the flour, coating lightly on all sides, and then in the beaten eggs.

Slip the chicken pieces into the hot oil and fry, turning as needed, until golden on all sides and cooked through, about 20 minutes. Using tongs, transfer briefly to paper towels to drain, then arrange on a platter. Serve hot with lemon wedges.

Scaloppine di Tacchino Rebecca
TURKEY SCALLOPS WITH HERBS

Here is another dish named after Rebecca, the ubiquitous Jewish housewife. Economical and low-fat sliced turkey breast and boneless chicken breasts have become the veal scaloppine of the nineties. This authentic Italian turkey scaloppine was way ahead of the trend. A similar dish made with veal is also named after Rebecca.

SERVES 3 OR 4

1 pound boneless turkey breast, sliced ⅔ inch thick, or boneless, skinless chicken breast halves

All-purpose flour for coating

Salt and freshly ground black pepper to taste

2 tablespoons olive oil

1 cup dry white wine

3 tablespoons chopped fresh flat-leaf parsley

3 tablespoons chopped green onions

Juice of 1 lemon

One at a time, place the turkey or chicken breasts between 2 sheets of plastic wrap and pound to a uniform thickness of about ⅓ inch. Do not pound too thin or the meat will tear. Spread the flour on a plate and season with the salt and pepper. Dip the pounded breast meat in the flour, coating both sides lightly.

Warm the olive oil in a large sauté pan over medium-high heat. Add the breast meat and sauté, turning once, until golden and cooked through, about 6 minutes. Transfer to a warmed platter and keep warm.

Add the wine to the pan over medium-high heat and let it reduce a bit, scraping up any brown bits on the bottom of the pan. Add the parsley, green onions, and lemon juice and cook for 3 to 4 minutes to let the flavors blend. Pour the sauce over the scaloppine and serve at once.

 Pollo Arrosto all'Arancia, Limone, e Zenzero
Roast Chicken with Orange, Lemon, and Ginger

Pollo Arrosto all'Arancia, Limone, e Zenzero

ROAST CHICKEN WITH ORANGE, LEMON, AND GINGER

Ginger arrived in Italy with Arabic traders or North African Jewish immigrants, so it's likely that this is a Sicilian or Livornese recipe. Most Italians would use ground ginger, but since fresh ginger is so plentiful at our markets, why not use it?

SERVES 4

1 lemon

1 roasting chicken, about 5 pounds

Grated zest of 1 lemon, then lemon cut into quarters

Grated zest of 1 orange, then orange cut into quarters

3 tablespoons peeled and grated fresh ginger root

Salt and freshly ground black pepper

5 tablespoons margarine, melted, or olive oil

4 tablespoons fresh lemon juice

½ cup fresh orange juice

3 tablespoons honey

Orange sections for garnish

Preheat an oven to 350 degrees F.

Cut the lemon into quarters. Rub the outside of the chicken with one of the lemon quarters, then discard. In a small bowl, stir together the lemon and orange zests and 1 tablespoon of the grated ginger. Rub this mixture evenly in the cavity. Put the lemon and orange quarters inside the bird. Place the chicken on a rack in a roasting pan. Sprinkle it with salt and pepper. In the now-empty small bowl, combine the melted margarine or olive oil, lemon and orange juices, honey, and the remaining 2 tablespoons ginger. Mix well.

Place the chicken in the oven and roast, basting with the citrus juice mixture at least 4 times during cooking, until the juices run clear when the thigh is pierced with a knife, about 1 hour.

Transfer to a serving platter and let rest for 10 to 15 minutes. Carve the chicken. Garnish with orange sections.

VARIATION:

Use 4 tablespoons pomegranate juice in place of the lemon juice.

Carne
Meat

Polpette alla Giudia   *Meatballs, Jewish Style*

Luganega   *Beef Sausage*

Cuscussù alla Livornese   *Livornese Couscous with Meatballs, White Beans, and Greens*

Stufadin di Zuca Zala   *Braised Meat with Butternut Squash*

Hamin Toscana di Fagioli con Polpettone   *Casserole of White Beans and Meat Loaf from Tuscany*

Cavolo Ripieno per Simhà Torà   *Stuffed Cabbage*

Stracotto di Manzo   *Braised Beef in Red Wine*

Scacchi   *Passover Meat and Matzoh Pie*

Rotolo di Vitello coi Colori   *Veal Stuffed with Peppers and an Omelet*

Involtini di Vitello   *Veal Rolls Stuffed with Meat*

Scaloppine di Vitello alla Lattuga   *Veal Scallops with Lettuce*

Spalla di Montone con le Olive   *Braised Lamb Shoulder with Olives*

Agnello Arrosto al Rosmarino, Aglio, e Limone   *Roast Lamb with Rosemary, Garlic, and Lemon*

Agnello Ripieno di Riso   *Lamb Stuffed with Rice*

Capretto e Carciofi all'Uova e Limone   *Kid and Artichokes with Egg and Lemon*

Carne

In keeping with the classic Italian diet, meat was traditionally served on Jewish Italian tables only for special meals such as birthdays, the Sabbath, and holidays. Of course, bits and pieces of cooked meat were used to flavor other dishes, such as soups, pastas, and some vegetable stews. But if meat was not part of the daily regimen, why is the written recipe repertoire so large? The reason is simple: because meat was not served every day, the recipes were not committed to memory, unlike more commonly prepared fare. Thus, it was wise to write down family favorites, so no crucial ingredient would be forgotten when a special meal was planned.

Pork, of course, as well as rabbit, horse, and game, is forbidden to the Jews. (Farm-raised game killed in the kosher manner would be acceptable today, but there are no traditional recipes for it, as farm-raised game is a recent phenomenon.) Only animals that chew their cud and have cloven hooves can be consumed. The slaughtering of animals is done by a rabbi according to Jewish rituals that prescribe careful bleeding. Then, to remove all traces of blood, the meat must be soaked in cold water for an hour, sprinkled with kosher salt, left to stand for another hour, and finally rinsed three times before cooking. This technique has a tendency to dry out the meat, so fattier cuts are generally preferable. Liver can escape this purging by being broiled or flame-seared.

Most of the traditional meat recipes were for beef and veal, usually braised, formed into meatballs and meat loaf. Lamb and veal shoulder or breast were used for festive meals. According to the laws of kashrut, the leg and hindquarters were forbidden unless the sciatic nerve was removed. If the butcher can remove the nerve and sinews, these cuts of meat are permitted. And always, trimmings and leftovers found their way into pasta fillings, soups, and small pastries.

Polpette alla Giudia

Meatballs, Jewish Style

In the Italian Jewish kitchen, the same meat mixture is often used for meatballs and meat loaf. Both make for inexpensive and tasty meat-based meals. In the spirit of thrift, and according to long Sephardic tradition, cooked vegetables are added to extend the meatball mixture. And thanks to Sephardic Jews, tomato sauce is the ubiquitous accompaniment. Mashed potatoes would not be out of place, but mashed with olive oil, not milk, of course. Rice or polenta would also be a good partner.

Serves 4 to 6

For the meatballs:

1 pound ground beef

³⁄₄ cup fresh bread crumbs, soaked in beef broth or water and squeezed dry

4 tablespoons chopped fresh flat-leaf parsley

2 tablespoons chopped fresh mint (optional)

2 or 3 cloves garlic, minced

1 or 2 eggs, lightly beaten

Salt and freshly ground black pepper to taste

Freshly grated nutmeg to taste

For the sauce:

Olive oil

2 to 3 cups Tomato Sauce (page 163)

1 tablespoon grated lemon zest (optional)

¹⁄₄ cup chopped fresh basil (optional)

*1 tablespoon sugar dissolved in
2 tablespoons red wine vinegar*

Preheat an oven to 350 degrees F.

To make the meatballs, in a bowl, combine the beef, bread crumbs, parsley, mint (if using), and garlic. Mix in 1 egg; if the mixture is too dry, add the second egg. Season with the salt, pepper, and nutmeg. Form into walnut-sized balls.

Warm the olive oil in a large sauté pan over high heat. Add the meatballs and fry, turning as necessary, until golden on the outside but still a bit undercooked in the center, 8 to 10 minutes. Transfer to an ovenproof baking dish or deep saucepan.

In a saucepan, warm the tomato sauce and season with the lemon zest and basil, if desired, and/or sugar-vinegar mixture. Pour enough of the sauce over the meatballs to cover them, then cover the dish or pan.

Bake until the sauce is slightly thickened and bubbly, 15 to 20 minutes. Serve hot.

Variations:

To stretch the meat mixture, you may add any one of the following to the ground beef: About 2 pounds leeks, white part only, chopped, cooked in water or olive oil until tender, then chopped again, and 3 eggs (from Tullia Zevi); 1 large eggplant, baked until very tender and then mashed with minced garlic to taste, 2 onions that have been chopped and sautéed in olive oil until tender, and 2 eggs; or about ³⁄₄ pound zucchini, coarsely chopped, and 1 large onion, chopped, sautéed in olive oil until tender, and 2 eggs.

Luganega
Beef Sausage

As Jews were forbidden to eat pork, they developed a sausage made from beef. It is called *luganega*, related to *lucanica*, a sausage from Basilicata in the south. Arabic influence is revealed in the use of savory sweet spices. The flavorful mixture can be stuffed into well-washed beef sausage casings purchased from your butcher, but it is just as easy to shape the mixture into long sausages, wrap them in aluminum foil or plastic wrap, and refrigerate for up to 5 or 6 days. When you need some sausage, you can just cut off the amount you want. You can also shape this mixture into patties or meatballs for cooking. This recipe is based on a description from *La cucina veneziana* by Giuseppe Maffioli.

Serves 8 to 10

2 pounds boneless beef shoulder, finely ground

1/2 pound beef kidney fat, finely ground

6 to 8 cloves garlic, finely minced

1 cup dry white wine

1 tablespoon salt

2 teaspoons freshly ground black pepper

1 tablespoon cracked black peppercorns

1 teaspoon ground cinnamon

1/4 teaspoon ground cloves

1/2 teaspoon freshly grated nutmeg

1 teaspoon ground coriander

2 eggs, lightly beaten, if making patties or meatballs

Olive oil for frying

In a bowl, combine all the ingredients except the eggs and olive oil and mix well. Divide into 2 or 3 equal portions and shape each portion into a sausage about 1 1/2 inches in diameter.

Wrap each sausage well in aluminum foil or plastic wrap and refrigerate.

If you want to cook this mixture as patties or meatballs, just after making, bind it with the eggs, then fry in olive oil until golden on both sides and cooked through, 8 to 10 minutes. If you have stored it in the refrigerator, slice off lengths as needed, and fry them in olive oil until golden.

Cuscussù alla Livornese

LIVORNESE COUSCOUS WITH MEATBALLS, WHITE BEANS, AND GREENS

Geographical proximity is always a logical explanation for the migration of food and recipes. Therefore, we might safely assume that the famous *cuscussù* of Trapani was carried to Sicily from North Africa, which was quite close by ship. But couscous in Livorno? That's another story indeed. It traveled there with North African Jews in the 1270s. In fact, so many Jews from Algeria, Tunisia, and Morocco settled in Livorno that the town was nicknamed Little Jerusalem. It is now safe to assume that most of the couscous dishes in Italy—in Sicily, in Sardinia where it took the form of *fregula* or *casca*, in Liguria and Tuscany—came with the North African Jews. They used lamb, however, while the Italians substituted veal, beef, or fish, often in the form of little meatballs. *Cuscussù* was usually served on Friday nights, and the room-temperature leftovers were eaten at the Sabbath midday meal.

Cuscussù is still served in Livorno. At the Restaurant La Gibigiana, Signora Zuccherofino's version has drifted away from the authentic and kosher, with her addition of Parmesan cheese to the meatballs. Versions of this recipe in Italian cookbooks often include the cheese as well. While *cuscussù* looks like quite a bit of work, all the parts can be prepared separately, then reheated together. The white bean ragout is very much like the Tuscan classic *fagioli all'uccelletto*. The vegetable stew is not unlike a North African vegetable *tagine*. And meatballs are common in Italian Jewish *cuscussù* as well as in North African. Ground meat was a thrifty cut, and even then it was often stretched by the addition of cooked leeks, celery, or zucchini. This is, of course, a model Mediterranean meal, with grain as the base, lots of vegetables and beans, and meat as a flavor accent—economical and satisfying.

The couscous was prepared in the classic manner, raked with cold water, steamed in a *coussoussière* atop the stew, raked again, rested, steamed. It was cooked, covered, in the Jewish manner. Today, however, most of us will be using the precooked instant couscous that is readily available in our markets. So I will give you two sets of cooking instructions, and you can prepare the one you prefer. A *coussoussière* or colander or a perforated double boiler will be needed to prepare the couscous traditionally.

SERVES 6 TO 8

For the beans:

2 cups dried white beans, picked over and rinsed

6 cups water

2 cloves garlic, smashed, plus 2 cloves, minced

2 teaspoons salt, plus more to taste

2 tablespoons olive oil

2 onions, chopped

2 cups chopped canned plum tomatoes

Salt and freshly ground black pepper to taste

For the meatballs:

1 pound ground beef

1 small onion, grated

4 slices bread, soaked in water or broth, then squeezed dry

4 tablespoons finely chopped fresh flat-leaf parsley

1 egg, lightly beaten

1 cup finely chopped cooked zucchini, leeks, or celery (optional)

Salt and freshly ground black pepper to taste

Olive oil for frying

1 ½ cups meat broth for poaching

recipe continues on page 144

Cuscussù alla Livornese

LIVORNESE COUSCOUS WITH MEATBALLS, WHITE BEANS, AND GREENS

For the vegetable stew:

3 tablespoons olive oil

2 onions, chopped

3 carrots, peeled and chopped

3 celery stalks, chopped

2 cups chopped canned plum tomatoes

1 small head green cabbage, cut into halves or quarters, core removed, and cut crosswise into narrow strips

1 head escarole, cored and cut into narrow strips

1 cup English peas

3 small zucchini, diced

Water or meat broth, as needed

Salt and freshly ground black pepper to taste

3 tablespoons chopped fresh mint or basil

For the couscous:

2 cups couscous

3 1/2 cups water, or part water and part meat broth

1 tablespoon olive oil, if steaming instant way

Salt to taste

Yellow Squash Condiment (page 167)

To make the beans, place the beans in a saucepan with the water. Bring to a boil and simmer for 2 minutes. Remove from the heat, cover, and set aside for 1 hour. Drain the beans, return them to the pan, and add fresh water to cover by 2 inches. Bring slowly to a boil over medium heat. Add the smashed garlic and the 2 teaspoons salt. Cover, reduce the heat to low, and cook slowly until the beans are tender, 45 to 60 minutes.

Warm the olive oil in a sauté pan over medium heat. Add the onions and sauté until tender,

about 10 minutes. Season with salt and add the minced garlic and tomatoes. Simmer for 5 minutes. Stir into the cooked beans and adjust the seasonings with salt and pepper. Reheat at serving time.

To make the meatballs, in a bowl, combine the beef, onion, bread, parsley, egg, cooked vegetables (if using), salt, and pepper. Pinch off a nugget and fry in a little olive oil. Taste and adjust the seasonings, then form into marble-sized meatballs. Refrigerate until needed. (If you want to cook the meatballs in advance, gently poach in the meat broth until cooked through, about 10 minutes, then keep covered in a little liquid so they don't dry out.)

To make the stew, warm the olive oil in a large sauté pan over medium heat. Add the onions, 1 carrot, and 1 celery stalk and sauté, stirring, until tender, about 10 minutes. Add the tomatoes and simmer for 5 minutes to blend the flavors. Add the 2 remaining carrots and 2 celery stalks, the cabbage, escarole, peas, and zucchini. Cook, stirring occasionally, until all the vegetables are almost completely tender, about 20 minutes. Add the water or meat broth and simmer until tender, 5 to 8 minutes. Season with salt and pepper. Stir in the mint or basil just before serving.

Meanwhile, prepare the couscous. To make it in the traditional way, spread the couscous grains in a baking pan. Sprinkle with water and rake with oiled fingers to break up lumps. Transfer to the top portion of a *couscoussière* or perforated double boiler or colander. Bring the water (or water and broth) to a simmer in the lower pan or saucepan, place the couscous on top, cover tightly, and steam until doubled in bulk, about 30 minutes. Return the couscous to the baking pan and rake again to break up any lumps. Return to the perforated top, re-cover, and steam the couscous until fully puffed, about 30 minutes longer.

To make couscous the instant way, spread the couscous in a shallow baking pan. Bring the liquid to a boil and add the olive oil and salt. Pour over the couscous. Cover the pan tightly with aluminum foil and place in a warm spot for 15 minutes. Fluff the couscous with a fork or small whisk. (You may keep the couscous warm in a colander over the stew, if you like.)

About 10 minutes before the couscous is ready, poach the meatballs in the broth until cooked through. If you have precooked them, reheat them in broth. Add the meatballs to the white bean stew and simmer together for 5 to 7 minutes to blend the flavors.

To serve, place the couscous in a mound in the center of a large platter. Top with the bean-and-meatball mixture and surround the couscous with the vegetables. If you like, serve accompanied with the yellow squash condiment.

Notes: For *cuscussù di pesce*, or fish couscous, omit the meatballs and poach a cod or simple white fish in fish broth (see page 114). Serve with the white beans, vegetables, and couscous. Or make fish balls using the mixture for the cakes on page 119 and poach them in broth.

Stufadin
di Zuca Zala
BRAISED MEAT WITH BUTTERNUT SQUASH

As many Ashkenazic Jews emigrated to the Veneto, it's not surprising to find a Venetian recipe for a stew reminiscent of the familiar Ashkenazic *tsimmes*, in which sweet potatoes or squash are paired with meat for a savory one-dish meal. In Mantua, a similar dish made with a beef rump roast is called *brasato Rachele*.

Despite the use of the squash and Marsala, the *stufadin* is not overly sweet.

SERVES 4 TO 6

4 tablespoons olive oil

2 large onions, chopped

1 clove garlic, minced

1 tablespoon chopped fresh rosemary

2 pounds cubed veal for stew

Salt to taste

1 cup Marsala or other sweet wine

1 butternut squash, about 1 pound, halved, seeds and fibers removed, peeled, cut into 1/2-inch cubes, and parboiled in salted water for 5 minutes

1 1/2 cups meat or chicken broth, or as needed

Freshly ground black pepper to taste

Warm 2 tablespoons of the olive oil in a sauté pan over low heat. Add the onions, garlic, and rosemary and sauté until tender and translucent, about 8 minutes. Remove from the heat and set aside.

Warm the remaining 2 tablespoons olive oil in a heavy pot over high heat. Add the meat and brown well on all sides, sprinkling with a little salt after it has browned. Add the wine and let it bubble up. Add the sautéed onions, the butternut squash, and the broth to cover and bring to a boil. Cover, reduce the heat to low, and simmer gently until the meat is tender and the squash has formed a puree, 1 to 1 1/4 hours. Season with salt and pepper before serving.

VARIATION:

You can use 3/4 pound carrots, peeled and grated, in place of the squash.

Hamin Toscana di Fagioli con Polpettone

CASSEROLE OF WHITE BEANS AND MEAT LOAF FROM TUSCANY

Hamin, literally "oven," is comfort food at its best—incredibly satisfying, but very filling. A Sabbath *cholent* dish, or one-pot slow-cooked stew (sort of like a primitive Crock-Pot), this recipe pairs the classic Tuscan bean dish, *fagioli all'uccelletto*, with meat loaf. To cut the richness, serve with braised Swiss chard or another robust, clean-tasting green, or with Braised Spinach Stems (page 85).

Edda Servi Machlin prepares a version of *hamin* made with brisket or flanken of beef, first well browned on all sides and then simmered with the beans over very low heat for 5 hours. She adds chicken meatballs that have been simmered with Swiss chard for the last 20 minutes or so. They all are served together, making for a cross between the *cuscussù* on page 142 and a *cholent*.

SERVES 6

For the beans:

1 ½ cups dried cannellini or other dried white beans, picked over and rinsed

6 cups water

3 tablespoons olive oil

1 large onion, chopped

2 or 3 cloves garlic, minced

3 or 4 fresh sage leaves

1 ½ to 2 cups Tomato Sauce (page 163)

Salt and freshly ground black pepper to taste

For the meat loaves:

1 ¼ pounds ground beef

2 eggs, lightly beaten

½ cup fresh bread crumbs or matzoh meal

4 tablespoons chopped fresh flat-leaf parsley

1 ½ teaspoons salt

½ teaspoon freshly ground black pepper

Freshly grated nutmeg or ground cinnamon to taste (optional)

All-purpose flour seasoned with salt and freshly ground black pepper to taste

½ cup olive oil, or as needed

Water, broth, or additional Tomato Sauce, if needed

To cook the beans, place in a large saucepan with the water. Bring to a boil and simmer for 2 minutes. Remove from the heat, cover, and set aside for 1 hour. Drain the beans, return them to the pan, and add fresh water to cover by 2 inches. Bring slowly to a boil over medium heat.

Meanwhile, warm the olive oil in a sauté pan over medium heat. Add the onion and garlic and sauté for a few minutes to soften. Add to the beans along with the sage leaves, Tomato Sauce, salt, and pepper. Cover, reduce the heat to low, and cook slowly until the beans are tender, about 1 hour.

Meanwhile, make the meat loaves: In a bowl, combine the beef, eggs, bread crumbs or matzoh meal, parsley, salt, pepper, and the nutmeg or cinnamon, if using. Form into 2 oval meat loaves (or giant meatballs). Spread the seasoned flour on a plate and coat the loaves with it.

Pour the olive oil to a depth of ¼ inch into a large sauté pan over medium-high heat. Add the meat loaves and brown well on all sides. Transfer the meat loaves to the tender beans and continue to simmer until the loaves are cooked through, 20 to 30 minutes. Check the amount of liquid; if the beans seem dry, add water, broth, or more Tomato Sauce. The dish should be somewhat brothy.

Carefully remove the meat loaves from the pan. Let them rest for about 10 minutes. Slice the meat loaves and serve with the beans.

Cavolo Ripieno per Simhà Torà
Stuffed Cabbage

Stuffed cabbage is not just an Ashkenazic, or even American Jewish deli, specialty. This particular recipe is adapted from two different Italian Jewish recipes, both of which are traditionally served on Simchat Torah, which falls at the end of Sukkot and joyfully celebrates the Torah. One recipe is from Mira Sacerdoti and the other is my interpretation of a recipe found in Cia Eramo's *La cucina mantovana*. Eramo braises the cabbage whole, slipping the filling between the leaves. Mira Sacerdoti stuffs the individual cabbage leaves and calls them *rotoli de verze*, a Jewish version of the Levantine Sephardic dolma. Thrifty Italian Jews readily embraced such a dish, which makes something delicious and special out of a few humble ingredients. This same filling can be stuffed into eggplant, peppers, and zucchini.

Serves 4 to 6

1 pound ground beef

1 large onion, grated or finely chopped

1 cup fresh bread crumbs or half-cooked white rice

1 egg, lightly beaten

Salt and freshly ground black pepper to taste

*1 large head green cabbage, 1 ½ to 2 pounds
(12 to 18 large leaves)*

3 to 4 cups meat broth, or as needed

In a bowl, combine the ground beef, onion, bread crumbs or rice, egg, salt, and pepper. Mix well and set aside.

To serve a whole cabbage, carefully spread the leaves and spoon some of the meat mixture down near the bottom between each layer of leaves. Reform the leaves into the head and tie with kitchen string to keep the filling in place. Place the cabbage in a large pot. Add the broth to cover and bring to a simmer over low heat. Cover and simmer until tender, about 1 ½ hours. (Alternatively, place the covered pot in an oven preheated to 300 degrees F for 1 ½ hours.)

To make individual cabbage rolls, bring a large pot two-thirds full of salted water to a boil. Cut out the core of the cabbage with a sharp knife. Slip the cabbage into the water, reduce the heat so the water simmers, and cook until the cabbage leaves soften, about 10 minutes. Drain carefully and remove the outer large leaves. You should have 12 to 18 leaves. Reserve the remaining cabbage for another use.

Spread out the cabbage leaves on a work surface. Place a few tablespoons of the meat mixture on the center of a leaf, fold over the top, then fold in the other 3 sides, to make a dolmalike package. Secure closed with toothpicks. Repeat until all the meat mixture is used. Place the packages, seam side down, in a large pot. Add the broth to cover and bring to a simmer over low heat. Cover and simmer until tender, 1 to 1 ½ hours. (Alternatively, place the covered pot in an oven preheated to 300 degrees F for 1 to 1 ½ hours.) Transfer the whole cabbage or the cabbage rolls, toothpicks removed, to a warmed platter. Cut the whole cabbage into wedges. Serve hot.

Variation:

Sauté 1 large onion, chopped, in olive oil until tender, about 10 minutes. Add the onion and 2 cups chopped canned plum tomatoes to the broth for braising the cabbage rolls.

 Stracotto di Manzo
Braised Beef in Red Wine

Stracotto di Manzo

Braised Beef in Red Wine

Stracotto means "overcooked." Although one shouldn't take this too literally, long cooking is nonetheless necessary to make a tough and inexpensive cut of meat tender. Some Roman versions of this hearty pot roast, like the one in Donatella Limentani Pavoncello's book *Dal 1880 ad oggi: la cucina ebraica della mia famiglia*, use no wine, only tomatoes, or use tomatoes and water. Other recipes for braised beef cut the meat into cubes instead of keeping it in one piece. A recipe for a similar stew, called *la tegamata* in *La cucina maremmana*, recommends marinating the meat overnight in wine and spices. I agree. I prefer the wine and spice version, as I think it results in a more interesting flavor. Not every cook browns the meat first, so you can skip this step entirely if you like. Accompany with polenta or potatoes.

Serves 6

3 tablespoons olive oil

1 beef roast, about 2 pounds, tied into a compact shape, or 2 pounds stewing beef, cut into 1 1/2- to 2-inch cubes

2 large onions, diced

3 carrots, peeled and chopped (optional)

2 celery stalks, chopped (optional)

4 cups peeled, seeded and chopped tomatoes (fresh or canned)

3 or 4 garlic cloves, cut into slivers

1 lemon zest strip, about 3 inches long

1 cinnamon stick

A few whole cloves (optional)

3 to 4 cups dry red wine, or as needed

Salt and freshly ground pepper to taste

Warm the olive oil in a large sauté pan over high heat. Add the roast or the meat cubes in batches and brown well on all sides. Transfer to a heavy pot. Add the onions, the carrots and celery, if using, the tomatoes, the garlic, the lemon zest, the cinnamon stick, and the cloves, if using. Pour in the wine to cover. Bring to a boil over medium-high heat, cover, reduce the heat to low, and simmer until the meat is *stracotto*, or very tender, and the pan juices are well thickened, about 2 hours.

Remove the cinnamon stick, lemon zest, and cloves (if used) and discard. Season the beef with salt and pepper. Transfer to a warmed serving plate or dish. If you have used a roast, slice to serve. Save any extra meat juices for tossing with pasta.

Variations:

You can sauté the onions, carrots, and celery in olive oil until tender before adding them to the pot. For a fuller flavor, marinate the meat overnight in the wine, garlic, lemon zest, and cinnamon, then drain, reserve the marinade, dry, and brown. Use the reserved marinade for braising the meat. If there is not enough liquid for braising, add water or meat broth as needed. You can also use beef brisket in place of the beef roast.

Scacchi
Passover Meat and Matzoh Pie

Scacchi are matzoh pies made with vegetables and meat or meat juices—sort of a Passover lasagna. In *Celebrating Italy*, Carol Field has an excellent recipe for *scacchi* in which layers of meat and matzoh alternate with layers of cooked spinach, artichokes, and mushrooms, a filling and complex dish. Here is a simpler version, also known as *tortino di carne e azzime*, that uses just meat. It is meant to be accompanied with many vegetable dishes. If you don't want an all-meat *scacchi*, you may use the same filling that goes into the Double-Crusted Vegetable Pie on page 34. For another view of a layered matzoh dish, see the recipe for Passover Matzoh Soup on page 42.

Serves 4 to 6

4 tablespoons olive oil

2 onions, chopped

¹⁄₂ cup pine nuts

1 ¹⁄₂ pounds ground beef

¹⁄₂ cup raisins, plumped in hot water and drained

1 teaspoon ground cinnamon

1 ¹⁄₂ teaspoons salt

¹⁄₂ teaspoon freshly ground black pepper

4 tablespoons chopped fresh flat-leaf parsley

4 matzohs

3 eggs

¹⁄₂ cup beef broth, or as needed

Warm 3 tablespoons of the olive oil in a large sauté pan over medium heat. Add the onions and pine nuts and sauté until the onions are softened, about 5 minutes. Raise the heat to medium-high and add the beef, raisins, and cinnamon. Sauté, stirring often, until the meat loses its redness and starts to brown, about 10 minutes. Season with salt and pepper and remove from the heat. Stir in the parsley.

Preheat an oven to 350 degrees F. Brush a baking pan with the remaining 1 tablespoon olive oil.

Soak the matzohs in water to cover to soften, about 15 minutes, then drain. Line the prepared baking pan with 2 softened matzohs, top with the meat mixture, and cover with the other 2 matzohs. In a bowl, whisk together the eggs and ¹⁄₂ cup broth and pour evenly over the surface, then shake the pan to distribute the liquids evenly. Add more broth, if needed, to cover.

Bake until golden, 30 to 40 minutes. Remove from the oven and let stand for 10 minutes before serving.

Rotolo di Vitello coi Colori
Veal Stuffed with Peppers and an Omelet

In this Sabbath specialty from Padua, breast of veal is boned, butterflied, and stuffed with an omelet seasoned with peas and roasted peppers, then rolled, tied, browned in olive oil, and braised in white wine and broth. As described in *La cucina padovana*, the dish is traditionally served cold, thinly sliced. Today, we'd probably serve it warm, accompanied with rice or fresh pasta dressed with the pan juices. If you are not keeping strictly kosher, you may use a boned leg of veal, as there will be more meat than with the breast. A variation from neighboring Ferrara stuffs the veal with an herbed omelet and a center layer of braised spinach—also delicious (see variation).

SERVES 6

6 eggs

Salt and freshly ground black pepper to taste

6 tablespoons olive oil

1 cup cooked English peas

2 cups mixed red and green roasted peppers,
cut into narrow strips

1 veal breast, boned and butterflied,
or 1 leg of veal, 2½ to 3 pounds, boned, butterflied,
and well trimmed of nerves and sinews

2 or 3 cloves garlic, cut into slivers (optional)

1½ cups dry white wine

2 cups chicken, beef, or veal broth

In a bowl, lightly beat the eggs with a fork and season with salt and pepper. Warm 3 tablespoons olive oil in a large, wide sauté pan over medium heat. Add the peas and roasted peppers and stir to coat with the oil. Pour in the eggs and stir well. As the eggs cook, using a fork, gently pull the runny center of the omelet out toward the edge of the pan to allow the uncooked eggs to flow underneath. Cook until the eggs are set, about 4 minutes. Turn the omelet out onto a kitchen towel or lightly oiled baking sheet.

Place the veal between 2 sheets of plastic wrap and pound lightly to an even thickness of ¾ inch. Sprinkle with salt and pepper. Lay the omelet over the veal, roll up the veal, and tie the roll with kitchen string at 1-inch intervals to secure. If desired, make shallow slits in the veal and slip the garlic slivers into them.

Heat the remaining 3 tablespoons olive oil in a large sauté pan over high heat. Add the veal and brown well on all sides. Transfer to a heavy pot with a tight-fitting lid. Add the wine and broth and bring to a boil over high heat. Cover, reduce the heat to low, and simmer until tender, 1½ to 2 hours.

If serving warm, transfer the veal to a cutting board and let rest for about 15 minutes. Snip the strings, then slice about ¼ inch thick, arrange the slices on a platter, and spoon the pan juices over the meat. If serving cold, remove the veal from the pot, let cool, snip the strings, cover, and chill well. Reserve the pan juices for another use. Thinly slice the chilled veal, arrange on a platter, and serve.

VARIATION:

To make a Ferrarese version, cook 1 pound spinach, drain, chop finely, and drain well again. Season with salt and freshly ground black pepper. Flavor the omelet with lots of chopped fresh flat-leaf parsley and thyme. Place the omelet over the butterflied leg of veal and then top with the spinach. Roll, tie, and cook as directed.

Involtini
di Vitello
VEAL ROLLS STUFFED WITH MEAT

Veal rolls are usually served with potatoes (even better are olive oil–mashed potatoes), but polenta or rice would work as well. This recipe can be made with beef or veal. Sometimes the rolls are stuffed with the mixture for meatballs (see page 140), but here is a milder version inspired by one in Giuliana Ascoli Vitali-Norsa's *La cucina nella tradizione ebraica*.

SERVES 4

8 veal scallops, about 1 pound

½ pound ground veal

*¼ cup fresh bread crumbs, soaked in water,
then squeezed dry*

1 egg, lightly beaten

Salt and freshly ground black pepper to taste

Extra-virgin olive oil, as needed

1 cup dry white wine

*1 ½ cups beef, veal, or chicken broth,
or as needed to cover meat*

Place the veal scallops between 2 sheets of plastic wrap and pound to an even thickness of ⅓ inch. In a bowl, combine the ground veal, bread crumbs, egg, salt, and pepper. Mix well. Spread the ground meat mixture on the veal scallops, dividing it evenly. Roll up and skewer closed with toothpicks or tie with kitchen string.

Warm enough olive oil to form a film in a large sauté pan over high heat. Add the veal rolls and brown well on all sides. Add the wine and cook until it evaporates. Add the broth to cover the rolls, cover the pan, reduce the heat to low, and cook until the filling is cooked through

and the rolls are tender, about 20 minutes.

Transfer the rolls to a warmed platter and remove the toothpicks or snip the strings; keep warm. Raise the heat and reduce the pan juices until slightly thickened. Spoon the pan juices over the veal rolls and serve at once.

Involtini di Carciofi
VEAL ROLLS STUFFED WITH ARTICHOKES

Milka Passigli's mother used to make these. Make a *battuto* of 1½ tablespoons minced garlic, 6 tablespoons chopped flat-leaf parsley, salt, pepper, and 1 tablespoon grated lemon zest. Clean 6 artichokes, cut into quarters or eighths, remove chokes, and sauté in 3 tablespoons olive oil and a little water until tender, about 8 to 10 minutes. Season with salt and pepper. Spread 6 slices of veal with *battuto* and then top with pieces of artichoke. Roll and tie. Sear over high heat in 3 tablespoons olive oil and deglaze the pan with 1 cup of meat broth. Reduce the sauce slightly, and serve spooned over the rolls.

 Involtini di Carciofi

VEAL ROLLS STUFFED WITH ARTICHOKES

Scaloppine
di Vitello alla Lattuga
Veal Scallops with Lettuce

The early Romans believed that lettuce was good for digestion. This Roman recipe was not originally a scaloppine as we know it. According to Donatella Pavoncello in *Dal 1880 ad oggi: la cucina ebraica della mia famiglia*, slices of veal were fried in meat fat, then layered with lettuce leaves and baked. As our veal is very lean and has a tendency to dry out quickly, I think it is best to treat this dish as a scaloppine and add the lettuce to the sauce. Try it both ways and see which you prefer. I took liberty with seasoning as well. Because the dish is a little bland for our contemporary palates, I suggest the addition of grated lemon zest and juice—turning it into a kind of *piccata* with greens. A more full-flavored green such as escarole could be used in place of the romaine. Serve with potatoes.

Serves 4

8 veal scallops (about 1 pound)

½ cup all-purpose flour

1 teaspoon salt, plus salt to taste

*½ teaspoon freshly ground black pepper,
plus pepper to taste*

¼ teaspoon freshly grated nutmeg

Olive oil, as needed

Juice of 1 large lemon

½ cup veal, beef, or chicken broth

*12 large leaves romaine lettuce, left whole if baking and
chopped if sautéing*

Grated lemon zest to taste (optional)

Place the veal scallops between 2 sheets of plastic wrap and pound to an even thickness of ¼ inch. Stir together the flour, salt, pepper, and nutmeg on a plate. Dip the veal in the seasoned flour, coating both sides lightly.

Warm enough olive oil to form a film in a large sauté pan over high heat. In batches, quickly brown the veal scallops on both sides. Transfer to a plate and keep warm. The veal should not be completely cooked, only seared. Add the lemon juice and broth and deglaze the pan, scraping up any browned bits from the pan bottom. Remove from the heat.

To make the classic version, preheat an oven to 400 degrees F. Place 4 slices of seared veal on the bottom of an oiled baking dish. Top with half of the lettuce leaves. Sprinkle with salt and pepper and the lemon zest, if using. Top with the remaining veal slices, and then the remaining lettuce leaves. Drizzle with the pan juices and 2 tablespoons olive oil. Bake until tender, about 30 minutes. Serve hot.

To treat this as a leafy veal scaloppine, sauté the veal as directed, but cook it fully. Transfer to a warmed platter and keep warm. Deglaze the pan with broth as described for the baked version (do not add lemon juice at this time). Then add the chopped romaine and wilt quickly. Season with salt, pepper, and the lemon juice and zest. Spoon over the veal and serve at once.

Variation:

In the baked version, omit the lemon zest. In its place, sprinkle a *gremolata* mixture of 1 tablespoon minced garlic, 2 tablespoons grated lemon zest, and 3 to 4 tablespoons chopped fresh flat-leaf parsley over the lettuce leaves.

Spalla di Montone con le Olive

BRAISED LAMB SHOULDER WITH OLIVES

Leg of lamb can be costly, even today. Leave it to the thrifty ghetto Jews of Rome to come up with the economy version. Traditionally, a boned shoulder of lamb was rubbed with salt, pepper, cloves, and cinnamon, then rolled and tied. Mira Sacerdoti's family made this without the cinnamon but added a bay leaf and thyme. The best way to prepare the rather tough lamb shoulder is to braise it until it is meltingly tender. In addition, instead of boning, rolling, and tying the shoulder, it is far easier to cook it as a stew.

SERVES 6

3 pounds boneless lamb shoulder,
well trimmed and cut into 2-inch pieces

⅛ teaspoon ground cloves

¼ teaspoon ground cinnamon

Olive oil, as needed

3 onions, sliced

2 cups meat broth, or as needed

½ cup dry white wine (optional)

6 large carrots, peeled and cut into 2-inch chunks

1 tablespoon chopped fresh rosemary (optional)

1 or 2 tablespoons grated orange zest (optional)

1 cup Mediterranean-style green olives,
pitted and coarsely chopped

Salt and freshly ground black pepper to taste

In a bowl, rub the cubed meat with the cloves, cinnamon, and a little olive oil. Cover and let stand for 2 hours at room temperature or as long as overnight in the refrigerator.

Warm enough olive oil to form a film in a sauté pan over high heat. Add the meat cubes and brown well on all sides. Using a slotted spoon, transfer the meat cubes to a large, heavy pot. To the fat remaining in the sauté pan, add the onions and sauté until tender and translucent, about 8 minutes. Transfer to the pot. Add about ½ cup of the broth or the white wine, if using, to the sauté pan and deglaze the pan, stirring to scrape up all the browned bits. Add to the pot. Add enough broth just to cover the meat, bring to a boil, cover, reduce the heat to low, and simmer for 1 hour.

Add the carrots and the rosemary or orange zest, if using, and cook for 25 minutes. Then add the green olives and simmer until the meat is tender, about 25 minutes longer. Season with salt and pepper, then serve.

Agnello Arrosto al Rosmarino, Aglio, e Limone

ROAST LAMB WITH ROSEMARY, GARLIC, AND LEMON

In the old days, braised lamb shoulder was considered a festive cut of meat. Leg of lamb was forbidden unless the sciatic nerve was removed. Today, most of us look upon leg of lamb as a festive cut, and the fattier, tougher shoulder has been relegated to stews. If you are not keeping strictly kosher, use a bone-in leg of lamb. A 5- to 6-pound bone-in leg will feed 6 people nicely. The amount of garlic and rosemary is up to you. Rosemary is a powerhouse of an herb and a little goes a long way, so be judicious. It is nice if you have a little lamb broth for pan juices to spoon over the roast meat. It can be thickened with a puree of roasted or braised garlic. Potatoes can be roasted in the pan along with the lamb. Although they will not be crisp, they will be succulent from cooking in the lemony pan juices.

SERVES 6

1 boned lamb shoulder, 3 1/2 to 4 pounds, or 1 bone-in leg of lamb, about 6 pounds

3 cloves garlic, cut into slivers, plus 1 tablespoon chopped

Leaves from 2 or 3 small fresh rosemary sprigs, plus about 1 tablespoon chopped

Juice of 2 large lemons (about 1/2 cup)

4 tablespoons extra-virgin olive oil

Salt and freshly ground black pepper to taste

For the sauce:

3 cups lamb broth

Minced garlic to taste

Chopped fresh rosemary to taste

Freshly ground black pepper to taste

12 braised or roasted garlic cloves, pureed (optional)

Preheat an oven to 375 degrees F. Make shallow slits all over the lamb and insert the garlic slivers and rosemary leaves into the slits.

In a bowl, stir together the lemon juice, olive oil, chopped garlic, and the 1 tablespoon chopped rosemary to use for basting the meat as it roasts.

Sprinkle the lamb with salt and pepper and place in a roasting pan. Roast, basting occasionally with the oil-lemon mixture, 1 to 1 1/4 hours, or until an instant-read thermometer inserted into the thickest part registers 120 degrees F.

While the lamb is roasting, make the sauce: In a saucepan boil the lamb broth until reduced to 1 1/2 cups, then season with a little garlic, chopped rosemary, and black pepper. Alternatively, thicken the reduced broth with the pureed garlic.

Remove the lamb from the oven and let sit for 10 to 15 minutes. Slice and serve on a warmed platter. Spoon the sauce over the top.

VARIATION:

To use a boned leg of lamb, 4 to 4 1/2 pounds, combine about 2 tablespoons minced garlic, 2 tablespoons fresh rosemary leaves, grated zest of 1 lemon, and an ample amount of freshly ground black pepper. Rub this mixture on the inside of the lamb leg, roll up the leg, and tie securely with kitchen string. Make slits in the outside of the rolled leg and insert garlic slices and rosemary leaves into it as directed for the bone-in leg. Roast as directed, let rest for 10 to 15 minutes, snip the strings, slice, and serve on a warmed platter. Spoon the sauce of reduced lamb broth over the top.

 Agnello Arrosto al Rosmarino, Aglio, e Limone

Roast Lamb with Rosemary, Garlic, and Lemon

Agnello Ripieno di Riso

Lamb Stuffed with Rice

Another Passover dish, this Sephardic recipe was originally made with a boned lamb shoulder into which a pocket was cut. Leg of lamb is much easier to bone, stuff, and roll, however, and is kosher, as long as the sciatic nerve is removed. The filling resembles a traditional dolma stuffing and would be delicious spooned into tomatoes, eggplant, or zucchini for an inexpensive meal.

Serves 6

1 ⅓ cups white rice

Leg of lamb, about 5 pounds, boned, butterflied, and well-trimmed of nerves and sinews

Salt and freshly ground black pepper to taste

1 teaspoon ground cinnamon

2 tablespoons olive oil, plus oil for browning

1 onion, chopped

¾ pound ground lamb

2 to 3 cups meat broth or water, or as needed

Place the rice in a bowl and add water to cover. Let stand for 30 minutes.

Meanwhile, lay the lamb leg flat. Cut away any excess fat and tendons. Using a meat pounder, flatten the lamb to a relatively uniform thickness. Season with salt, pepper, and half of the cinnamon.

Warm the 2 tablespoons olive oil in a sauté pan over medium heat. Add the onion and sauté until tender, about 8 minutes. Add the ground lamb and cook, stirring often, until the meat loses its redness, about 5 minutes. Transfer the lamb and onions to a bowl. Drain the rice and add to the bowl; stir to combine. Season with salt, pepper, and the remaining ½ teaspoon cinnamon.

Pat the rice mixture onto the flattened lamb leg in an even layer. Roll up the lamb and tie in several places with kitchen string.

Heat enough olive oil to form a film in a large sauté pan over high heat. Add the meat and brown well on all sides. Transfer to a heavy pot, add broth or water to cover, and bring to a boil. Cover, reduce the heat to low, and simmer until the lamb is tender, about 1 ½ hours.

Transfer the lamb to a cutting board and snip the strings. Let rest for 10 to 15 minutes. Meanwhile, reduce the pan juices to 1 cup over high heat, scraping up any browned bits from the bottom of the pot. Cut the lamb into slices ⅓ to ½ inch thick and arrange on a warmed platter, stuffing back in any rice filling that falls out. Spoon the pan juices over the meat and serve immediately.

Capretto e Carciofi all'Uova e Limone

KID AND ARTICHOKES WITH EGG AND LEMON

Egg-and-lemon-enriched sauces appear throughout Italian cuisine and are most likely of Sephardic origin. These *bagna brusca* dishes are reminiscent of the well-known Greek *avgolemono*. This recipe from Calabria uses kid (baby goat), as does *capretto alla giudia* from Rome. *Spezzatino d'agnello con salsa di uova per Pasqua* and *agnello brodettato*, Passover recipes of Lazio and Tuscany respectively, are practically identical to this recipe as well except for their use of lamb. In non-Jewish versions, lard or prosciutto fat is used instead of olive oil. The artichokes can be cooked separately and added during the last 10 minutes. Peas may also be added, as well as favas and asparagus. You can also make this stew with chicken.

SERVES 6

½ cup olive oil, or as needed

3 ½ pounds kid or lamb, cut into 2-inch pieces

1 large onion, chopped

4 tablespoons chopped fresh flat-leaf parsley

Salt and freshly ground black pepper to taste

2 tablespoons all-purpose flour (optional)

1 cup dry white wine

1 lemon, plus juice of 2 large lemons (about ½ cup)

6 small artichokes

3 egg yolks

1 tablespoon chopped fresh marjoram or mint

Warm the olive oil in a large saucepan or wide sauté pan over high heat. Add the kid or lamb, onion, and half of the parsley, and sauté until the lamb is golden, 8 to 10 minutes. Sprinkle with salt, pepper, and the flour and mix well. Add the wine and bring to a boil. Cook over high heat for about 5 minutes, then cover, reduce the heat to low, and simmer for 35 to 40 minutes.

Meanwhile, prepare the artichokes: Fill a large bowl with water, cut the lemon in half, and squeeze the juice into the water. Working with 1 artichoke at a time, remove all the tough outer leaves until you reach the pale green heart. Pare away the dark green area from the base and any tender stem. Cut the artichoke in half lengthwise and scoop out and discard the choke from each half. Cut each half in half again lengthwise and drop into the lemon water.

When the meat has simmered for about 40 minutes, drain the artichokes, add them to the pot, re-cover, and continue to simmer until the meat and artichokes are tender, about 25 minutes longer. Taste and adjust the seasonings.

In a bowl, whisk together the egg yolks, lemon juice, the remaining 2 tablespoons parsley, and the marjoram or mint until foamy. Remove the stew from the heat and beat in the egg-lemon mixture, stirring constantly. Re-cover the pan and let stand off the heat until the eggs thicken the sauce, about 3 minutes. Serve at once.

Notes: Quartered fennel bulbs or heads of lettuce may be added during the last 10 minutes of cooking. Another variation on this dish braises lamb rib chops with the artichokes.

Salse
SAUCES

Tre Salse Fondamentale della Cucina Ebrea Italiana   *Three Basic Sauces from the Italian Jewish Kitchen*

1. Salsa Besciamella   *Classic Cream Sauce*

2. Salsa Maionaise   *Mayonnaise*

3. Salsa di Pomodoro   *Tomato Sauce*

Sugo Finto   *False Sauce*

Salsa di Noce   *Walnut Sauce*

Salsa Verde   *Green Sauce*

Bagna Brusca   *Egg-and-Lemon Sauce*

Salsa Tonnato   *Tuna Sauce*

Thurshi   *Yellow Squash Condiment for Couscous*

Haroset   *Passover Fruit Condiment*

Salse

These sauces form part of the basic Italian Jewish pantry. Everyone has a family tomato sauce recipe or a special touch with the nutmeg grinder for the *besciamella*. Mayonnaise is made fresh and has a golden hue due to the deep yellow-orange yolks that also color fresh pasta. Piquant *salsa verde* is spooned over cold poached fish and chicken, vegetables, and boiled beef. And the rich *salsa di noce* is used as an accompaniment for cooked fish.

Sweet-and-sour sauces remain popular today. Pine nuts and raisins are added to many pan sauces, along with a pinch of sugar and a dash of vinegar. These sauces are usually of Arabic or Levantine origin, transmitted via the cuisine of Sicily or the Sephardim. *Bagna brusca*, the frothy mixture of eggs and lemon juice bound with broth, is related to Greek (Sephardic) *avgolemono* sauce and was traditionally used as a creamy thickener in soups, stews, and pan sauces in dishes where non-Jews would have added cream or mounted a sauce with butter.

For Passover, every family has its version of *haroset*, the condiment of dried fruits and nuts macerated in sweet wine or fruit juice. Some cooks add chestnuts, others poppy seeds, and still others a few pieces of fresh diced apple.

Tre Salse Fondamentale della Cucina Ebrea Italiana

THREE BASIC SAUCES FROM THE ITALIAN JEWISH KITCHEN

What follows are three sauces that are the corner-stones of the Italian and Italian Jewish kitchens. The first is the classic cream sauce known as *besciamella*, which is better known by its French name, béchamel. It acts as a thickener or liaison in soups, puddings, and gratins, as well as a sauce. Obviously it cannot be used in any dish that has meat, or even in a meal where any meat is served. It provides a note of rich-ness at dairy dinners.

The mayonnaise is pareve; it can be used at both dairy- and meat-based meals. Always made with golden yellow yolks from eggs that are not fertilized, that is, without blood spots, mayonnaise is served with cold cooked fish, tuna or chicken loaf, hard-boiled eggs, and cooked vegetables. It should have enough lemony tartness to cut through the inherent richness of the emulsified yolk-and-oil-based sauce. You may use all pure olive oil or part extra-virgin oil for fruitier taste. Using all extra-virgin olive oil may make the mayonnaise too strong in flavor, however, thus possi-bly overpowering the dish it is to accompany.

Tomato sauce is ubiquitous in the Italian cooking repertoire. For pasta it is an essential condiment. For braised meats and stews it acts as a thickener and fla-vor enhancer to the meat juices. The first tomato sauce recipe is a light and simple one, not cooked too long. In some regions of Italy it is known as *pommarola*. In summer, ripe plum tomatoes can be used, but most of the year canned plum tomatoes will form the basis of this sauce.

Salsa Besciamella
CLASSIC CREAM SAUCE
MAKES ABOUT 2 CUPS

2 cups milk

3 to 4 tablespoons unsalted butter

3 tablespoons all-purpose flour

Salt and freshly ground black pepper to taste

Freshly grated nutmeg to taste

Pour the milk into a small saucepan and bring to just below a boil over medium heat. Meanwhile, melt the butter in another small saucepan over low heat. Add the flour and cook, stirring, for about 5 minutes; do not let the mixture color. Whisk in the hot milk and continue to whisk until thickened and all the raw flour taste is gone, 8 to 10 minutes. Season with salt, pepper, and nutmeg.

Salsa Maionaise
MAYONNAISE
MAKES ABOUT 2 CUPS

2 egg yolks (see Note)

3 to 4 tablespoons fresh lemon juice

2 cups pure olive oil, or part extra-virgin

Salt and freshly ground black pepper to taste

Place the egg yolks in the container of a blender or food processor. Add a little of the lemon juice and then process until combined. With the motor running, gradually add the olive oil, a few drops at a time, until a thick emulsion begins to form. Then add the remaining oil in a very thin, slow stream until all the oil is incorporated and the mixture is thick. Add lemon juice to taste and season with salt and pepper. If the mayonnaise is too thick, thin with a little water. Of course, you may also make this in a bowl with a whisk. The resulting texture will be a little lighter.

Note: If you are concerned about salmonella, look for pasteurized egg yolks.

VARIATIONS:

You can flavor the mayonnaise in a variety of ways. Among the possible additions are 2 tablespoons capers, rinsed and chopped; 4 olive oil–packed anchovy fillets, drained and chopped; 1 tablespoon grated lemon or orange zest, or to taste; 2 cloves garlic, mashed to a fine paste with salt. For *salsa agliata*, add lemon juice and garlic to taste plus ½ cup finely chopped toasted walnuts.

Salsa di Pomodoro
TOMATO SAUCE

MAKES ABOUT 6 CUPS

2 cans (28 ounces each) plum tomatoes, with their juices

1 cup tomato puree

Salt and freshly ground black pepper to taste

2 to 3 tablespoons unsalted butter, cut into small pieces (optional)

2 to 3 tablespoons extra-virgin olive oil (optional)

Pinch of sugar (optional)

Place the tomatoes and their juices in a food processor and process until finely chopped but not liquified. Transfer to a heavy saucepan. Stir in the tomato puree and place over low heat. Bring to a simmer and cook, stirring often, until the sauce is hot and slightly thickened, about 20 minutes. Season with salt and pepper.

If desired, stir in the butter, olive oil, or sugar to balance the flavors. The sauce will keep for up to 4 days in the refrigerator.

Sugo Finto
FALSE SAUCE

This tomato sauce, called by the Romans *sugo finto* or "false sauce," gets its name because it is enriched with chopped vegetables and cooked longer than the first sauce. It is thick and rich and resembles a meat-based sauce, or *sugo*. *Sugo finto* may be passed through a food mill for a more uniform texture. Non-Jewish Romans use lard instead of olive oil for making it, and some add meat juices after cooking. In the Italian Jewish kitchen, the sauce may be enriched by meat juices, but then the sauce may only be used at a meat-based meal.

MAKES ABOUT 6½ CUPS

3 tablespoons olive oil

2 carrots, peeled and chopped

2 celery stalks, chopped

1 large onion, chopped

1 clove garlic, minced (optional)

½ cup chopped fresh flat-leaf parsley

4 tablespoons chopped fresh basil

Salt and freshly ground black pepper to taste

½ cup dry red wine

2 cans (28 ounces each) plum tomatoes, with their juices

Heat the olive oil in a large saucepan over medium heat. Add the carrots, celery, onion, garlic (if using), parsley, basil, salt, and pepper and sauté until the *battuto* is pale gold, about 10 minutes. Add the wine and cook until it evaporates. Then add the tomatoes with their juices, stir well, reduce the heat to low, and simmer gently, uncovered, until thickened, about 1 hour.

Pass the sauce through a food mill if you want a smoother texture. This sauce will keep for up to 5 days in the refrigerator.

Salsa di Noce
Walnut Sauce

This rich sauce is a cross between an Italian *salsa verde* and a Sephardic nut sauce. It usually is served with cooked fish, but it is also tasty spooned over cooked vegetables or hard-boiled eggs. Note that unlike other nut-based sauces, this one has no acid—no lemon or vinegar. It is quite fragrant and voluptuous without it, but if you are craving a bit of tartness, add the capers, as their brininess will cut some of the richness. Some recipes use almonds or pine nuts in place of the yolks. If you are pressed for time, you can pulse the ingredients in a food processor, although the result will not be as good.

Makes about 2 cups

3 hard-boiled egg yolks, chopped

1 cup walnuts, toasted and chopped

3/4 cup chopped fresh flat-leaf parsley

2 cloves garlic, finely minced

1 cup extra-virgin olive oil

Salt and freshly ground black pepper to taste

4 tablespoons chopped, pitted Mediterranean-style black olives (optional)

1 tablespoon capers, rinsed and chopped (optional)

In a bowl, combine all the ingredients and whisk to mix well.

Note: Giuliano Bugialli refers to a Renaissance *salsa agresto* with walnuts in his excellent first cookbook, *The Fine Art of Italian Cooking*. It probably has Jewish origins. Chopped toasted walnuts and almonds are combined with a little finely diced red onion, parsley, garlic, bread crumbs, and lemon juice and zest, but instead of mixing them with olive oil, the recipe uses warm chicken or meat broth in the manner of a *bagna brusca* (see page 166).

Salsa Verde
Green Sauce

This classic parsley sauce is much beloved by the Italian Jews. It brightens and refreshes bland foods and adds flavor interest when spooned over cooked fish, chicken, vegetables, or boiled beef. It is best if all the ingredients are chopped by hand and whisked together in a bowl. If time is of the essence, however, you may put the ingredients in a food processor and pulse to combine.

Makes about 1 1/2 cups

4 olive oil–packed anchovy fillets, drained and finely minced

1 hard-boiled egg, peeled and chopped

4 tablespoons capers, rinsed and chopped

4 tablespoons pine nuts, toasted and chopped

2 cloves garlic, finely minced

1/2 cup chopped fresh flat-leaf parsley

2 to 3 tablespoons fresh lemon juice

1/2 cup extra-virgin olive oil

Fine dried bread crumbs

Pinch of red pepper flakes (optional)

Salt and freshly ground black pepper to taste

In a bowl, combine the anchovies, hard-boiled egg, capers, pine nuts, garlic, parsley, lemon juice, and olive oil. Whisk to mix well. If the mixture is too thin or tart, add bread crumbs as needed for balance and thickness. Add the red pepper flakes, if desired, and season with salt and pepper.

 Salsa di Noce

WALNUT SAUCE

Bagna Brusca
Egg-and-Lemon Sauce

Brusca means "tart" or "sour," and *bagna* comes from *bagnare*, "to wet" or "to bathe." This sauce is related to the Sephardic *agristada*, made with sour grape juice (*verjus*), and it resembles the familiar Greek and Turkish egg-and-lemon *avgolemono* sauces used for thickening meat and vegetable stews at the last minute.

Edda Servi Machlin calls this same sauce *brodo brusco* (sour broth) because she uses beef broth as the basis for the thickener of egg and lemon or egg and grape juice and serves it as an accompaniment for cooked meat or tosses it with noodles. In the Veneto, where it is served with meat or fish, it is sometimes called *salsetta garba*, and is prepared like *zabaglione*, in the top of a double boiler. In the Marches, it is used as an accompanying sauce for a dish of room-temperature fresh *tagliolini* dressed with juices from roast meats (*tagliolini con la bagna brusca o agresto all'uso marchigiano*). To confuse us further, there are even sauces called *bagna brusca* that are built around anchovies and tomatoes.

Serves 4

1 whole egg plus 2 egg yolks

Juice of 2 lemons

1 cup beef, chicken, or fish broth (see page 114)

In the top pan of a double boiler, combine the whole egg, egg yolks, and lemon juice. Bring the water to a very gentle simmer in the bottom pan and place the top pan over (not touching) the barely simmering water. Beat the egg mixture until foamy. Gradually beat in the broth, and continue to whisk briskly until the mixture thickens, about 10 minutes.

Note: Bottled sour grape juice, often labeled *verjus* in the United States and called *agresto* in Italian, is available in some markets. You may use it in place of the lemon juice in all *bagna brusca* recipes. To approximate the flavor of the grape juice, you can substitute balsamic vinegar or a combination of balsamic vinegar and lemon juice. You can also make your own sour grape juice: Puree 8 pounds sour grapes in a blender. Strain the juice through a fine-mesh sieve into a saucepan. Place over medium heat and cook until reduced by half. Pour into a bottle and refrigerate for up to 1 month.

Salsa Tonnato
Tuna Sauce

Spoon this sauce over Tuna Loaf (page 27), cooked tuna, hard-boiled eggs, or cooked veal. It would be good on green beans or boiled potatoes as well.

Makes about 1 ½ cups

1 can (6 ½ ounces) olive oil–packed tuna, preferably Italian (see recipe introduction, page 24), drained

1 egg

2 tablespoons capers, rinsed

4 olive oil–packed anchovy fillets, drained

Juice of ½ lemon

2 teaspoons grated lemon zest (optional)

1 cup olive oil

Salt and freshly ground black pepper to taste

Put the tuna, egg, capers, anchovies, lemon juice, lemon zest (if using), and olive oil in a blender or food processor. Process until smooth. Season with salt and pepper.

Thurshi

Yellow Squash Condiment for Couscous

Edda Servi Machlin recommends serving couscous (see page 142) with *thurshi,* a puree of yellow squash. I believe the condiment is of Tunisian origin, probably having made its way to the Italian Jewish kitchen from Livorno, where so many North African Jews settled. The caraway is the giveaway, a signature spice in *tabil,* the classic Tunisian seasoning mixture. This condiment also resembles a North African squash puree dish called *hlou,* where dried apricots are often added to the squash. I've increased the spices and added lemon juice to punch up the sweet-and-sour aspects of the dish, thus producing a better contrast to the richness of the couscous ensemble.

Makes about 2 ½ cups

1 thick-skinned yellow squash such as acorn, butternut, or banana, about 2 pounds

2 cups water

6 cloves garlic, finely minced

1 teaspoon caraway seeds, toasted in a dry pan and lightly crushed

½ teaspoon ground cinnamon

¼ to ½ teaspoon cayenne pepper

½ cup fresh lemon juice

Grated zest of 2 lemons

½ cup olive oil

Salt and freshly ground black pepper to taste

Halve the squash, scoop out and discard the seeds and fibers, and then peel away and discard the skin. Cut into 1-inch cubes. Place in a saucepan with the water, cover, and bring to a simmer over low heat. Cook, stirring from time to time and mashing down the squash with a spoon as it softens, until the squash and liquid form a coarse puree, 20 to 30 minutes.

Add the garlic, caraway, cinnamon, cayenne, lemon juice and zest, and the olive oil. Stir well. Remove from the heat and season with salt and pepper. Serve warm. You can make this ahead of time and gently reheat. Adjust the seasonings before serving.

Haroset
PASSOVER FRUIT CONDIMENT

Haroset is the condiment served at the Passover Seder that symbolizes the mortar used for building the pyramids—a sweet symbol of a bitter memory. Some versions are cooked briefly; others are a mixture of finely chopped dried fruits and nuts, bound together in wine or juice with no time on the stove. Here are three versions of this special Passover condiment.

COOKED HAROSET FROM PADUA
This recipe is from Mira Sacerdoti's Zia Ulda.

MAKES ABOUT 12 CUPS

2 cups dried chestnuts, cooked in water to soften, or 2 cups fresh-cooked shelled chestnuts

3 cups chopped apples

1 1/2 cups chopped walnuts

1 1/3 cups chopped pitted dates

1 1/3 cups chopped pitted prunes

1 1/3 cups raisins

1 cup fresh orange juice

1 cup sweet wine

1 teaspoon ground cinnamon, or to taste

Combine all the ingredients in a saucepan. Bring just to a boil over medium-high heat, reduce the heat to low, and simmer, uncovered, for about 15 minutes to blend the flavors. Transfer to a bowl, cover, and refrigerate until serving. Serve at room temperature.

UNCOOKED HAROSET FROM ANCONA

MAKES ABOUT 5 CUPS

Not all harosets must be cooked. Some call just for chopping together the ingredients and serving the mixture as a paste, like this one from Ancona, an adaptation of a recipe from Mira Sacerdoti's *Italian Jewish Cooking.*

3 cups pitted and chopped dates

1 2/3 cups chopped almonds

1/3 cup raisins

2 apples, cored and grated

Juice of 2 large oranges

Combine all of the ingredients in a bowl. Stir well, cover, and refrigerate until serving. Serve at room temperature.

UNCOOKED HAROSET FROM THE VENETO

MAKES ABOUT 5 CUPS

1 cup chestnut puree

1/2 pound dates, pitted

1/2 pound dried figs, coarsely chopped

2 tablespoons poppy seeds

1/2 cup walnuts, coarsely chopped

1/2 cup almonds, chopped

Grated zest and juice of 1 orange

1/2 cup golden raisins

1/2 cup sweet wine

Honey to taste

Combine all the ingredients in a food processor and process to chop to a coarse paste. Transfer to a bowl, cover, and refrigerate until serving. Serve at room temperature.

 Cooked Haroset from Padua

PASSOVER FRUIT CONDIMENT

Dolci
DESSERTS

Torta di Carote e Zenzero *Double-Crusted Carrot and Ginger Tart*

Torta di Carote del Veneto *Carrot Cake from the Veneto*

Torta di Zucca Barucca *Pumpkin Cake from the Veneto*

Crostata di Marmellata di Visciole e Mandorle *Sour Cherry Jam and Almond Tart*

Bianco Mangia *Almond-Filled Pastries I*

Spongata di Brescello *Double-Crusted Fruit-and-Nut Tart*

Buricche di Mandorle *Almond-Filled Pastries II*

Frittelle di Zucca *Squash Fritters from the Veneto*

Bocca di Dama *Passover Almond Sponge Cake*

Bocca di Dama II *Yom Kippur Almond Sponge Cake*

Scodelline *Almond Pudding*

Pan di Spagna alle Nocciole *Passover Hazelnut Sponge Cake*

Budino di Mandorle e Cioccolata *Almond and Chocolate Pudding*

Cassola *Ricotta Soufflé Pancake*

Timballo di Ricotta *Warm Ricotta Soufflé Pudding*

Crema Fritta *Fried Cream*

Crostata di Ricotta e Visciole *Cheese Tart with Sour Cherry Preserves*

Dolce di Tagliatelle *Noodle Pudding*

Frutta Caramellata *Caramelized Fresh Fruit*

Fichi Caramellati *Caramelized Figs*

Mele Cotogne in Giulebbe *Quince in Syrup*
Pizza Dolce *Sweet Pizza*
Bolo *Ring-Shaped Sweet Bread*
Roschette Dolce *Ring-Shaped Cookies*
Orecchie di Amman *Haman's Ears*
Sfratti *Nut-Filled Cookie Sticks*

Dolci

A piece of fruit or a fruit compote was the traditional daily sweet on most Italian Jewish tables. Yet, the largest written recipe section in every Italian Jewish cookbook is for desserts—often double or triple the size of the other chapters. Desserts are divided into pareve (those that can be served at dairy- or meat-based meals) and those suitable for dairy meals. There are special holiday pastries, served only on that day or at that time of year, and finally there's a whole section dedicated to the desserts and pastries of Passover, when no leavening agents are allowed. Baking according to kosher laws is a complex matter.

Most of the pastries have a certain rustic charm. Dried fruits, candied citron and lemon and orange peels, nuts of all kinds, and almond paste are used in abundance. Some of the most interesting desserts are those of Sephardic origin that call for pumpkin and carrots. And some of the best sweets use creamy fresh ricotta.

The desserts come with a variety of wonderful names and the story is often almost better than the sweet. *Orecchie di Amman*, or Haman's Ears, rounds of thin dough deep-fried and sprinkled with sugar, are served at Purim. *Sfratti*, honey-and-nut cookies, represent the sticks that were wielded by the evil landlord when he came to evict tenants who couldn't pay rent. *Buccellato* means "a bracelet," the perfect name for a ring-shaped sweet bread. *Scodelline* are "little plates," rich almond-and-egg sweets that should only be served in tiny portions. *Bocca di dama* is "the mouth of a woman," just the place this delicious almond cake is certain to end up.

 Torta di Carote e Zenzero
Double-Crusted Carrot and Ginger Tart

Torta di Carote e Zenzero

DOUBLE-CRUSTED CARROT AND GINGER TART

Sephardic Jews love desserts and confections made with sweetened squash and even carrots. This double-crusted tart filled with carrot puree perfumed with ginger is inspired by a description in Giuseppe Maffioli's *La cucina padovana*. The top crust is decorated with the tines of a fork in the form of a Star of David. As a little note of irony, a variation on this recipe made with pumpkin squash is in the Roux brothers' book, *French Country Cooking*, where it is listed as a classic Provençal tart served at Christmas!

SERVES 6 TO 8

For the pastry:

2 ¼ cups all-purpose flour

½ cup sugar

Pinch of salt

¾ cup plus 2 tablespoons (1 ¾ sticks) chilled unsalted butter

1 egg

1 teaspoon vanilla extract

1 teaspoon fresh lemon juice

2 tablespoons cold water

For the filling:

2 pounds sweet carrots, peeled and coarsely grated (7 to 8 cups)

1 ½ cups sugar

6 tablespoons finely chopped candied ginger

1 egg beaten with 2 tablespoons water, for egg wash (optional)

To make the pastry, in a bowl, combine the flour, sugar, and salt. Cut in the butter with a pastry blender until the mixture has the consistency of coarse meal. Add the egg, vanilla, lemon juice, and water, and stir and toss with a fork until the mixture just holds together. Remove the dough from the bowl and gather it into a ball. (The dough can also be made in a food processor, pulsing to cut in the butter and processing to bring the dough together.) Divide the dough into 2 portions, one slightly larger than the other, and flatten each half into a disk. Cover with plastic wrap and refrigerate for 1 hour.

To make the filling, combine the carrots and sugar (and a tablespoon or two of water if needed) in a heavy enameled cast-iron pan over medium heat. Cook down, stirring occasionally, until you have a thick conserve, 18 to 20 minutes, adding a tablespoon or two of water if the mixture begins to scorch. Stir in the candied ginger and remove from the heat. Let cool. (This filling can be made a day ahead of time.)

Preheat an oven to 375 degrees F.

On a lightly floured board, roll out the larger pastry disk into a round 11 inches in diameter and ⅛ inch thick. Carefully transfer the round to a 9-inch pie pan, pressing it gently into the pan. Spoon in the carrot filling. Roll out the second disk in the same way and position it over the filling. (Or, if desired, create a lattice.) Trim the edges evenly, dampen with water, turn under to form a slight rim, and press to seal. Press the edges with the tines of a fork to create an attractive rim, then inscribe the Star of David in the center of the tart. Brush the top with the egg wash, if desired.

Bake until golden brown, 20 to 25 minutes. Transfer to a rack to cool completely before serving.

Torta di Carote del Veneto

Carrot Cake from the Veneto

It seems carrot cake is not an American invention. Granted, this version lacks the ubiquitous cream cheese frosting, but there's no reason it cannot be served with a dollop of mascarpone cheese.

This recipe is a combination of three carrot cakes from the Veneto, all of which had something good and something not quite right about them. Two were from Fernanda Gosetti's *I dolci della cucina regionale italiana*, and one was from Giovanni Capnist's *I dolci del Veneto*. I also found one in Milka Passigli's *Le ricette di casa mia*. I tried all of them a few times, but there were problems of dryness and unpleasant texture. I think you will find this one to be free of such shortcomings. The only caveat is that you must use the sweetest, most flavorful organic carrots—not starchy giants. Otherwise, this cake will be a big "so what."

Serves 8

½ cup (1 stick) unsalted butter

1 cup granulated sugar

2 eggs

½ teaspoon almond extract

1 teaspoon vanilla extract

Grated zest of 1 large lemon

2 cups all-purpose flour

2 teaspoons baking soda

1 teaspoon ground cinnamon

½ teaspoon freshly grated nutmeg

Pinch of salt

4 cups finely grated carrots (about 1 pound)

½ cup ground toasted almonds

Confectioners' sugar for topping

Preheat an oven to 350 degrees F. Butter a 9-inch cake pan, line it with parchment paper, and butter the parchment.

In a bowl, beat together the butter and granulated sugar until light and fluffy. Add the eggs and almond and vanilla extracts and lemon zest and beat until thoroughly incorporated. In another bowl, sift together the flour, baking soda, cinnamon, nutmeg, and salt. Fold the flour mixture into the batter, then fold in the carrots and almonds. Pour into the prepared cake pan.

Bake until golden and the top springs back to the touch, 45 to 60 minutes. Remove from the oven and cool on a wire rack. When cool invert the cake, lift off the pan, peel off the parchment, and turn upright on a serving platter. Sift a light dusting of confectioners' sugar over the top.

Note: For Passover, omit the flour and baking soda. Increase the ground toasted almonds to 2 cups, add 4 tablespoons matzoh cake meal, and stir together with the spices and salt. Separate the 2 eggs. Add the yolks as directed for the whole eggs. Add 4 additional egg whites to the whites, and beat them until stiff peaks form, and fold them into the batter before pouring it into the pan.

Torta di Zucca
Barucca
Pumpkin Cake from the Veneto

Dense and creamy at the same time, this cake comes from the town of Treviso in the Veneto. Once again, the use of pumpkin indicates Sephardic origins.

Serves 8

1 sugar pumpkin or butternut squash, about 2 pounds

³⁄₄ cup (1 ¹⁄₂ sticks) unsalted butter

³⁄₄ cup plus 2 tablespoons sugar

¹⁄₂ cup ground almonds

¹⁄₂ cup candied citron, minced

¹⁄₃ cup raisins, plumped in 3 tablespoons plum grappa or wine

Grated zest of 2 large lemons

¹⁄₂ cup all-purpose flour

2 teaspoons baking powder

1 teaspoon ground cinnamon

Pinch of salt

3 eggs, separated

Halve the butternut squash or pumpkin, scoop out and discard the seeds and fibers, and cut into ¹⁄₂-inch dice. You should have about 4 cups.

Melt the butter in a large sauté pan over low heat. Add the squash, cover, and cook until it is falling-apart tender, and lump-free, about 25 minutes. Meanwhile preheat an oven to 325 degrees F. Butter a 9-inch cake pan, line it with parchment paper, and butter the parchment.

Remove the squash from the heat and turn it into a bowl. Whisk in the sugar, almonds, citron, raisins, and lemon zest. In another bowl, sift together the flour, baking powder, cinnamon, and salt. Add the flour mixture to the squash mixture, mixing well, then beat in the egg yolks until thoroughly combined. In yet another bowl, beat the egg whites until stiff peaks form. Fold the whites into the squash mixture just until no white streaks remain. Pour into the prepared pan.

Bake until a toothpick inserted into the center emerges clean, 45 to 60 minutes. Remove from the oven and cool on a rack. When cool invert the cake, lift off the pan, peel off the parchment, and turn upright onto a serving platter.

Crostata di
Marmellata di Visciole e Mandorle
Sour Cherry Jam and Almond Tart

Jam-filled tarts are very popular throughout Italy, but this sour cherry jam *crostata* is a Roman favorite. The recipe is from Miriam Piperno and was part of a series of Italian Jewish menus called *Le feste ebraiche*, published in Rome in 1987. Usually these jam tarts have a lattice top. I find it's faster and easier to roll out the crust, spread jam over most of it, and roll up the sides to make an overlapping *galette*-style crust. You may, however, want to roll up only a slight edge and make lattice strips, as they look so pretty. In that case, you will need to divide the dough in half and roll the halves separately for the top and bottom crusts. *Visciole* are a variety of sour cherries, but any sour cherry jam will work here. If you can't find sour cherry jam, apricot or orange marmalade can be used.

Serves 8

For the pastry:

2 ¼ cups all-purpose flour

½ cup sugar

½ teaspoon salt

¾ cups plus 2 tablespoons (1 ¾ sticks) chilled margarine or unsalted butter

1 egg

Grated zest of 1 lemon

2 tablespoons cold water or sweet wine

For the filling:

2 cups sour cherry preserves, or as needed

1 cup toasted sliced almonds

1 egg yolk beaten with 1 tablespoon heavy cream or water, for egg wash (optional)

Vanilla sugar

To make the pastry, in a bowl, combine the flour, sugar, and salt. Cut in the butter with a pastry blender until the mixture has the consistency of coarse meal. Add the egg, lemon zest, and water or wine, and stir and toss with a fork until the mixture just holds together. Remove the dough from the bowl and gather it into a ball. (The dough can also be made in a food processor, pulsing to cut in the butter and processing to bring the dough together.) Flatten it into a disk. Cover with plastic wrap and refrigerate for 1 hour.

Preheat an oven to 375 degrees F. Line a baking sheet with parchment paper.

On a lightly floured work surface, roll out the pastry disk into a round about 15 inches in diameter and ⅛ inch thick. Transfer to the prepared baking sheet.

To make the filling, spread the cherry jam evenly over the round, leaving a 3-inch border uncovered. Sprinkle the jam with the almonds. Fold the uncovered border up over the filling, pleating it as necessary to make a *galette* edge. If desired, glaze the pastry edges with the egg wash.

Bake until the crust is golden brown, about 30 minutes. Remove from the oven and, keeping the tart on the parchment, carefully slide them together onto a rack to cool. Transfer the tart to a serving platter, and sprinkle with a dusting of vanilla sugar.

Bianco Mangia
Almond-Filled Pastries I

Bianco mangiare is usually a bland almond custard. This Roman recipe, however, gives the name to little almond paste–filled pastries similar to the sweet almond *buricche* from Emilia-Romagna. Versions of this recipe appear in Donatella Limentani Pavoncello's book *Dal 1800 ad oggi: la cucina ebraica della mia famiglia*, in *Le feste ebraiche*, in Fernanda Gosetti's *I dolci della cucina regionale italiana*, and in *La cucina nella tradizione ebraica*.

Makes about 32 pastries

For the dough:

4 cups all-purpose flour

Pinch of salt

$\frac{1}{2}$ cup (1 stick) unsalted butter or margarine, at room temperature, plus $\frac{1}{2}$ cup unsalted butter or margarine, melted

5 tablespoons vegetable oil

1 cup warm water

For the filling:

2 $\frac{1}{4}$ cups chopped blanched almonds

$\frac{3}{4}$ cup granulated sugar

Grated zest of 1 large lemon

$\frac{1}{2}$ teaspoon ground cinnamon, or to taste

2 tablespoons chopped candied orange peel

2 tablespoons chopped candied citron

1 egg

Vegetable oil for deep-frying

Confectioners' sugar for topping

To make the dough, in a bowl, combine the flour, salt, the room-temperature butter or margarine, the vegetable oil, and the warm water. Stir together to form a soft and elastic dough. On a lightly floured board, roll out the dough into a large rectangle about $\frac{1}{4}$ inch thick. Brush the dough with some of the melted butter or margarine and fold into thirds. Roll out again and brush with more butter or margarine. Fold again. Repeat this process at least 4 times, using up all the melted butter or margarine, then wrap the folded dough in plastic wrap and refrigerate for 1 hour.

To make the filling, grind the almonds in a food processor with the granulated sugar. Add the lemon zest and cinnamon, mix briefly, then add the candied citrus and pulse to combine. Add the egg and pulse briefly. Remove to a bowl and set aside.

Divide the dough in half. On a lightly floured board, roll out half of the dough into a rectangle $\frac{1}{8}$ inch thick. Cut into 4-inch squares. Put about 1 tablespoon of the filling on each square at an angle, bring up the sides to meet in the middle, and press closed. Roll out the remaining dough half and cut and fill in the same way. (These can be made up to 1 day in advance and refrigerated until frying.)

Pour oil to a depth of 3 inches in a wide saucepan. Heat to 350 degrees F. When the oil is hot, add the pastries, a few at a time, and fry until golden, about 4 minutes. Using a slotted spoon, transfer to paper towels to drain briefly. Keep warm until all the pastries are cooked. (Alternatively, bake in an oven preheated to 350 degrees F until golden, about 20 minutes.)

Arrange on a platter and sift a dusting of confectioners' sugar over the top. Serve warm.

Spongata di Brescello

DOUBLE-CRUSTED FRUIT-AND-NUT TART

Ironically now a Christmas classic in many cities of Emilia-Romagna, especially Parma and Brescia, *spongata* is said to have been brought to Italy by the Spanish Jews at the end of the fifteenth century. The Jewish Muggia family of Brescia made this rich tart their specialty from 1867 until 1990. Sometimes the dessert is called *spongata di Busseto*, as Busseto is the birthplace of Giuseppe Verdi, whose picture appears on packages of the commercially made pastries. Some versions use *mostarda di frutta* (candied fruit in mustard syrup) in the filling instead of marmalade. Others use fresh fruit, cooked down into a jam. Still others use prepared conserves. Lynn Rossetto Kasper, in her celebrated cookbook *The Splendid Table*, has a version of the tart filled with dried fruits and nuts, but no jam.

SERVES 8 TO 10

For the pastry:

2 ¹/₂ cups all-purpose flour

¹/₂ cup plus 2 tablespoons superfine sugar

Pinch of salt

³/₄ cup (1 ¹/₂ sticks) chilled unsalted butter

1 whole egg plus 2 egg yolks

Grated zest of 1 lemon

¹/₄ cup cold water or sweet wine

For the filling:

²/₃ cup pine nuts, toasted and coarsely chopped

1 cup almonds, toasted and coarsely chopped

¹/₄ cup candied citron, chopped

¹/₄ cup candied orange peel, chopped

1 ¹/₄ cups apricot jam

³/₄ cup toasted bread crumbs

¹/₂ cup raisins, plumped in hot water and drained

1 cup honey

¹/₂ cup water

1 teaspoon ground cinnamon, or to taste

Confectioners' sugar for topping

To make the pastry, combine the flour, sugar, and salt. Cut in the butter with a pastry blender until the mixture has the consistency of coarse meal. Add the egg and egg yolks, lemon zest, and water or wine, and stir and toss with a fork until the mixture just holds together. Remove the dough from the bowl and gather it into a ball. (The dough can also be made in a food processor, pulsing it to cut in the butter and processing to bring the dough together.) Divide the dough in half and flatten each half into a disk. Cover with plastic wrap and refrigerate for 1 to 2 hours.

To make the filling, in a bowl combine the pine nuts, almonds, citron, orange peel, apricot jam, bread crumbs, and raisins. Mix well. In a small saucepan, combine the honey and water over medium heat. Gradually bring to a boil, stirring from time to time. When the mixture boils, pour the honey over the fruit-and-nut mixture and stir well. Season with the cinnamon. (This mixture can be made several days in advance, but warm it a bit to make it spreadable before assembling the tart.)

Preheat an oven to 375 degrees F. Line a baking sheet with parchment paper.

On a lightly floured board, roll out 1 disk into a round 10 inches in diameter and ¹/₄ inch thick. Transfer to the prepared baking sheet. Spread the fruit-and-nut mixture over the round, leaving a 1-inch border uncovered. Roll out the second disk of dough in the same way. Dampen the uncovered border of the filled round with water, and carefully cover the filling with the second round. Trim away any excess pastry and press the edges together well to seal.

Bake until golden, about 20 minutes. Remove from the oven and, keeping the tart on the parchment, slide them together onto a pastry rack to cool. Transfer the tart to a serving platter, and sift a dusting of confectioners' sugar over the top.

Buricche di
Mandorle
ALMOND-FILLED PASTRIES II

This dough is a simpler shortcrust than the one on page 177, and may be easier to shape. But the first is the best.

MAKES ABOUT 32 PASTRIES

For the dough:

3 cups all-purpose flour

¾ cup granulated sugar

½ cup (1 stick) chilled unsalted butter

3 egg yolks, or 1 whole egg plus 1 egg yolk

Grated zest of 1 lemon

2 tablespoons cold water, if needed

For the filling:

2 ¼ cups chopped blanched almonds

¾ cup granulated sugar

Grated zest of 1 large lemon

½ teaspoon vanilla extract

½ teaspoon ground cinnamon

4 tablespoons chopped candied citron and/or candied lemon or orange peel

1 egg

1 egg white, lightly beaten

Confectioners' sugar for topping

To make the dough, in a bowl, combine the flour and granulated sugar. Cut in the butter with a pastry blender until the mixture has the consistency of coarse meal. Add the egg yolks, lemon zest, and the water, if needed, tossing and stirring with a fork until the ingredients come together into a smooth dough. Press the dough into a disk, wrap in plastic wrap, and chill for 1 hour.

To make the filling, combine the almonds and granulated sugar in a food processor and process to grind. Add the lemon zest, vanilla, and cinnamon and mix briefly, then add the candied citrus and pulse to combine. Add the egg and pulse again. Set aside.

Preheat an oven to 350 degrees F. Butter 1 or 2 baking sheets.

On a lightly floured board, roll out the chilled dough as thin as possible. Cut into 2-by-4-inch rectangles or into 3-inch rounds. Place about 1 tablespoon of the almond mixture into the center of each rectangle or round and fold the rectangle into a square, similar to an envelope fold, or the round into a half-moon. Place on the prepared baking sheet(s). Brush the pastries with the egg white.

Bake until golden, about 20 minutes. Remove from the oven and transfer to a wire rack. Sift a dusting of confectioners' sugar over the top. Serve warm.

Note: The dough can be refrigerated for up to 2 days before assembling the pastries.

 Frittelle di Zucca

Squash Fritters from the Veneto

Frittelle di Zucca
Squash Fritters from the Veneto

At Hanukkah, Italian Jews are not "latke people," but they do serve all manner of fried foods on this holiday, to commemorate the lamp oil that burned for eight nights. These Venetian pumpkin fritters are the perfect Hanukkah dessert.

A few words about measurements: It's hard to find a squash that will weigh exactly 1 ¼ pounds. Just be sure the cubed squash is covered with milk, and then add enough flour to make a mixture that is as thick as sour cream. You will need to adjust the sugar to taste, as squashes vary in sweetness. Butternut is usually sweeter than kabocha or pumpkin.

This recipe is an adaptation of two recipes, one from Capnist's *I dolci del Veneto* and the other from Milka Passigli's *Le ricette di casa mia.*

Serves 6

1 butternut squash or pumpkin, about 1 ¼ pounds

2 cups milk, or as needed

1 ½ cups all-purpose flour, or as needed

2 teaspoons baking soda dissolved in 2 teaspoons water

2 eggs

Pinch of salt

⅔ cup granulated sugar, or to taste

Grated zest of 1 or 2 oranges

½ cup candied citron, cut into small dice

⅓ cup golden raisins

½ cup pine nuts, toasted

Peanut oil for deep-frying

Confectioners' sugar for topping

Halve the squash or pumpkin, scoop out and discard the seeds and fibers, peel, and cut into ½-inch dice. You should have 3 to 3 ½ cups. Place in a saucepan, add milk to cover, and place over medium heat. Bring to a simmer and cook until the squash breaks down into a smooth puree, about 30 minutes. Don't worry if the mixture looks curdled; it will smooth out.

Stir in the 1 ½ cups flour and continue to stir until the mixture is thick, about 5 minutes, adding more flour as needed to bind. Beat in the dissolved baking soda, and then the eggs, one at a time, beating well after each addition. Add the salt, granulated sugar, orange zest, citron, raisins, and pine nuts. Remove from the heat. Let stand for about 15 minutes until most of the moisture has been absorbed.

Pour oil to a depth of 3 inches in a deep frying pan or wok and heat to 375 degrees F. In batches, drop the batter by small (1 inch diameter) teaspoonfuls into the hot oil. (These should not be too large or the center will not cook.) Fry until golden, 3 to 5 minutes. Using a slotted spoon, transfer to paper towels to drain briefly. Keep warm until all the fritters are cooked.

Arrange the fritters on a platter and sift a heavy dusting of confectioners' sugar over the top. Eat while hot or very warm.

Bocca di Dama
PASSOVER ALMOND SPONGE CAKE

Bocca di dama means "mouth of a woman." It is also the name for a classic Italian almond cake. This adaptation of Emma Belforte's recipe from *La cucina livornese* is obviously for Passover, as it is flourless and uses matzoh meal and almonds.

SERVES 8 TO 10

1 ½ cups finely chopped blanched almonds

1 ½ cups granulated sugar

12 eggs, separated

6 to 8 tablespoons matzoh meal

Grated zest of 2 oranges

½ teaspoon almond extract

Preheat an oven to 350 degrees F. Butter a 10-inch springform pan. In a food processor, combine the almonds and ⅓ cup of the granulated sugar and process until ground. Set aside.

In a bowl, beat together the egg yolks and the remaining granulated sugar until pale and thick. Gradually add the matzoh meal, the ground almond mixture, the orange zest, and the almond extract. In another, larger bowl, beat the egg whites until stiff peaks form. Gently stir one-third into the almond batter until evenly distributed, then fold in the remaining batter just until no white streaks remain. Spoon into the prepared pan.

Bake until a toothpick inserted into the center of the cake emerges clean, 45 to 50 minutes. Remove from the oven and let cool completely on a rack. Release the pan sides and slide the cake onto a serving platter.

Bocca di Dama II
YOM KIPPUR ALMOND SPONGE CAKE

This version of *bocca di dama* served to break the fast at Yom Kippur. It is similar to the sponge cake baked for Passover, but flour and confectioners' sugar are used.

SERVES 8 TO 10

1 ⅔ cups finely chopped blanched almonds

1 cup plus 2 tablespoons granulated sugar

8 whole eggs plus 3 additional egg yolks

1 ¼ cups plus 2 tablespoons all-purpose flour

Grated zest of 2 lemons

Confectioners' sugar for topping (optional)

Preheat an oven to 350 degrees F. Butter a 10-inch springform pan.

In a food processor, combine the almonds and ⅓ cup of the granulated sugar and process until ground. Set aside.

In a bowl, beat together the whole eggs, egg yolks, and remaining sugar until very thick and pale. Gradually add the flour, the ground almond mixture, and the lemon zest. Spoon into the prepared pan.

Bake until a toothpick inserted into the center of the cake emerges clean, 45 to 50 minutes. Remove from the oven and let cool completely on a rack. Release the pan sides and slide the cake onto a serving platter. If you like, sift a dusting of confectioners' sugar over the top.

Scodelline
Almond Pudding

The Portuguese Jews brought this pudding to Livorno. It is reminiscent of Portuguese sweet egg custards such as *ovos moles* (soft eggs), but with almonds added at the end as if making *toucinho do ceu* (bacon from heaven). In Portugal, the pudding is used as a filling for pastries or spooned over cakes. It never sets up, but is meant to have a soft texture. It is also very, very rich and should be put into tiny ramekins or pots for pot de crème, if you have them. (The name tells you what to do. *Scodelline* means "small plates." This dessert is also called *le tazzine*, or "little cups.") You could also spoon this pudding from one large bowl onto individual plates and serve it with fresh fruit, or take a hint from the Portuguese and serve it with a slice of sponge cake (see page 182). In the Veneto, this same sweet dish is known as *rosada con le mandorle* and is a Purim specialty.

Serves 12

10 egg yolks

1 ½ cups sugar

½ cup water

1 ½ cups ground or grated toasted blanched almonds

1 tablespoon orange flower water

2 teaspoons grated lemon zest (optional)

1 teaspoon ground cinnamon

In a bowl, using an electric mixer, lightly beat the egg yolks until blended. Set aside. Combine the sugar and water in a heavy-bottomed saucepan and place over low heat. Stir until the sugar dissolves. Raise the heat to medium and cook until the mixture reaches the soft-ball stage (234 to 240 degrees F on a candy thermometer); do not let it color. (If you lack a thermometer, test the mixture by dropping a tiny bit into ice water; it should form a pliable ball when rubbed between your fingers.) Gradually pour the hot syrup into the egg yolks and beat until the mixture is thick and holds a 3-second slowly dissolving ribbon when the beaters are lifted, about 5 minutes. Return the mixture to the saucepan and warm over low heat, stirring often, until thickened, about 5 minutes. Do not allow it to boil. When thickened, stir in the almonds, orange flower water, and the zest, if using.

Pour into twelve 3-ounce ramekins and refrigerate until cool, about 1 hour. Cover with plastic wrap if not serving immediately. The pudding will keep for up to 2 days in the refrigerator. Sprinkle with the cinnamon at serving time.

Pan di Spagna alle Nocciole

PASSOVER HAZELNUT SPONGE CAKE

Here is another flourless nut cake for Passover. This one is fragrant with sweet toasted hazelnuts. San Francisco Bay Area resident Nelda Cassuto's Passover nut cake recipe was given to me by Esther Prigioni, the wife of the Italian consul in San Francisco. Cassuto's version uses 2 cups walnuts, ½ cup almonds, 8 eggs, 1 ½ cups sugar, 2 tablespoons rum or maraschino liqueur, and 2 tablespoons orange or cherry marmalade.

SERVES 8 TO 10

10 eggs, separated

1 cup sugar

Grated zest and juice of 1 orange

Grated zest and juice of 1 lemon

1 ½ cups finely ground toasted and peeled hazelnuts

6 tablespoons matzoh cake meal, sifted

2 tablespoons potato starch

Pinch of salt

1 teaspoon vanilla extract

In a bowl, combine the egg yolks, ½ cup of the sugar, and both the zests and juices. Beat with an electric mixer until the mixture is thick and pale and holds a 3-second slowly dissolving ribbon when the beaters are lifted.

In a second bowl using clean, dry beaters, beat the egg whites until foamy. Gradually beat in the remaining ½ cup sugar, and continue to beat until stiff peaks form. Gently fold the whites into the egg mixture, then fold in the hazelnuts, the matzoh meal, potato starch, salt, and vanilla. Pour the batter into an ungreased 10-inch tube pan and smooth the top.

Place the pan in a cold oven. Turn on the oven to 325 degrees F and bake until a toothpick inserted into the center of the cake emerges clean, about 45 minutes. Invert the cake still in the pan onto a wire rack. Let cool completely, then lift off the pan and transfer the cake to a serving platter.

Budino di Mandorle e Cioccolata

ALMOND AND CHOCOLATE PUDDING

This traditional Livornese dessert is, despite the name, more like a chocolate pudding cake with a moist center—ironically a trendy contemporary dessert. According to Claudia Roden, the use of chocolate in Livornese desserts came about because of trade between Livornese Jews and some Marrano Jews in Amsterdam who had started a chocolate factory. Emma Belforte's original recipe, as noted in Aldo Santini's *La cucina livornese*, did not advise baking this in a bain-marie, but the cake seemed very dry and was more like an overcooked brownie. With the bain-marie the texture is creamier and more voluptuous. I've also increased the sugar just a bit.

SERVES 8

½ cup plus 1 tablespoon unsalted butter

4 ½ ounces bittersweet chocolate

1 ¼ cups chopped blanched almonds

½ cup plus 1 tablespoon sugar

4 eggs, separated

Whipped cream for serving (optional)

Preheat an oven to 300 degrees F. Butter a 9-inch cake pan or eight ¾-cup ramekins.

Combine the butter and chocolate in the top

pan of a double boiler placed over (but not touching) hot water in the lower pan. Heat, stirring occasionally, just until melted and smooth. Meanwhile, grind the almonds with the sugar in the container of a food processor. Transfer the almonds to a bowl and whisk in the chocolate mixture and the egg yolks.

In another bowl, beat the egg whites until medium-firm peaks form. Stir one-third of the egg whites into the chocolate mixture to lighten it, then fold in the remaining whites just until no white streaks remain. Spoon into the prepared pan or ramekins. Place in a baking pan, and add hot water to come halfway up the sides of the cake pan or ramekins. Cover the baking pan with aluminum foil.

Bake until the center seems just set but not wet, 35 to 45 minutes for the larger pudding or 25 minutes or so for the small puddings. Remove from the oven and let cool completely on a rack. Invert onto a serving platter or individual plates to unmold. Serve with whipped cream, if you like.

Cassola
Ricotta Soufflé Pancake

Although this Roman ricotta pudding, also called *channa*, can be baked in the oven (325 degrees F for 20 to 25 minutes), it is usually cooked on top of the stove—sort of a cheese pancake. In her book *Italian Jewish Cooking*, Mira Sacerdoti adds 2 cups white rice cooked in 4 cups milk to the basic cheese mixture, resulting in a cross between a cheese pancake and rice pudding.

Serves 8

15 ounces (scant 2 cups) ricotta cheese

4 eggs, separated

½ cup sugar, or a bit more

2 tablespoons all-purpose flour or cornstarch

2 tablespoons liquor or wine of choice such as dark rum, cognac, or sweet Marsala (optional)

Grated zest of 1 large lemon (optional)

Pinch of salt

2 tablespoons pure olive oil

Spoon the ricotta into a sieve placed over a bowl and let drain in the refrigerator for 1 to 2 hours.

In a bowl, using an electric mixer, beat together the egg yolks and sugar until very thick and pale. Beat in the drained ricotta and the flour or cornstarch. In another bowl, beat the egg whites until soft peaks form. Fold into the ricotta mixture. Stir in the liquor or lemon zest, if using, and the salt.

Preheat a broiler. Warm the olive oil in a flameproof 9-inch nonstick frying pan over medium heat. Add the ricotta mixture and cook until the bottom has set, 15 to 20 minutes. Slip under the broiler until glazed and golden, about 5 minutes. Serve warm.

Note: Michele Scicolone has a version of this recipe in her book *La dolce vita*. She puts the ricotta mixture into an oiled 8-inch frying pan and starts the cooking over low heat on the stove top. After 20 minutes, she slips the pan into an oven preheated to 350 degrees F and bakes the pancake until it is golden, about 12 minutes longer. After it has cooled a bit, she unmolds it and serves it with fresh fruit.

 Timballo di Ricotta

WARM RICOTTA SOUFFLÉ PUDDING

Timballo di
Ricotta

Warm Ricotta Soufflé Pudding

Be sure to use fresh, moist ricotta for this classic Roman Jewish cheese dessert. I've doubled the sugar, as the original recipe seemed very flat. I also added a tablespoon of flour for a smoother texture; in another version of this recipe, called *cassola* or *channa* (see page 185), flour is added, too. I halved the cognac as the finished pudding was too alcoholic-tasting. You might want to try dark rum or Marsala instead. Serve the pudding with berries or other fresh fruit.

Serves 8 to 12

1 pound (2 cups) fresh ricotta cheese

4 eggs, separated

1 cup sugar

1 tablespoon all-purpose flour

2 tablespoons cognac

Grated zest of 2 lemons

¹/₂ teaspoon ground cinnamon (optional)

Spoon the ricotta into a sieve placed over a bowl and let drain in the refrigerator for 1 to 2 hours.

Preheat an oven to 300 degrees F. Butter twelve ³/₄-cup ramekins or one 2-quart soufflé dish.

In a bowl, using an electric mixer, beat together the egg yolks and sugar until very thick and pale. Add the drained ricotta, flour, cognac, lemon zest, and the cinnamon, if using.

Mix gently until well combined. In another bowl, beat the egg whites until stiff peaks form. Stir about one-fourth of the egg whites into the cheese mixture to lighten it, then fold in the remaining whites just until no white streaks remain. Pour into the prepared ramekins or soufflé dish. Place in a baking pan and pour hot water into the pan to reach halfway up the sides of the ramekins or dish. Cover the pan with aluminum foil.

Bake until set but still a little jiggly, 25 to 30 minutes for the ramekins and about 40 minutes for the large mold. Remove from the oven and place on a rack. Serve warm.

Crema Fritta
FRIED CREAM

I've always thought of this as an old-time San Francisco dessert, but its origins are in the Veneto and Liguria, home of many of the Italians who settled in the city. I've played with many versions of the recipe, from a variety of sources, and this one won the family taste test.

SERVES 8

4 cups milk

1 vanilla bean

Zest of 1 lemon

1 1/4 cups plus 2 tablespoons all-purpose flour

3/4 cup granulated sugar

8 egg yolks

Pinch of salt

4 egg whites

Fine dried bread crumbs

Clarified butter or vegetable oil, as needed

Confectioners' sugar or cinnamon sugar for topping

Place a marble board or baking pan (about 8 by 10 inches) in the freezer to chill well.

In a saucepan, combine the milk, vanilla bean, and lemon zest and bring to a boil over medium heat. Reduce the heat to low and simmer for 10 minutes. Remove from the heat and let steep for 1 hour.

Strain the milk through a sieve and return it to the saucepan. Whisk in the flour, granulated sugar, egg yolks, and salt and bring slowly to a boil over low heat, stirring often. Cook, continuing to stir, until thickened, about 10 min-

utes. Remove from the heat and pour the mixture onto the chilled marble or into the chilled baking pan. Spread the mixture to an even thickness of 1 inch. Cover and chill in the refrigerator until fully set, about 2 hours.

To serve, cut the cream into diamonds. In a shallow bowl, beat the egg whites until foamy. Spread bread crumbs on a plate. Warm clarified butter or vegetable oil to a depth of 1/2 inch in a sauté pan over medium heat. In batches, dip the diamonds in the egg whites, coating evenly, and then in the bread crumbs, again coating evenly. Add to the pan and fry, turning once, until golden on both sides, 6 to 8 minutes total. Using a slotted spoon, transfer to paper towels to drain briefly.

Keep warm until all the diamonds are fried, then arrange on a platter. Sprinkle with confectioners' sugar or cinnamon sugar and serve hot.

Crostata di
Ricotta e Visciole
CHEESE TART WITH SOUR CHERRY PRESERVES

A recipe in Donatella Pavoncello's *Dal 1880 ad oggi: La cucina ebraica della mia famiglia* inspired this version of a traditional Italian cheese tart with a surprise layer of cherry jam. Lemon zest is in the crust, but you might want a little in the filling as well. I've added the almond extract, which accents the cherries nicely. It's wise to brush the crust with egg wash to hasten browning and thus prevent the overcooking of the filling.

SERVES 8

For the pastry:

2 1/2 cups all-purpose flour

²/₃ cup sugar

Pinch of salt

1 cup (2 sticks) chilled unsalted butter

2 eggs

Grated zest of 1 lemon

¹/₄ cup cold water, or as needed

For the filling:

*1 pound (2 cups) ricotta cheese, drained in
a sieve in the refrigerator for 1 to 2 hours*

¹/₂ cup sugar

4 eggs

1 tablespoon all-purpose flour

¹/₂ teaspoon almond extract (optional)

Grated zest of 1 lemon (optional)

1 cup sour cherry jam

*1 egg beaten with 2 tablespoons water,
for egg wash (optional)*

To make the pastry, in a bowl, combine the flour, sugar, and salt. Cut in the butter with a pastry blender until the mixture has the consistency of coarse meal. Add the eggs, lemon zest, and water, and stir and toss with a fork until the mixture just holds together. Remove the dough from the bowl and gather it into a ball. (The dough can also be made in a food processor, pulsing it to cut in the butter and processing to bring the dough together.) Divide the dough into 2 portions, one slightly larger than the other. Flatten each into a disk. Cover with plastic wrap and refrigerate for 1 to 2 hours.

To make the filling, in a bowl, whisk together the ricotta, sugar, eggs, flour, and the almond extract or lemon zest, if using. Have the cherry jam ready.

Preheat an oven to 350 degrees F.

On a very lightly floured board, roll out the larger disk into a round 12 to 13 inches in diameter. Carefully transfer it to a 9-inch cake pan with a removable bottom or to a 10-inch tart pan with a removable bottom. Press it gently into the pan. Trim off excess dough and turn the edges under to a neat rim.

Spread a thin layer of jam on the crust bottom, then pour in the ricotta mixture. Roll out the second disk in the same way, cut into 1 inch-wide strips, and cover the ricotta filling with the strips, arranging them in a lattice pattern. Press the edges of the strips to the bottom crust, sealing with a bit of water. Brush the lattice strips with the egg wash, if desired.

Bake until the crust is golden, about 50 minutes. Remove from the oven and let cool on a rack. Serve warm or at room temperature.

Note: One time I made this *crostata* with sour cherries packed in liqueur, the classic brandied Amarene. I drained 1 cup of the cherries, placed them on the bottom of the tart, and saved the syrup for another day. When that day came, I used the syrup to enrich a rather lackluster cherry jam for the same tart. *Molto buono.*

Dolce di Tagliatelle
NOODLE PUDDING

Although Jews think of noodle pudding as *kugel*, an Ashkenazic sweet, this is an inevitable dessert for Italian Jews, who have leftover noodles to spare. The name *tagliatelle* is used in the region of Emilia-Romagna, and it is a synonym for what is called *fettuccine* elsewhere. This recipe was inspired by *La cucina nella tradizione ebraica* and is usually served at Sukkot. The apples add moisture and the pudding puffs up nicely, but, to my palate, it is a bit dry in the absence of milk or cream. So, like any good cakey noodle or rice pudding, it's wonderful dressed with a little cream or a thin custard sauce, if served at a dairy meal.

SERVES 4

7 to 8 ounces fresh **tagliatelle** *or fettuccine*

3 eggs, separated

⅓ cup sugar

½ cup almonds

½ cup raisins, plumped in hot water and drained

2 apples, peeled, cored, and grated

½ teaspoon ground cinnamon

Heavy cream for serving

Preheat an oven to 350 degrees F. Oil a 9-inch springform pan.

Bring a large pot of water to a boil, add the pasta, stir well, and cook until al dente.

Meanwhile, in a bowl, beat the egg whites until stiff peaks form.

Drain the noodles and place in a bowl. Add the egg yolks, sugar, almonds, raisins, apples, and cinnamon. Mix well. Fold the whites into the noodle mixture, then pour into the prepared pan.

Bake until golden and just set, about 40 minutes. Remove from the oven and place on a rack to cool a bit. Release the pan sides and slide the pudding onto a serving platter. Serve warm. Pass a pitcher of cream at the table.

Frutta Caramellata
CARAMELIZED FRESH FRUIT

One of my favorite desserts, this simple sweet brings back childhood memories of candied apples. The crisp, crunchy sugar-coated fruits are refreshing and festive after a filling meal, and are especially good as an accompaniment to Passover Hazelnut Sponge Cake (page 184). These are also known as *golosezzi veneziani*, but I first read about them in Donatella Pavoncello's book of Roman Jewish recipes, so I have given them the Roman name. She uses apples, pears, and oranges, but strawberries make a nice addition to the mix. One version in *La cucina nella tradizione ebraica* calls for stuffing almond paste into dates and prunes; another sandwiches the paste between walnut halves.

SERVES 8 TO 10

2 tablespoons unsalted butter or margarine, melted

4 cups sugar

4 tart apples, cored and cut into eighths

24 strawberries, hulled

Brush the butter or margarine on a baking sheet.

Put the sugar in a wide, heavy-bottomed saucepan. Place over medium heat and heat until the sugar melts and caramelizes to a golden amber. Stir away any lumps with a wooden spoon, being careful that the sugar doesn't spatter and burn you. Have a bowl of ice water nearby in case you burn your hands.

Be sure the fruits are dry. Thread them onto wooden skewers, if you like, or use tongs or chopsticks and dip individual pieces. *Carefully* dip the fruit skewers, one at a time, into the hot caramel. Then place on the greased baking sheet or on a wire rack until set, 10 to 15 minutes. Caramelize the fruits as close to serving time as possible so that they remain crisp.

Note: To make an easier syrup for dipping, combine 1 cup sugar, $\frac{1}{2}$ cup light corn syrup, and $\frac{1}{4}$ cup water in a heavy-bottomed saucepan and place over medium heat. Cook, stirring, until the sugar dissolves, then continue to cook until golden, 8 to 10 minutes.

a lemon zest strip into each slit. Sprinkle the sugar over the figs. Add water, or part water and part rum, to a depth of $\frac{1}{4}$ inch in the pan. Put a vanilla bean in the center of the pan.

Place over high heat and bring to a boil. Reduce the heat to medium and simmer, uncovered, until the sugar caramelizes, 15 to 20 minutes. Serve warm.

Note: Another version of this dish calls for making a medium-thick sugar syrup, allowing it to cool a bit, and then pouring it over the uncooked figs. A few drops of rum are added. The dish is then tightly sealed for a few hours so the figs absorb the syrup.

Fichi Caramellati
Caramelized Figs

Here's a simple baked fig dessert based on a recipe from Donatella Pavoncello's *Dal 1880 ad oggi: la cucina ebraica della mia famiglia.* Pears can be prepared the same way: peel, halve, and core, then poach in syrup or wine with strips of lemon zest or vanilla bean. They will take longer to cook than the figs.

Serves 8

2 pounds ripe figs

Lemon zest strips, 1 inch long and $\frac{1}{4}$ inch wide, as needed

2 cups sugar

Rum, as needed (optional)

Vanilla bean

Arrange whole figs in a deep, wide saucepan. Cut a small slit at the top of each fig and insert

Mele Cotogne
in Giulebbe
Quince in Syrup

Poached quinces in a clove-and-cinnamon-scented syrup are served at Rosh Hashanah and to break the fast at Yom Kippur. In this version, the quinces are left unpeeled for the preliminary cooking in water, and then peeled and cooked in syrup. In *La cucina livornese*, Pia Bedarida recommends peeling the quinces, letting them rest to take on a reddish brown color as they oxidize, and then cooking them in syrup. Other cooks peel the quinces and cook them in syrup immediately, but suggest saving the peels and seeds and cooking them along with the sliced quinces. Still another recipe uses wine instead of water.

Serves 6

2 pounds quinces

For the syrup:

2 cups sugar

1 cup water, or as needed

2 whole cloves

2 cinnamon sticks

In a large saucepan, combine the quinces with water to cover. Bring to a boil over high heat and cook, uncovered, until barely tender, 10 to 15 minutes. Drain the quinces and, when cool enough to handle, peel, halve, core, and cut into slices.

To make the syrup, in a saucepan large enough to accommodate the sliced quinces, combine the sugar, 1 cup water, cloves, and cinnamon sticks. Place over medium heat and bring to a simmer, stirring to dissolve the sugar. Add the quinces and additional water if needed to cover. Simmer for 5 minutes. Then, over the course of 12 hours, bring the quince slices to a boil in the syrup 3 times, boiling them for 5 minutes each time. This helps to bring up the rich red color of the fruit and allows them to absorb the syrup over time.

Transfer to a serving dish and refrigerate. Serve chilled.

 Bocca di Dama e Mele Cotogne in Giulebbe
ALMOND SPONGE CAKE AND QUINCE IN SYRUP

Pizza Dolce
Sweet Pizza

In Giuliana Ascoli Vitali-Norsa's *La cucina nella tradizione ebraica*, this recipe is described as an ancient one, "still in use today for all the familiar holidays." The fruit-studded "pizza" is a specialty of the Jewish bakery in Rome on Via Portico d'Ottavia, the main street of the city's ghetto. It's rather dense and usually a little overbaked and quite dark around the edges. Nonetheless, people love it. Actually it's a giant cookie, ideal with a cup of tea. I've made the candied cherries optional because not too many people are fond of them (especially me). You might want to add a little vanilla extract or grated lemon zest to the dough. Claudia Roden has a version of this pastry in her excellent and scholarly cookbook *The Book of Jewish Food*, but she forms the dough into individual little cakes.

Makes 24 large cookies

1 cup (2 sticks) unsalted butter, margarine, or olive oil

4 cups all-purpose flour

1 cup granulated sugar

3/4 cup almonds

2/3 cup raisins, plumped in 1 cup Marsala or other sweet wine, drained, and, in the spirit of thrift, the wine reserved for the dough

1/2 cup chopped candied citron, or part citron and part candied lemon or orange peel

3 tablespoons candied cherries (optional)

Pinch of salt

Confectioners' sugar (optional)

Preheat an oven to 350 degrees F.

In the bowl of a stand mixer fitted with the paddle attachment (or in a food processor), combine the butter, margarine, or olive oil with the flour and granulated sugar and beat until mixed. Beat in the almonds, raisins, citron or citron and citrus peel, the cherries, if using, and the salt. Add the reserved wine as needed to form a soft dough. Turn out onto a baking sheet and press into a 9-by-13-inch rectangle.

Bake until golden, about 25 minutes. Remove from the oven and cut into strips or lozenges while still warm. Transfer to a wire rack and sift a dusting of confectioners' sugar over the tops, if you like. Store in an airtight cookie tin for up to 1 week. I find that these cookies taste better on the second, third, or fourth day, when the flavors of the candied fruits and nuts have a chance to permeate the dense dough.

Bolo

Ring-Shaped Sweet Bread

Bolo is Spanish for "ball" or "bun." This dessert, also called *bollo,* has been thoroughly assimilated into the Italian baking repertoire. Every region seems to have a version of the fabulous sweet bread. It is called *bussola* in the Veneto, *buccellato* in most of Tuscany, and *ciambella* in the town of Lucca. *Buccellato* means "bracelet," and the name comes from the fact that the cake is traditionally formed into a ring. I have found recipes for this in Tunisian cookbooks as well, due to the many Livornese Jews who settled there.

The cake's Jewish origins are revealed in finding some versions that call for milk instead of water and butter instead of oil, depending upon whether the sweet is to be served at a dairy meal or not. Some recipes add a bit of orange flower water or Marsala to scent the dough. Bolo is usually served at Sukkot. I like it toasted for breakfast!

Serves 12 generously

For the sponge:

1 cup all-purpose flour

1 ½ envelopes (4 teaspoons) active dry yeast

½ cup warm water (about 105 degrees F)

For the dough:

3 cups all-purpose flour

1 cup sugar

⅔ cup warm water (about 105 degrees F)

½ teaspoon salt

Grated zest of 1 lemon

Grated zest of 1 orange

4 eggs

4 tablespoons olive oil

⅔ cup raisins

2 tablespoons aniseeds

To make the sponge, place the flour in a small bowl. In another small bowl, stir the yeast into the warm water, then add the mixture to the flour. Cover with plastic wrap and let rest in a warm place until frothy and doubled in size, about 30 minutes.

To make the dough, in the bowl of a stand mixer fitted with the paddle attachment, combine the flour, sugar, warm water, salt, citrus zests, eggs, and olive oil. Beat to mix well. Add the sponge and beat on low speed until smooth and elastic, about 5 minutes. Add the raisins and aniseeds and mix gently. Turn into an oiled bowl, cover with plastic wrap, and let rise in a warm place until doubled in size, about 3 hours.

Line 2 baking sheets with parchment paper. Turn the dough out onto a lightly floured board. Punch down and fold the dough over onto itself a few times. Divide the dough in half. Using your palms, roll half the dough into a log 20 to 24 inches long. Place on a prepared baking sheet and connect the ends of the log to form a circle. Repeat with the other half of the dough and place on the other baking sheet. (You can also make 1 giant ring, forming the dough into a single log of 30 inches long and then connecting the ends to form a circle.) Cover with a kitchen towel and let rise until doubled in size, about 3 hours.

Preheat an oven to 375 degrees F.

Bake until golden, 35 to 40 minutes. Remove from the oven and transfer to a rack to cool completely. To store, cool, then wrap in plastic wrap and store at room temperature for up to 5 days.

Roschette Dolce
Ring-Shaped Cookies

Here are more bracelet-shaped pastries. These are traditionally served at Purim. This recipe is based on one
in Emma Belforte's *La cucina livornese*, but with a few additions.

Makes twenty-four 3-inch rings

For the sponge:

1 cup all-purpose flour

2 teaspoons active dry yeast

1 cup warm water (105 degrees F)

For the dough:

2 cups all-purpose flour

³/₄ cup sugar

3 eggs

¹/₂ cup olive oil

4 tablespoons milk or water

Grated zest of 1 lemon

¹/₄ teaspoon ground cinnamon

1 teaspoon vanilla extract or orange flower water

Vegetable oil for deep-frying

For the coating:

1 egg white

3 tablespoons honey

3 tablespoons water

To make the sponge, place the flour in a large
bowl. In a small bowl, stir the yeast into the warm
water, then add the mixture to the flour. Cover
with plastic wrap and let rest in a warm place until
frothy and doubled in size, about 30 minutes.

To make the dough, add the flour, sugar, eggs,
olive oil, milk or water, lemon zest, cinnamon,
and vanilla extract or orange flower water to the
sponge and stir well to form a dough. Transfer
to a lightly floured work surface and knead
until elastic, 5 to 10 minutes. Cover and let
rise in an oiled bowl until doubled, 2 to 3
hours.

Line 2 baking sheets with parchment paper.
Turn out the dough onto a lightly floured
board. Punch down and fold the dough over
onto itself a few times. Divide the dough into
24 equal pieces. Using your palms, roll each
piece into a log 6 to 8 inches long. Place on a
prepared baking sheet and bring the ends
together to form a ring. Cover loosely with a
kitchen towel and let rise until doubled again,
about 1 ¹/₂ hours. (Some recipes call for forming the rings but not waiting for a second rising.)

Pour vegetable oil to a depth of 3 inches in a
deep saucepan. Heat to 375 degrees F.

While the oil is heating, make the coating: In a
shallow bowl, whisk together the egg white,
honey, and water until blended.

In batches, drop the dough rings into the hot
oil and fry in oil until golden, about 5 minutes. Using a slotted spoon, transfer to paper
towels to drain briefly, then dip in the egg
white mixture and place on a rack to cool. Serve
warm.

Notes: You may also bake these rings in an
oven preheated to 350 degrees F for 20 minutes, then, while they are still warm, dust them
with confectioners' sugar. Traditionally, however, they are fried.

An unyeasted version called *ciambellette* appears
in Donatella Pavoncello's book. It calls for
orange zest in place of the orange flower water.

Orecchie di Amman
Haman's Ears

These cookies, which are served at Purim, represent the ears of the wicked minister Haman. A strip of dough is formed into a circle or a butterfly to look like an ear, then fried in oil.

Makes about 24 cookies

3 whole eggs, or 2 whole eggs and 2 egg yolks

4 tablespoons granulated sugar

½ teaspoon salt

2 teaspoons grated lemon zest or orange zest

3 tablespoons olive oil

3 tablespoons brandy

½ teaspoon vanilla extract

2 ½ to 3 cups all-purpose flour

Vegetable oil for deep-frying

Confectioners' sugar for topping

In a bowl, using a whisk or wooden spoon, beat together the eggs (or whole eggs and egg yolks), granulated sugar, salt, citrus zest, olive oil, brandy, and vanilla until well combined. Gradually add the flour, stirring only enough for the mixture to come together in a soft dough.

Turn out onto a lightly floured board and knead for 5 minutes until smooth. Roll out into a thin sheet and, using a pastry wheel, cut into strips about 1½ inches wide by 4 to 6 inches long. Pinch together the ends of the longer strips to form rings and pinch the centers of the shorter strips to form butterflies.

Pour vegetable oil to a depth of 3 inches into a deep frying pan or saucepan. In batches, slip the pastries into the hot oil and fry until golden, about 3 minutes. Using a slotted skimmer, transfer to paper towels to drain briefly. Keep warm until all the cookies are cooked. Arrange on a platter and sift a dusting of confectioners' sugar over the top while still warm. Eat at once.

Sfratti
Nut-Filled Cookie Sticks

Sfratti means "evicted." The name comes from Italian landlords of long ago who used sticks to chase away poor tenants who had not paid their rent. Some of them were probably poor Jews. The cookies are stick-like, and Jewish cooks have turned their origins around, making them instead sweet symbols of eviction. These honey-and-nut-filled cookies are served at Rosh Hashanah. As described in Aldo Santini's *La cucina maremmana*, they are made with pastry moistened with sweet wine instead of water. Butter or margarine is used, depending upon whether the rest of the meal is dairy or not. My family thinks these are better than *rugelach!*

MAKES FORTY-EIGHT 2-INCH-LONG COOKIES

For the pastry:

3 cups all-purpose flour

1 cup sugar

Pinch of salt

$\frac{1}{3}$ cup chilled margarine or unsalted butter

$\frac{2}{3}$ cup sweet wine

For the filling:

$\frac{2}{3}$ cup honey

1 teaspoon ground cinnamon

$\frac{1}{4}$ teaspoon ground cloves

2 cups walnuts, coarsely chopped

1 tablespoon grated lemon zest

1 tablespoon grated orange zest

Pinch of freshly ground black pepper

All-purpose flour or fine dried bread crumbs for dusting

1 egg yolk beaten with 2 tablespoons water, for egg wash

Chill a pastry board.

To make the dough, in a bowl, combine the flour, sugar, and salt. Cut in the margarine or butter with a pastry blender until the mixture has the consistency of coarse meal. Add the wine and stir and toss with a fork until the mixture just holds together. Remove the dough from the bowl and gather it into a ball. (The dough can also be made in a food processor, pulsing it to cut in the butter and processing to bring the dough together.) Divide the dough in half and flatten each half into a disk. Cover with plastic wrap and refrigerate for 1 to 2 hours.

To make the filling, pour the honey into a heavy-bottomed saucepan over medium-high heat. Bring to a boil, add the cinnamon and cloves, and boil until it forms a ribbon when a spoon is lifted, about 10 minutes. Add the nuts, citrus zests, and pepper and simmer for 10 minutes. Remove from the heat and let cool until you can touch the mixture without burning yourself.

Dust the chilled board with flour or bread crumbs. Pour the filling onto the board and, using your hands, roll it into 6 long, thin ropes, each 12 to 14 inches long. Act quickly as the mixture sets up fast!

Preheat an oven to 375 degrees F. Butter 1 or 2 baking sheets or line with parchment paper.

On a lightly floured board, divide the dough into 6 equal pieces. Roll out each piece into a 4-inch-wide strip that is 12 to 14 inches long. Place a strip of nut paste on the center of each piece of dough, and roll up the dough, fully enclosing the nut paste. Cut into finger-length cookies. Place on the prepared baking sheet(s). Brush the sticks with the egg wash glaze. Bake until golden, about 20 minutes. Transfer to a rack to cool. These keep well but you won't have them long!

 Sfratti
Nut-Filled Cookie Sticks

Bibliography

Alhadeff, Nora Pinto. *Quaderna di cucina, profumi, sapori, e ricordi di una vita di viaggi.* Verona: Arnaldo Mondadori, 1993.

Ascoli Vitali-Norsa, Giuliana. *La cucina nella tradizione ebraica.* Florence: ADEI-WIZO-La Giuntina, 1987.

Bassani, Giorgio. *The Garden of the Finzi-Contini.* Translated by William Weaver. New York: Harvest Books, 1977.

Belgrado Passigli, Milka. *Le ricette di casa mia: La cucina casher in una famiglia ebraica italiana.* Florence: La Giuntina, 1993.

Calimano, Ricardo. *The Ghetto of Venice.* Milan: Rusconi, 1988.

Capnist, Giovanni. *I dolci del Veneto.* Padua: Franco Muzzio, 1983.

Eramo, Cia. *La cucina mantovana.* Padua: Franco Muzzio, 1980, 1985.

Le feste ebraiche. Rome: Logart Press, 1987.

Field, Carol. *Celebrating Italy.* New York: William Morrow, 1990.

——. *Italy in Small Bites.* New York: William Morrow, 1993.

Fortis, Umberto. *Jews and Synagogues.* Venice: Storti Edizioni, 1973.

Galluzzo, Maria Allesandra Iori, Narsete Iori, and Marco Inotta. *La cucina ferrarese.* Padua: Franco Muzzio, 1989.

Gossetti, Fernanda. *I dolci della cucina regionale italiana.* Milan: Fabbri Editori, 1993.

Gosetti della Salda, Anna. *Le ricette regionale italiane.* Milan: Casa Editrice Solares, 1967.

Kaspar, Lynn Rossetto. *The Splendid Table.* New York: William Morrow, 1992.

Machlin, Edda Servi. *The Classic Cuisine of the Italian Jews.* 2 vols. New York: Dodd, Mead and Co., 1981 (vol. 1). Croton on Hudson: Giro Press, 1992 (vol. 2).

Maffioli, Giuseppe. *La cucina veneziana.* Padua: Franco Muzzio, 1987.

——. *La cucina padovana.* Padua: Franco Muzzio, 1980.

Midor Ledor: vita e cultura ebraica nel Veneto. Padua: Edizioni Scritti Monastici—Abbazia di Praglia—Bresseo di Teolo, 1988.

Milano, Attilo. *Storia degli ebrei in Italia.* Torino: Einaudi, 1963, 1992.

Pavoncello, Donatella Limentani. *Dal 1880 ad oggi: la cucina ebraica della mia famiglia.* Rome: Carucci Editore, 1982.

Roden, Claudia. *The Book of Jewish Food.* New York: Alfred Knopf, 1996.

Roth, Cecil. *The History of the Jews in Italy.* Philadelphia: Jewish Publication Society of America, 1946.

Sacerdoti, Annie. *Emilia-Romagna-itinerari ebraici.* Venice: Marsilio, 1992.

——. *Veneto-itinerari ebraici.* Venice: Marsilio, 1996.

Sacerdoti, Annie, and Luca Fiorentino. *Italian Jewish Travel Guide.* Brooklyn: Israelowitz Publications, 1993.

Sacerdoti, Mira. *Italian Jewish Cooking.* London: Robert Hall, 1992.

Santini, Aldo. *La cucina livornese.* Padua: Franco Muzzio, 1988.

——. *La cucina maremmana.* Padua: Franco Muzzio, 1991.

Scicolone, Michele. *La dolce vita.* New York: William Morrow, 1993.

Segre, Bruno. *Gli ebrei in Italia.* Milan: Fenice 2000, 1993.

Stille, Alexander. *Benevolence and Betrayal.* New York: Summit Books, New York, 1991.

Tas, Luciano. *Storia degli ebrei italiani.* Rome: Newton Compton, 1987.

Zanini de Vita, Oretta. *Il Lazio a tavola: Guida gastronomica tra storia e tradizioni.* Rome: Alphabyte Books, 1994.

Index

Table of Equivalents

The exact equivalents in the following tables have been rounded for convenience.

LIQUID AND DRY MEASURES
U.S. to Metric

1/4 teaspoon = 1.25 milliliters

1/2 teaspoon = 2.5 milliliters

1 teaspoon = 5 milliliters

1 tablespoon (3 teaspoons) = 15 milliliters

1 fluid ounce (2 tablespoons) = 30 milliliters

1/4 cup = 60 milliliters

1/3 cup = 80 milliliters

1 cup = 240 milliliters

1 pint (2 cups) = 480 milliliters

1 quart (4 cups, 32 ounces) = 960 milliliters

1 gallon (4 quarts) = 3.84 liters

1 ounce (by weight) = 28 grams

1 pound = 454 grams

2.2 pounds = 1 kilogram

LENGTH MEASURES
U.S. to Metric

1/8 inch = 3 millimeters

1/4 inch = 6 millimeters

1/2 inch = 12 millimeters

1 inch = 2.5 centimeters

OVEN TEMPERATURES
Fahrenheit to Celsius to Gas

250°F = 120°C = 1/2

275°F = 140°C = 1

300°F = 150°C = 2

325°F = 160°C = 3

350°F = 180°C = 4

375°F = 190°C = 5

400°F = 200°C = 6

425°F = 220°C = 7

450°F = 230°C = 8

475°F = 240°C = 9

500°F = 260°C = 10

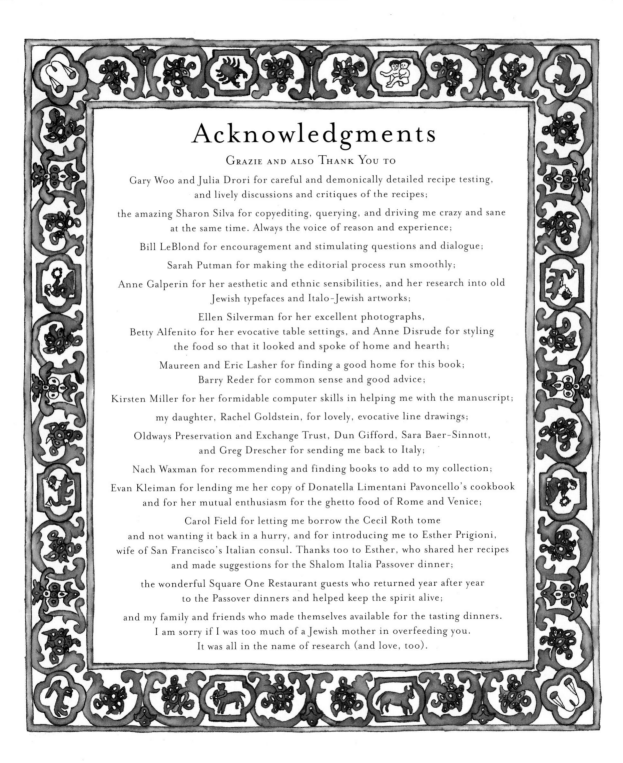

Acknowledgments

GRAZIE AND ALSO THANK YOU TO

Gary Woo and Julia Drori for careful and demonically detailed recipe testing,
and lively discussions and critiques of the recipes;

the amazing Sharon Silva for copyediting, querying, and driving me crazy and sane
at the same time. Always the voice of reason and experience;

Bill LeBlond for encouragement and stimulating questions and dialogue;

Sarah Putman for making the editorial process run smoothly;

Anne Galperin for her aesthetic and ethnic sensibilities, and her research into old
Jewish typefaces and Italo-Jewish artworks;

Ellen Silverman for her excellent photographs,
Betty Alfenito for her evocative table settings, and Anne Disrude for styling
the food so that it looked and spoke of home and hearth;

Maureen and Eric Lasher for finding a good home for this book;
Barry Reder for common sense and good advice;

Kirsten Miller for her formidable computer skills in helping me with the manuscript;

my daughter, Rachel Goldstein, for lovely, evocative line drawings;

Oldways Preservation and Exchange Trust, Dun Gifford, Sara Baer-Sinnott,
and Greg Drescher for sending me back to Italy;

Nach Waxman for recommending and finding books to add to my collection;

Evan Kleiman for lending me her copy of Donatella Limentani Pavoncello's cookbook
and for her mutual enthusiasm for the ghetto food of Rome and Venice;

Carol Field for letting me borrow the Cecil Roth tome
and not wanting it back in a hurry, and for introducing me to Esther Prigioni,
wife of San Francisco's Italian consul. Thanks too to Esther, who shared her recipes
and made suggestions for the Shalom Italia Passover dinner;

the wonderful Square One Restaurant guests who returned year after year
to the Passover dinners and helped keep the spirit alive;

and my family and friends who made themselves available for the tasting dinners.
I am sorry if I was too much of a Jewish mother in overfeeding you.
It was all in the name of research (and love, too).